Topics in Sociology

Paul Trowler

and Mike Riley

University Tutorial Press

Published by University Tutorial Press Limited
842 Yeovil Road, Slough, SL1 4JQ

ISBN 0 7231 0875 7

Published 1984

Typeset in Great Britain at The Pitman Press, Bath

Preface

In this book we deal with some of the areas in Sociology which have been either inadequately covered by earlier texts or are new to the "A" level Sociology syllabuses of the main examining boards. The book will also be useful for undergraduates and for Sociology based professional courses. In it we attempt to give the reader a full understanding of each subject by succinctly summarising the major studies within the context of a general account of important themes.

Although the book is divided into the traditional topic chapters, we have indicated areas of overlap between these and other concerns of the discipline. We assume that the examination oriented reader has some familiarity with these other subdisciplines, or has access to one of the main texts which covers them. We hope that this volume will not only provide the reader with a grounding in the subjects we deal with here but will deepen and widen his or her understanding of other areas of Sociology.

The work was divided up as follows: the chapters on Development, Youth Culture, Health and Mass Media were written by me, the chapter on Race by Mike Riley. I would like to express my appreciation for the valuable criticism of and comment on the work by my wife, Terry Wareham. I would also like to thank Nan Bray and Ann Chapman for their rapid and efficient typing work. Mike Riley wishes to thank his wife, Alex, for her patient support and advice during the time spent in preparing his contribution. Alex's labour of typing and comments on style were essential to the outcome. Mike and I wish to thank Ann Hawkins and Carol Bryson at the Milton Keynes College library, Bletchley, for their considerable help and forbearance during the period this book was being written. The authors, of course, accept full responsibility for all weaknesses the book may contain.

The authors and publisher wish to thank those who gave permission to use copyright material, the sources of which are listed in the bibliographies at the end of the chapters. The three tables from the HMSO publications *Social Trends* and *Household Food Consumption and Expenditure* in the Health chapter are reproduced with the permission of the Controller of Her Majesty's Stationery Office.

Paul Trowler

To
My Parents and
Eve

Contents

4 The sociology of health

5 The sociology of the mass media

1 The sociology of development

Introduction

One of the most obvious features of the modern world is its division into three distinct parts; the First, Second and Third Worlds. The First World consists of the industrialised democracies such as the USA and the countries of the EEC. The Second World comprises the communist countries such as the USSR and its satellites in the Eastern Bloc. The Third World refers to all those countries which are not, or not yet, industrialised. In geographical terms the First World can be thought of as the North West, the Second as the North East and the Third as the South. Some countries are rather difficult to place. China and Cuba could be said to be Second *or* Third World countries; while Libya, Saudi Arabia and Kuwait are wealthy but do not seem to belong in the same category as other wealthy and industrialised non-communist countries.

The distinction between the First and Second Worlds is a political one. An economic characteristic creates a clearly identifiable Third World. Lack of capital for investment in industry and the presence of widespread poverty with its associated hunger, disease and social problems are prevalent in the Third World. The Third World has 70% of the population alive today but only 17% of the world's income. 55% of the population of the Third World are un- or under-employed and 60% are without health care. A recent World Bank estimate suggests that 800 million people are in absolute poverty today, another 100 million may be added to that number by 1990 unless the rich countries of the world take decisive action.

The continent of Africa is a representative part of the Third World. Its gross domestic product (the total amount of goods and services produced per year) increased by an average of 4% between 1960 and 1967. However, when this is translated into growth per head of the population the rate is reduced to about 1% per annum. The difference is due to the high rate of population growth which Africa shares with other countries of the Third World. While 1% seems to compare reasonably with the UK figure of 1.8% GDP growth per head between 1968 and 1978, we must remember that 1% of a small figure is less than 1% of a large figure. In real terms, the gap between the UK and Africa is widening rapidly. Even in those countries within the continent where the GDP is greater than that of the already-developed countries, the time periods involved before the catch-up is completed are enormously long. Malawi, for example, will catch up to the USA in 727 years time, according to the Nat West Bank review of February 1970.

Within Third World countries there are great inequalities. The 1980 World Development Report estimates that in Brazil the poorest 20% of the population get 2% of the income while the richest 20% get 67%. In Malaysia the figures are 3% and 57%. In Britain the poorest 20% get 6% of the income while the richest get 39%. It is well known that in terms of wealth (as opposed to income) some of the richest people in the world come from the poorest nations. Within the developed world too, there remain great inequalities of wealth ownership, with 5% of the population owning 50% of the wealth according to some estimates. In the Third World there are a wide range of other inequalities, for example in terms of access to comfortable housing, to health services and in levels of literacy.

The word development encompasses more than simply an increase in the gross domestic product of a country and its more equitable distribution. It also implies social, cultural and political changes. The Brandt Commission on International Development Issues began its study of the relationship between the rich and the poor countries of the world in early 1978 and reported its findings in *North-South: a Programme for Survival* in 1980. It defines development as "desirable social and economic progress"(1). Peter Donaldson, the economist and Third World specialist, defines the process of development as:

> "bringing about basic changes in the underlying social fabric of attitudes and motivations so that the objectives of society can be more fully realised."(2)

Although objectives are usually the cause of much disagreement and conflict, there are some objectives which most members of most societies do share. Improvements in nutritional standards, housing conditions, health and levels of education for the mass of the population, the transport and communication networks and stabilisation of the demographic characteristics of the country are usually agreed to be part of the development process. In addition to the simple increase in the productivity of a developing country there is usually expected to be a decrease in the large differences in income and wealth distribution usually found in Third World countries. In terms of international trade, a developed country is usually considered to have roughly balanced imports and exports with neither exclusively devoted to one type of product. One striking characteristic of the Third World is that its exports mainly consist of agricultural produce and minerals while it mainly imports manufactured goods. The costs of the latter are usually far greater than the income from the former. A developing country is one that moves away from primary production (mineral extraction and agriculture) and towards manufacturing on a large scale, eventually moving into the service sector such as banking and communications (the secondary and tertiary sectors of the economy respectively). This change transforms the occupational structure from the shape of a pyramid, with the bulk of the population at the bottom doing unskilled manual work and only a few in white collar jobs. The shape changes to that of a light bulb, with a large proportion in the middle class white collar or skilled manual sectors. A further change associated with the development of a country is a move away from the dictatorial type of political regime largely found in the Third World to the democratic types found in the most industrialised countries.

The list of countries which have developed during the course of this century or are developing at the moment according to the above criteria of development is, in fact, rather small. In the early part of this century we can point to the USSR and Japan. Since the Second World War the list contains Taiwan, South Korea, Mexico, Brazil and Argentina on the capitalist side; with China, Cuba and North Korea on the communist. The extent to which these countries have merely industrialised rather than developed in the much broader sense is a matter for discussion.

Before moving away from the discussion of the nature of development some of the problems associated with the use of the concept need to be examined. The words developed and development imply good and mature, while definitions of such words (like Brandt's above) often contain value-laden concepts like progress and progressive which suggest that the old form of society is 'bad' and the new form 'good'. There is, in other words, a value judgement inherent in the terminology itself. Most sociologists would argue that as value judgements should be avoided wherever possible, so should words which themselves carry such a judgement. A second problem is that the verb 'to develop' implies a gradual and slow change. In fact in societies like those of Latin America and Africa, change tends to come about in an abrupt, often violent way. Thirdly, and perhaps most importantly, the verb 'to develop' implies that the society is following a pre-defined path of change into some new and known state. Thus the word itself gives unjustified force to those theories which suggest that societies do 'develop' along pre-defined and identifiable lines.

During this chapter some of the major perspectives which attempt to explain the nature of the process of development and the reasons for its presence or absence in particular countries will be examined. These will be divided into four general categories: Determinist theories, Voluntarist theories, Modernisation theories and Structural theories.

Determinist theories argue that the process of social change occurs due to immutable laws largely outside the control of men and women. In this section we will look at two *materialist* writers, ie ones who stress that material factors such as the type of technology and the system of production employed determine other features in society such as its belief systems and its political system.

Voluntarist theories argue that the pattern of social change is not pre-set and that its direction and shape are in the hands of men and women. We will examine the work of two *idealist* writers, ie ones who maintain that ideas and beliefs can shape the more concrete factors such as the nature of the economy.

Modernisation theory sees development as the product of a range of social and economic changes that can spur social development towards modernism, by which is meant the Western pattern of society. These changes sometimes occur spontaneously, as in Britain; or are induced by countries that have already achieved the modern pattern. Modernisation theory includes a variety of writers and is such a broad school that it includes determinists, voluntarists, materialists and idealists.

Structuralism sees lack of development in the Third World as the product of exploitative international relationships, particularly market relationships. Its focus of attention is on the international structure. Once again the breadth of this school of thought is very great, including as it does writers of different political complexions.

The final section of this chapter will examine convergence theory. This is the view that once a society has achieved the early stages of industrialisation it begins to take on certain predictable characteristics as a necessary consequence of its industrial base and regardless of the nature of its culture or social structure prior to this stage in its history. All developed societies will increasingly become similar to each other in all important respects, in other words they will *converge*. This is one of the claims made by both modernisation theory and determinist theory and we will use this section as a test of their merits and those of voluntarist theory (for which no such convergence is necessary.) We will use Japanese development as a case study to put these perspectives to the test.

Determinist theories of social development

"The term determinism denotes the doctrine which claims that all objects or events, or all objects or events of some kinds (for instance, falling within the range of some scientific discipline) are determined, that is to say *must* be as they are and as they will be, in virtue of some laws or forces which necessitate their being so. . . . For instance, economic determinism tends to mean the doctrine that economic factors determine others."(3)

"In acquiring new means of production men change their mode of production, in changing the way of earning their living, they change all their social relations. The hand mill gives you the society with the feudal lord, the steam-mill, society with the industrial capitalist".(4)

Karl Marx and historical materialism

Marx's account of social development is important in the study of development because of its comprehensive nature, the issues it raises (primarily those of determinism and materialism – the notion that concrete material factors give rise to ideas and beliefs rather that vice versa) and because many developing countries adopt some form of Marxism in their scheme for development.

Before we can properly discuss Marx's ideas we need to make clear some of the terms he uses:

Means of production – the physical things which are central to the creation of goods (land, machinery, tools, factory buildings etc)
Relations of production – the social organisation upon which production is based (citizen and slave, nobleman and serf, capitalist and proletarian.)
Mode of production – the combination of the above two. Marx talks, for example of "the capitalist mode of production" which is a description both of the means and of the relations of production.

As time goes by there is, according to Marx, a progressive change in the mode of production of every society brought about by increasing efficiency of production which is in turn the result of improved technology. For example, when a simple society learns how to produce enough food for all its members without all of them having to spend time in food collection, then the possibility is present for a non-working, ruling class to develop. The technology which enabled this to happen would be, for example, the establishment of fixed areas of cultivation or the keeping of domestic animals. A change in the means of production has produced a change in the relations of production. As a result the whole mode of production has changed. A mode of production which was a primitive form of communism has become a class society simply because the technology of production has changed.

It would be unwise and incorrect to suggest that Marx was a complete economic determinist, as this example and the quote above would seem to suggest. He did recognise the importance of human actions in changing the shape of society and in accelerating or slowing down historical change:

> "History does nothing – it 'possesses no immense wealth', it 'wages no battles'. It is *man*, real living man, that does all that, that possesses and fights; 'history' is not a person apart, using man as a means for its own particular aims; history is *nothing* but the activity of man pursuing his aims."(5)

Social change is brought about not just passively through the gradual improvement of technology, but actively through class conflict which resolves the contradictory aims and interests of the social classes and results in a change of the relations of production, clearing the way for a new stage in social development:

> "Freeman and slave, patrician and plebian, lord and serf, guildmaster and journeyman, in a word, oppressor and oppressed, carried on an uninterrupted, now hidden, now open fight (which ended) either in a revolutionary reconstruction of society at large, or in the common ruin of the contending classes."(6)

In the development of his thought Marx seems to have moved from a broad materialist view of history which saw material factors such as technology as merely conditioning other social features in a rather weak way to a more narrow technological view. The fact that Marx said different things at different times to different audiences makes *the* correct reading of his work rather difficult to arrive at and even harder to defend. It is true that in the last analysis, the economic base of society is determinant in that it establishes possibilities for future development and contradictions in the present day, but it is for highly motivated groups of people to realise the possibilities and resolve the contradictions.

Marx maps the development of human societies as passing through five modes of production before the 'true' form of society, communism, is reached. The first stage is *Primitive Communism*. Here goods are held by the whole community, they do not belong to individual people. Apart from distinctions based on age and sex there is no stratification system. The means of production are extremely primitive; simply hunting wild animals and gathering fruit. In fact Marx calls this stage *primitive* communism precisely because the means of production are so limited – people cannot realise their true potential when their whole beings are devoted simply to staying alive.

An example of a society approximating Marx's primitive communist model is the Andaman Islands in the Pacific Ocean studied by the anthropologist Radcliffe-Brown(7). The Andaman economy was based on fishing, gathering shellfish, hunting animals and gathering the fruits and edible roots from the forest. There was no system of agriculture in the sense of animal husbandry or cultivation of crops, so a large amount of time and effort went on food gathering. The only division of labour was by sex: the men hunting and fishing, the women gathering food. There were no chiefs or nobles and indeed little idea of social rank except for the distinction between the old and the young. Private ownership of land did not exist and there was very little private property. The largest item which was privately owned was the canoe, though this was freely lent by its owner to anyone who needed it.

In the *Asiatic* mode of production (which is seen more as a possible alternative form of society rather than as a *necessary* step in social development) the common ownership of the means of production is institutionalised in what is an early form of 'nationalisation'. The state owns the means of production and assumes a dominating role. It takes for itself the profits from the labour of its people. This is one of the earliest forms of exploitative society and, as its name suggests, was found primarily in the East.

The *Ancient* form of society is predominantly urban and is the first form in which the individual can own property. The clearest example was in ancient Rome. The transition to this form from primitive communism is brought about by tribal invasion and conquest. The vanquished are taken as slaves by the victors. Agricultural techniques have now developed to such an extent that non-producers in the city can be supported by those working the land, while the urban ruling class attempt to extend their ownership of territory and the wealth it produces by wars of conquest. The number of slaves increases with the success of these imperialistic wars and the class divisions within the domestic society become more acute.

The social tension this creates, combined with the fact that the social relations of production embodied in the ownership of slaves are not able to properly exploit the potential for production created by changes in the means of production, brings about the downfall of the ancient mode of production which is replaced by feudalism.

Feudalism is based on ownership of the land and the exploitation of those who work it by its owners. The nobility extract the surplus produced by their tenants in the form of rent and tithes, and allow the tenants only enough to live on for themselves. In return, however, the land owners have certain obligations to the tenants, such as ensuring their economic security in times of difficulty (as when there is a poor harvest.) What starts off as a contractual arrangement between one owner and one tenant becomes, over the generations, enshrined in tradition so that the sons of the original tenant are automatically tied to the land of the sons of the original owner without the agreement of a contract on either side.

Capitalism develops from feudalism as a result of the increasing strength of the urban bourgeoisie. These are owners of the new industrial means of production and they employ wage labour towards whom they have none of the traditional feudal obligations. They are increasingly able to challenge the old order through the power which their wealth gives them. The process of change from feudalism to capitalism began in the 16th century.

Technological development of the type we know today began then, and this was followed by political changes (the increasing power of the bourgeoisie as opposed to the land owning classes) and religious ones (the Reformation which challenged the hegemony of the Catholic Chuch and destroyed the religious support for traditional conditions of ownership and working of the land). Within capitalism the wage labourers, the proletariat, are formally free to seek the highest return for their labour. The bourgeoisie, however, derive their profit from the proletariat by paying less in wages than the value that is created by the work of the labourer, allowing profit to be made over and above running costs. If any capitalist company did not do this it would quickly go out of business. Eventually, this mode of production creates unemployment through increasing mechanisation. It also creates monopolisation and centralisation of capital and thus great poverty and misery for the ever-expanding proletariat on the one side and extreme wealth for the other side of society, the few capitalists who remain after the process of monopolisation has cut down their numbers. More goods are produced by the ever-more efficient technology than can be consumed by the society, the rate of profit extracted by the capitalist declines as he employs fewer and fewer workers. As a result the mode of production undergoes a series of crises which, while not causing the downfall of capitalism, are a symptom of these contradictions. Eventually the proletariat, now virtually everybody in society, rise against their oppression and take control of the means of production. Having removed the exploiting capitalists and put the benefits derived from technology in the hands of the people it is now possible to build a new and liberating society. Thus the communist revolution is, according to Marx, only the beginning of a process which sees the development of a society founded on very advanced technology and where the material world is under the complete control of the human population which can now devote its attention to perfecting itself.

This path of history is a winding one and often comes to a sudden end or turns back on itself, yet eventually reaches the goal of communist and the beginning of *true* (ie non-exploitative) history. History is guided by contradictions, both economic (eg overproduction and underconsumption of goods) and social (class conflict.) Its path of development is *not* a simple one, regularly and automatically passing through the stages described above. There is no possibility for a type of society to arise outside of these stages which can last. Similarly, once one of these stages has been reached there must be further social change, either forward movement or regression to a previous state. The possibility of stability does not exist due to the moving force of the contradictions inherent in all societies other than the communist one.

Marx's account of the process of social change has been the subject of criticism from many quarters, though these criticisms often attack a form of 'vulgar Marxism', a crude form of materialism which Marx did not subscribe to.

As an accurate description of different forms of society Marx's account can be faulted on many points. M. Sahlins makes the point in his book *Stone Age Economics*(8) that simple forms of society were *not* devoted on a full time basis to the gathering of food. He argues, on the basis of anthropological and archaeological evidence, that stone age man and members of similar non-technological societies had more spare time than does modern man. Marx's description of primitive communism is, in fact, rather superficial. Claude Meillassoux argues(9) that this is due to the fact that Marx was not really interested in this and other pre-capitalist modes of production for themselves, but merely wished to trace the characteristics found within capitalism back in history. Thus Marx does not describe them fully, only commenting on what features of captitalism are present or absent in them. He does not work out the 'laws' by which they operate as he tries to do for capitalism, and, most importantly, he does not give us any adequate description or explanation of the transformation processes from one to the other (except for the passage from feudalism to capitalism.)

Many critics(10) have questioned the accuracy of Marx's account of developments within capitalism. Rather than becoming immiserated and pauperised, the working class are more affluent and live and work in far better conditions than they did in the past. Far from the middle classes disappearing as society polarises into bourgeoisie and proletariat, they are becoming the largest sector of the economy(11). Modern Marxists attempt to counter these criticisms by pointing to the *relative* pauperisation of the working class and suggesting that the period of large scale technological unemployment and resulting absolute poverty has only just begun.

The pre-eminent role of class in the Marxian account of social change has been the source of much criticism and debate too. H. Marcuse(12) suggests that the revolutionary potential of the working class has been sapped by their relative material affluence and comfort within capitalism and we must look to other groups, especially students for any radical social change. Feminists argue that in his concentration on class antagonisms in history Marx overlooked the oppression of women by men which predates the oppression of class by class. Some consider it possible to include this factor in his account by modifications of it(13) while others propose a new theory of social change to replace that of Marx(14). Certainly it would appear that as a means of analysis of the stratification systems of all forms of society and conflicts within them, the theory of class has serious limitations.

Marx's determinism has been subject to the fiercest and most sustained criticism. Marx believed that economic factors were the ultimate shaping forces of society. His voluntarist critics argue that human choices and beliefs are central factors in shaping society and that it is therefore impossible to 'map out' the necessary stages of human history because there is simply no necessity about any aspect of social development. Society can be precisely what men and women make it, it is not the subject of economic laws of change.

W. W. Rostow and the stages of growth

Like Marx, Rostow sees societies as undergoing a largely technologically determined path of change. Both writers subscribe to a form of materialist philosophy, seeing material factors as largely determining social, political and cultural features. Economic change leads to social development on a particular and identifiable path. The end point of this path for both is an equitable form of social and economic organisation. Despite the fact that Rostow's book is subtitled "A Non-Communist Manifesto", the writers have many similarities. Rostow writes:

> "It is possible to identify all societies, in their economic dimensions, as lying within one of five categories: the traditional society, the pre-conditions for take off, the take-off, the drive to maturity, and the age of high mass consumption."(15)

In *traditional* societies the production functions are limited, being mostly concerned with agriculture. Output levels are low. Science and technology are either not available or not systematically applied. Social mobility is low and politically these societies are centralised, though there is considerable regional autonomy due to poor communications.

In the stage of *pre-conditions for take off*, which occured in Europe during the late 17th and early 18th centuries, there is a transformation of economic production by science and technology. This transformation occurs within an expanding market environment, the volume of trade increasing in leaps and bounds. Britain was the first to benefit from this expansion of production potential due to its natural resources, its advantageous trading possibilities resulting from its geographical position, and its suitable social and political structure. It is important that for Rostow in the contemporary world societies reach the stage of the pre-conditions for take off *not* thanks to their own internal factors but due to externally introduced technology and the presence of foreign banks and other institutions for the mobilisation of capital. As we shall see later, structuralist approaches strongly disagree that the developed world play this 'helping hand' role.

The period of *take-off*, lasting about twenty years, sees the technological development of industry and agriculture, the build up of capital and the formation of an elite prepared to modernise the economy rather than simply looking after its own interests. Profits are reinvested, industry grows and sees the growth of an urban proletariat together with the services to support them. The society becomes increasingly urban as a result of this growth. Incomes increase and so do savings, allowing further investment to take place. A virtuous circle has been set in motion which is inevitably leading to the greater affluence and happiness of all.

The *drive to maturity* consists of a period of about 40 years of sustained progress with the extension of modern technology over all economic activity. The nation's economy finds its niche in the international economy of imports and exports and the majority of the population have access to large numbers and a great variety of consumer products and services. The social and geographical structure of the population progressively changes so that the unskilled working class declines in proportion to other strata and the majority of the population are beneficiaries of the extensive provision of welfare facilities. This is the end point of Rostow's model of economic and social development, *the age of high mass consumption*. Thus while Marx sees the necessity for a new form of society, Rostow considers what is in effect advanced capitalism to be the last stage. Rostow's theory is, literally, 'non-communist'.

Rostow fails to take into account the fact that 'late developers' face special problems which were not faced by the first countries to industrialise. Marx, too, ignores these problems, and because of their materialist orientation both would agree that an impediment to economic development is an impediment to social development. Unlike Britain and the USA, the countries of the South are not developing into an environment of 'traditional' societies. Many of the other countries in the world are already developed and this has the following implications for the newcomers:

1 The 'traditional' societies already have a niche in the world economy as the source of raw materials for the developed countries. Any move away from this role and towards industrial production would be at the expense of developed countries who would be deprived of the raw materials and food their industries and people require.

2 If today's underdeveloped countries expanded their secondary sectors, the goods they produced would be similar to, and therefore in competition with, those produced in today's developed countries. This would lead to a loss of jobs and a loss of markets for the developed nations.

3 It is exceedingly difficult to compete in a world economy dependent on advanced technology. Machines would have to be imported rather than produced by the domestic economy. This would mean that an important industrial sector would not develop in an industrialising country.

4 Third World investors tend to export their capital to the industrial capitalist world, engaging in speculation and investing in land, commerce and real estate to achieve a greater rate of return than is available in the domestic economy. Indigenous industrialisation of any scope based on domestic capital is therefore unlikely, while investors from abroad will be aware of the damaging effects that competing industries in the Third World would have on the industries at home.

5 Any development of the Third World would put an additional burden on the earth's already strained ecological structure and depleted resources:

> "With world population doubling time a little more than 30 years and decreasing, society will be hard put to meet the needs and expectations of so many more people in so short a period. We are likely to try to satisfy these demands by over-exploiting our natural environment and further impairing the life-supporting capacity of our earth."(16)

While it is true that as countries develop their birth rates tend to decline and therefore the expansion of the population begins to slow, this process takes many decades. We would find ourselves in the situation of a race between the decline in population growth of the Third World and the increasing demands placed on the world's resources and ecological systems by its industrialisation. Whatever the criticisms of the Club of Rome's report, it is clear that the question of the allocation of resources between North and South is complicated by the finite nature of these resources.

Andre Gunder Frank points out(17) that Rostow assumes that there were no other stages before the 'traditional' one, and that the 'developed' societies of today were once impoverished in the same way that the Third World is. Rostow fails to distinguish between traditional societies, including under that label many widely variant historical and contemporary societies in spite of the fact that the only thing they have in common is that they are neither industrialised nor 'modern' (ie like the USA). Rostow ignores the rich and diverse cultural patterns of non-developed societies and the destructive effects that mature societies have had on them. The history of Britain before industrialisation is quite different from that of the Third World countries because Britain had no already developed competitors. As for Rostow's third stage, take off, Frank suggests that the changes in institutions and investment patterns involved no real changes in the structure of under-development for reasons we will look at in more detail later. Argentina and India, both claimed by Rostow to be at the stage of take-off, are in fact becoming *more* structurally under-developed. Other critics have shown that Rostow attributes motivations and purposeful actions to such abstractions as 'the nation' and 'history'. Who or what is it that is doing the 'driving' to maturity? Only *people* can make this kind of decision and follow these kinds of courses of action, and they rarely do so without opposition. Rostow is completely ignoring the process of decision making and the conflicts between people and groups which go on before and after the decision is taken.

Finally, in the current climate of recession and unemployment, Rostow seems to be too optimistic about the future of the West:

> "There is every reason to believe, looking at the sensitivity of the political process to even small pockets of unemployment in modern

> democratic societies, that the sluggish and timid policies of the 1920's and 1930's with respect to the level of employment will no longer be tolerated in Western societies. And now the technical tricks of the trade – due to the Keynesian revolution – are widely understood. It should not be forgotten that Keynes set himself the task of defeating Marx's prognosis about the course of unemployment under capitalism; and he largely succeeded."(18)

Even in the North the 'tricks of the trade' seem to have been forgotten, or deliberately left aside. Cyclical crises and unemployment persist, as does poverty, even here in the so-called developed world.

Voluntarist theories of social development

> "Voluntarism in social science denotes any theory that stresses the place of choice, decision, purpose and norms in social action . . . In its crudest form voluntarism means that all social phenomena are directly traceable to the deliberate decisions of human beings."(19)
> "What people want, they somehow manage to get, in the main and on average, though other factors can modify the speed with which they get it."(20)

Voluntarism is that perspective on social change which stresses that change is under the control of men and women. Religious movements may arise from the preachings of just one person which encourage the population to work hard and accumulate capital or, just as likely, an anti-materialist ethic may arise which effectively stops any industrialisation. In either case the beliefs of the society have not been determined, according to the voluntarist approach, but are simply the results of human action and free will. Voluntarist approaches are often *idealist* ones.

One recent study uses a voluntarist perspective to explain the industrial 'success' of Japan and the 'failure' of China(21). In its passage from China to Japan the ideology of Confucianism changed in certain important respects. Obedience to one's lord became stressed in the Japanese version, rather than obedience to one's own conscience as in China. Benevolence was a central virtue of Confucianism in China, whereas no importance was attached to it in Japan. Filial piety (being faithful to one's parents and obeying their wishes) was all-important in China, but secondary to loyalty to one's lord in Japan. In short, the Japanese version was a perfect ideology for the creation of an obedient and well-disciplined work force while the Chinese version led to greater individuality and less discipline. The modifications to the doctrine of Confucianism were not accidental, according to the author, but were a natural result of the fact that Confucianism was imported by members of the ruling class and *deliberately* modified by them in their own interests.

Max Weber

The work of Max Weber is seen as important to development theory because he emphasises the danger of jumping to too-simple, single-cause explanations of social development, particularly the idea that social change is caused by technological development. For this reason much of Weber's work has been described as replying to the ghost of Marx – a reply to Marx's exaggerations, errors and omissions. However, on many issues they share common perspectives. For example, they are agreed that the main features of capitalism are as follows:

1 That there is an orientation towards specifically economic ends;
2 that the most efficient means for achieving these ends are utilised;
3 that there is a high degree of technological advancement;
4 with a highly developed division of labour; and
5 that there is a formally free wage-earning class which does not own the means of production.

In his discussion of the origin of this form of society, Weber is less concerned with its *institutional* features than Marx and more with its 'spirit'; the type of attitude which considers work and the accumulation of money not as a means to an end (eg a more comfortable, fulfilling or enjoyable lifestyle) but as an end in itself, indeed a moral duty:

> "The acquisition of more and more money, combined with the strict avoidance of all spontaneous enjoyment . . . is thought of so purely as an end in itself, that vis-a-vis the happiness of, or utility to, the particular individual, it appears as quite transcendental and wholly irrational. Man is dominated by acquisition as the purpose of his life; acquisition is no longer the means of satisfying his material needs. The reversal of what we might call the 'natural' situation, completely senseless from an unprejudiced standpoint, is as evidently a leading principle of capitalism as it is foreign to all peoples not under capitalistic influence."(22)

Weber is arguing that while greed and selfish hoarding may be found in all societies, it is only *under capitalism* that such accumulation becomes an end in itself and a moral duty. In *The Protestant Ethic and the Spirit of Capitalism*, Weber considers the nature of ascetic Protestant sects (Calvinist, Pietist, Methodist and Baptist) in Europe and America and the influence they had on social organisation. Protestants were those who attacked abuses and corruption of the priesthood of the medieval Roman church, while ascetism refers to the austerity and self-discipline which these sects advocated. Though it was Martin Luther who was the emotional instigator of the Protestant Reformation, John Calvin (1509–1564) was its intellectual leader and whose work Weber takes as the starting point of his investigation. Weber isolates the following features of Calvin's doctrine as of particular importance:

1 The notion that God does not exist for humanity, but the reverse, ie that humanity is God's agent here on Earth and that each individual has been assigned work to do for God (has been 'called' to a 'vocation') so that one must devote one's time not to one's own pleasures or desires but to the work allocated by God;
2 that the motives of God are beyond all human comprehension and influence;
3 only a small number of people have already been chosen ('elected') by God to achieve eternal grace in heaven and nothing that they do on earth will affect their future after death (the doctrine of predestination);
4 individuals stand alone before God – the clergy and religious ceremony which stand between the individual and God in Catholicism can offer him or her no support in facing God in Protestantism.

Being an interpretive sociologist, Weber stresses the psychological consequences of the Calvinist doctrine for the believer. The effect of Calvin's doctrine was to produce great insecurity, both because the individual is left alone to face God and because he or she is unsure about their place in heaven. A doctrine which produces this level of psychological unease cannot remain in its original form for long, it is simply too disturbing for believers. A subtle change began to occur in the doctrine and increased importance was given to the *faith* of the believer – the believer must now have faith in personal salvation, despite the incomprehensibility of God's will. Strong faith removed the feeling of insecurity for the believer, and proof of one's faith in one's own salvation is given by how diligently one works in one's calling and how far one denies oneself the pleasures of this world for the greater glory of God. It was only a small step from this for the believer to begin to identify these features – hard work and an ascetic way of life, not as proof of *faith* in election by God, but as proof of election *itself*. The diligent ascetic Puritan (ie member of one of the Protestant sects mentioned above) became self-righteous in his self-denial.

The economic effects of this doctrine were almost incidental as far as the Puritan was concerned. Naturally the effect of an emphasis on hard work and denial of consumption was the build-up of wealth. To the Puritan this wealth was a danger, an accidental result of spiritual ethics translated into the material world, the presence of which represented a temptation. At this point there was a further transformation of the ethic, from a concentration on *work* as an end in itself to *wealth* as an end. By now, however, the ethic of Protestantism had become divorced from Protestantism itself, having become secularised and vulgarised. This later stage of the ethic is exemplified by the writings and sayings of Benjamin Franklin (1706–1790), the American statesman and philosopher who significantly was *not* a Protestant himself. Franklin stresses, like the Puritans, that time-wasting and idleness is wrong, though he relates this wrongness to *money* rather than to God:

> "time is money . . . he that wastes idly a groat's worth of his time, loses five shillings, and might as prudently throw five shillings into the sea."(23)

The approach to money has become a moral judgment, it is morally wrong to waste money and morally right to save it (though by now the idea that it is 'in trust' for God is gone). This ethic is reflected in the organisation of commerce and social life. Every aspect of life and individual conduct are rationally orientated, ends and means are assessed and re-assessed for maximum profitability and efficiency; inefficiency is simply wrong.

In addition to his explanation of the development of the spirit of capitalism in Europe and the USA, Weber also examines the reasons for its lack of development elsewhere. Clearly, if the reasons for the non-appearance of some equivalent to the spirit of capitalism can be identified, then Weber has gone at least some way to explaining the lack of economic development of the Third World. Without a Protestant Ethic there would be no build-up of capital, without a spirit of capitalism, no disciplined and hard-working work force.

In India, he suggests that Hindu modes of thought and customs, especially the caste system which is central to that religion, had a conservative influence on the pre-capitalist social and economic system. Physical obstacles together with the spirit of the whole system made an economic and technological revolution almost impossible. However, it has proved possible for Europeans to exploit the labour of Indians:

> "it must . . . be considered extremely unlikely that the modern organisation of industrial capitalism would ever have *originated* on the basis of the caste system. A ritual law in which every change of occupation, every change in work technique, could result in ritual degradation is certainly not capable of giving birth to economic and technical revolutions from within itself, or even of facilitating the first germination of capitalism within its midst."(24)

Commentators on this part of Weber's work have noted that indigenous Indian industry *has* developed despite these difficulties, and that Indians abroad tend to be noticeably enterprising and efficient at rapidly accumulating capital while retaining their religious ideas (for example, in Burma, Malaya and in Britain). One writer, after a detailed study of the history of Bombay cotton mills, notes that "it was not difficult to create an industrial labour force in India", that despite possible commitments to rural life and the influences of religion it is comparatively easy to achieve discipline and regular work habits necessary in a modern factory(25).

A further criticism of Weber comes from Tawney who suggests that Weber has misunderstood Calvinist doctrine, or has exaggerated some parts of it at the expense of others. Tawney argues that there was not so much an emphasis on individualism in the sects of the Puritans but collectivist dictatorship, and that other Calvanists, such as Richard Baxter, prohibited living off the labour of others and hence were anti-capitalist. Weber's methodoligical device, the 'ideal type', leads him to emphasise those aspects of Puritanism which he considers to be its essential features and so he underplays other aspects of the creed.

The major issue of controversy around Weber's account is the question of cause and effect. Did the Protestant ethic *cause* the development of the spirit of capitalism and therefore, allow and promote capitalist organisation; or did an already developing capitalism create the right conditions for the Protestant Reformation to occur? Both Tawney (in *Religion and the Rise of Capitalism*) and Marx suggest that the material conditions of society, in the form of embryonic capitalism, were suitable for the formulation of the Protestant creed and account for its popularity and persistence. Marx, while admitting that 'hard word, saving and avarice' became the 'three cardinal virtues of society' (26) insists that in the final analysis consciousness and ideas are determined by social organisation and technological development. However, although Weber is sometimes portrayed as giving greatest importance to the realm of ideas (ie as subscribing to an idealist philosophy) and therefore of seeking to reject materialist determination of ideas, he explicitly rejects this position in the closing paragraph of the *Protestant Ethic and the Spirit of Capitalism*:

> "Protestant ascetism was in its turn influenced in its development and character by the totality of social conditions, especially economic."(27)

Moreover his concept of 'elective affinity' proposes that people will only elect to follow new ideas from charismatic leaders (or some selected and interpreted elements of them) if and when there is an affinity between the life and conditions of the people and the ideas proposed.

The *origin* of ideas is totally undetermined. If they are to achieve wide popularity, there must be some degree of 'fit' between their principles and the conditions in society at the time. If the fit is only partial then appropriate elements might be retained while inappropriate ones will be dropped or changed in some way (as in fact occurred to some aspects of Protestantism). Thus people *elect* to follow those ideas with which they have an *affinity*. This affinity is largely determined by the material conditions of society.

Raymond Aron(28) suggests that Weber is seeking to establish two propositions:

1 That the behaviour of men and women in various societies is explained only by understanding their ideas, attitudes, motives, much of which come from religious beliefs; but that

2 religious ideas are *one* determinant (only) of economic behaviour and therefore one of the causes of social and economic change.

His account of the Protestant ethic should not be seen simply as an argument against Marx's materialistic and deterministic themes, but as an attempt to add to it idealistic elements and multicausal explanations within the framework of an interpretive methodology. For Weber reality is too complex, the question of causation too tangled for simplistic single-cause deterministic explanations, and so he rejects the setting up of any single path of social development. For him there are no fundamental or essential driving forces that provide one particular direction for social change. Having said this, we *are* given the impression that the advance of rationalism is an inevitable (if sporadic) movement in the history of the Western World. Charismatic personalities may appear and temporarily stop this phenomenon, but when they die rationalisation sets in once again:

> "'The fate of our times', writes Weber, 'is characterised by rationalisation of intellectualisation and, above all, by the "disenchantment of the world", which means that "there are no mysterious incalculable forces that come into play, but rather that one can, in principle, master all things by calculation ... One need no longer have recourse to magical means in order to master or implore the spirits ... Technical means and calculations perform this service."'"(29)

David McLelland and 'The Achieving Society'

If Weber is right in that 'correct' attitudes can produce social change towards industrialisation, at least in conjunction with other necessary conditions, then clearly this has implications for the social policy of any governing group that wishes to stimulate the modernisation of their society. Attitudes and ideas which prevent the desired changes should be discouraged while functional equivalents of the Protestant ethic should be nurtured.

The psychologist David McLelland has built on Weber's premises and applied them to the developing societies of today by evolving techniques for the measurement of development-inducing attitudes and suggesting strategies for their encouragement. McLelland suggests that the most conducive psychological characteristic for social and economic development is ambitiousness, or what he calls the 'need for achievement' ('nAch.') By evolving tests which enabled the nAch present in the psychological make-up of an individual or in the culture of a society to be measured and expressed in a mathematical form (the nAch quotient) it was possible for McLelland to compare its presence in different societies at the present time and the same society over time with some interesting results. The tests were applied to written material such as folk tales and the literature of the society in question to estimate the degree to which nAch was encouraged in the socialisation of new generations. The resulting data indicated a correlation between the nAch quotient and the economic activity of the society concerned over time. There was a positive correlation between the nAch measured in popular literature in England between 1500 and 1800 and the quantities of coal shipped to London (a measure of economic activity). The two indices did not rise and fall simultaneously, there was a 'lead-in' time of 30–50 years between the first and the second during which the orientations expressed in the literature became propagated throughout society. Similarly the nAch measured in medieval Spain correlated with tonnage shipped to the New World. In the contemporary world, correlations were identified between nAch quotients and both the gross national products and electric power usage in different societies.

Relating his work to Weber's, McLelland suggests that the Protestant ethic led to an increased degree of nAch and thus to development. Third World countries are lacking in sufficient levels of nAch at the moment, and therefore what is needed is the correct attitudes to be taught to children and businessmen. Parents should expect a "self-reliant mastery" from their children by about the age of 8 years, ie they should be competitive, independent and active by then. Schools, textbook writers and authors of children's books clearly have an important role to play, as do leaders of all aspects of social life. Businessmen and women should be indoctrinated with nAch, women being particularly important because of their increasing role in the economy and the fact that they are central to the socialisation of the young. Courses to do this for business people were set up in India and it was found that those who had attended them invested twice as much money and created twice as many jobs as a comparable group who had not undergone such training(30).

McClelland's theory is fraught with a considerable number of problems. Perhaps it is true that the correct psychological attitude is a *necessary* factor which must be present if a society is to develop, but it certainly is not sufficient. Other necessary factors include:

material resources (raw materials and fuel);
the necessary skills and the educational resources to transmit them;
technological expertise in a wide range of areas;
sufficient markets for the sale of goods;
a favourable political system.

He also ignores the *special* problems faced by late developers discussed on pages 11–12. If, as the structuralists suggest, the Third World is actively underdeveloped by the First and Second then the attitudes which are found in underdeveloped countries are going to have little effect on an economy which is consistently suffering exploitation from abroad.

Modernisation theory

Modernisation theory is a name given to the approaches that stress that development is an interactive process involving all elements of society; not only the economy but religion, family structures and the political system for example. These elements are interlinked in a social system and any particular combination of them can either help or hinder future development. Modernisation is linked to convergence theory in that the former claims that 'to develop' necessarily means to achieve a similar socio-cultural pattern to that of societies which are already developed, particularly capitalist ones. 'Development' and 'becoming like the Western countries' amount to the same thing for modernisation theorists. Examples of writers in this category are N J Smelser, S N Eisenstadt, E E Hagen and T Parsons(31). Both idealists like McLelland and materialists like Rostow are often cited as modernisation theorists. They differ in their view of the main driving force of social change but they agree on the fact that particular types of social systems demand particular sets of mutually compatible characteristics and that the end product of development is 'modern' society, which is basically in the American mould. They agree on the fact that the First World can and should help the Third to develop. Let us now look at Gunnar Myrdal. He is a theorist who straddles the materialist/idealist divide.

In *Economic Theory and Underdeveloped Regions*(32) Myrdal makes a comparison between the position of the underdeveloped regions of the world and what he calls the 'Negro problem' of the United States. The continued lack of development of the Negro people and their subordinate position in the USA is the product of two causal factors: white prejudice and the 'low plane of living' of the Negro population:

> "poverty, ignorance, superstition, slum dwellings, health deficiencies, dirty appearance, bad odour, disorderly conduct, unstable family relations and criminality."(33)

White prejudice and low Negro standards are a cause of each other; the latter reinforcing the former and the former resulting in discriminatory practices which mean that the Negro population cannot escape their poverty. But:

> "If either of the two factors should change, this is bound to bring a change in the other factor, too, and start a cumulative process of mutual interaction in which the change in one factor would continuously be supported by the reaction of the other factor and so on in a circular way."(34)

Thus a vicious circle of poverty (the poverty trap) can be transformed into a benign circle by simply changing one or more of its components. Some changes will have rapid effects (for example a rise in levels of employment) while others (like improvements in health or education standards) will take longer to make their effects felt. Myrdal argues that it is useless to look for a basic factor, one more important than the rest, as all are mutually dependent. In this way he avoids both the materialist and idealist positions; the economic and cultural factors interlock.

Myrdal argues that the best way to achieve development in the Third World is to change as many factors as possible to attain a cumulative effect. Primitive religions in underdeveloped regions must be abolished because they sanction traditional mores and, being irrational, tend to hinder the adoption of rational economic methods. Health levels must be raised, schools provided, democratic institutions set up and defended(35), the nuclear family encouraged, capital invested, transportation and communication systems built and population levels reduced. Each will play its part in raising the level of society from traditional and backward to modern and advanced. Fortunately we can rely on the 'spread effects' to help in this process, ie the expansionary momentum of these patterns from centres of modernity (both domestic and international) to the regions. Aid and Third World projects can help tremendously in expanding the social and economic influence of the centres of modernity in impoverished countries. Myrdal's advice to the Third World, as to the American Negro is "become more like us in order to become more like us".

The roots of modernisation theories like Myrdal's lie in two sources; structural-functional theory and the practical observations of Western organisations and aid agencies who advise the newly independent countries on strategies for development. We will refer to this second strand as 'liberal theory' as it stresses the desire for real independence and equality for the Third World. From structural functionalist theory, such as that of Parsons, modernisation receives the concept of society as a system (that is a whole comprising interdependent parts) in which any single part must be understood by reference to its function in the whole structure. It also considers that the parts mutually support each other in the maintenance of the whole system. From this standpoint societies can be said to form discrete types, each with its own set of mutually compatible institutions. Parsons sees societies as undergoing an evolutionary process from Primitive (eg Australian aboriginal society) to Archaic (Ancient Egypt) to Historic (China, India) to Seedbed (Ancient Greece) to Modern (the USA.) The important changes in this progression are changes in the pattern variables from the traditional to the modern choice (see page 138), the increasing differentiation of institutions, the increasing adaptability of society to change, the inclusion of previously excluded groups into full participation in the social system and the spread of one set of values across the whole social system. Certain 'evolutionary universals' have to be attained before progression from one stage to the next can be achieved. These include written language, money, administrative bureaucracy and a politically independent class of literati, though each of these can be spread from higher to lower societies by the process of diffusion.

The second source of the modernisation approach, liberal theory, tends to adopt an approach which compares the rich countries with the poor and subtracts the differences. These then become defined as the pre-requisites for development. Clearly by this method one comes up with a list of *indicators* of development which come to be seen as the *conditions* for development. Ankie Hoogvelt comments:

> "This monumental theoretical error – which to be fair was not always commited by the [modernisation] theorists themselves – has in fact been made and continues to be made by modernisation policy makers such as those employed by Western governments, UN organisations, the World Bank and so forth."(36)

Development policies are then based on fostering the appearance of these factors (free enterprise, the multi-party system, urbanisation, literacy) in the Third World countries concerned. Aid is directed towards changing the socio-economic structure; educational institutions are built, political systems are constructed and defended, programmes of population control are instituted, food aid is given in return for work or entrepreneurial activity (37) and aid is withheld from unsuitable or unwilling recipients.

Hoogvelt argues that the actual outcomes of these liberal diffusionary policies have generally been more harmful than beneficial:

> "... crash programmes both of industrialisation and of agricultural modernisation set adrift a rural proletariat which flocked to towns causing over-urbanisation rather than urbanisation."(38)

Much money went into formal education for people who would then be unemployed (especially wasteful at the level of higher education). Undemocratic regimes were de-stabilised despite the fact that they were, perhaps, the best hope for escape from poverty, though not for modernisation (ie Westernisation). In giving support to such schemes modernisation theory has lent them academic legitimacy, but criticisms of it go much deeper than that. Writers like Hoogvelt and Andre Gunder Frank see modernisation theory as *ideological*, supporting attempts to camouflage imperialism under the name of modernisation:

> "The western capitalist system for its very own survival needed and still needs to *expand*. It had and has to spread its tentacles further and further across the globe, but the success of its expansion depends on its ability to reproduce, wherever it reaches out to, the structural conditions under which it operates at home. Thus Westernisation becomes a tool of imperialism."(39)

As we will see in the next section, those writers who stress the importance of the international structure in creating poverty and dependence in the

South see the penetration of the capitalist North into the countries of the South as the root cause of their economic and social problems. Modernisation theory and liberal policy combine to disguise exploitation as philanthropy.

The structural-functional heritage of modernisation theory has also been the target of considerable criticism by sociologists of development. Hoogvelt points out that structural functionalism presents a full picture of how societies cohere, elaborating as it does on the functionality of the parts for the maintenance of the whole, but gives no explanation of social change:

> "How very odd! How is it that a theory that has nothing to say about social change has become the dominant intellectual force behind theories of social change?"(40)

W E Moore in *Social Change*(41) is also aware of this apparent paradox. He suggests that both structural-functionalism and modernisation theory imply that traditional societies and modern societies are static entities. Only the intervening 'transitional' stage is dynamic. All the writers in these schools have this three – fold model at the heart of their writing and it gives the impression that modern societies, like the USA are at the final stage of development. They are the 'complete' society, impossible to improve on and not subject to the kind of internal tensions which may result in change in lower social forms. Certainly Parsons' scheme is based on this tripartite division: his five-fold scheme referred to earlier is a sub-classification of three basic types; Primitive, Intermediate and Modern.

Ernest Gellner in *Thought and Change*(42) highlights the fact that structural-functionalists and modernisation theorists share the view that the passage of time and social change necessarily bring improvement. Time for them is no longer ethically neutral; the past is bad and the future is good. Progress will bring what he calls "a kind of secularised salvation", the heaven on earth being, of course, the American social and economic system for those who are at present the world's poor. This highly ethnocentric view is also reflected in the attitudes of structural-functionalism and modernisation theorists towards 'non-modern' societies. These are simply grouped together under the title Traditional or Primitive when the only thing they have in common is the fact that they are not like Western societies.

Later in this chapter (page 36) we will examine and criticise in more detail modernisation theory's view that there is a necessary convergence of societies towards the Western model. First, let us review approaches to the study of development which are highly critical of the three we have so far covered. These critical writers may be grouped under the general name of the Structural Perspective.

The structural perspective on development and underdevelopment

The determinist, voluntarist and modernisation approaches to the study of social change have in common a focus on the internal characteristics of underdeveloped societies. In each case their discussion of the role of the developed world is simply in terms of its ability to give poor countries a 'push' in the right direction. Marx sees European capitalism as laying the infrastructural foundation for India's (autonomous) development. McLelland sees the need for the West to imbue the South with the right attitude of mind and then they can get on with their own development. Myrdal says we should tinker with the socio-economic characteristics of the Third World countries to initiate a 'benign circle' which will send them on their way.

The structural perspective takes a wider view. It examines the nature of the world-wide economic structure, the relationships between the North and the South. From this perspective it is no accident that part of the world is very rich and part very poor. The wealth of some is gained by the exploitation of others. While there are obvious similarities between this and Marx's view of exploitative relationships *inside* societies, many of these writers would not call themselves Marxists or even Neo-Marxists. Frank, for example, has denied being a Marxist because he sees exploitation of the Third World as being founded on market relations, not the relations of production (property relations). Illich is perhaps best described as an anarchist. In this section we will examine the work of a variety of structuralist writers.

Paul Baran

Baran notes that the catching up by the Third World countries to the First World ones which Marx predicted has not taken place. If anything the gap between the two has become wider. Baran's writing attempts to re-work that of Marx to account for the failure of this prediction. It also tries to reply to bourgeois theories of development, particularly modernisation theory, with an up to date conflict perspective on development issues.

In many ways Marx is out of date, especially due to the growth in power and importance of multinational corporations, the increasing importance of nationalistic rather than class movements in many Third World countries and the fact that Marx's scheme is clearly inapplicable to the mode of production of many of those countries. In most Third World countries the urban proletariat tend to form a minority and are relatively privileged. There tends to be no conflict between the landed class and the bourgeoisie so there seems to be little prospect of either bourgeois or proletarian revolution. The only potentially revolutionary group in these countries is the dispossessed, the peasantry, those in poverty (often living on the edges of large cities) for whom society has nothing to offer. For Marx these groups had no potential for social change whatever, he dismissed them as the 'lumpenproletariat' – a group with as much initiative and potential for united action as a sack of potatoes.

How, then, does the structuralist analysis deal with these modern features? Paul Baran argues that the Third World represented, in the early stages of capitalist development, a means of increasing the economic surplus (the difference between actual current output and the actual current consumption of a society) at the disposal of European countries. This economic surplus was useful in that it was concentrated in large amounts and therefore provided capital for investment in the further industrialisation of Europe.

Let us look at a specific example. In the period up to the 18th century, India had a relatively advanced economic substructure. It manufactured and exported muslins and other fabrics. Its cultural tradition was strong and the problem of over-population experienced today had not yet arrived. This problem is largely of the West's making. Before Western intervention in India the birth rate was particularly high, mainly because of the tradition of universal marriage and marriage before puberty for girls. Early marriage was encouraged by ancient Hindu scriptures and was copied by other religious communities. Even today there are an estimated 5 million children married despite its theoretical illegality(43). However, this fact was counterbalanced by a high death rate. The industrialising countries were able to lower their own death rates and, after a period of rapid population increase, also experienced a lowering of their birth rates. Having achieved a low death rate through knowledge and techniques of controlling disease they applied the same methods to India and other countries. This brought a sudden decline in *their* death rates but with no corresponding decline, either then or later, in the birth rate. This fact alone was enough to prevent an increase in the general standard of living in India and inhibit industrialisation:

> "If capital output is 3, ie 3 units of capital are required to produce one unit of income, then with a population growth of 2% per annum, 6% of the net income has yearly to be invested only to maintain the same level of living for the increased population. With a population growth of 3% per annum, 9% of national income has to be invested to reach the same result. The higher the rate of population growth, the harder becomes the task of breaking through a Malthusian trap. A vicious spiral is therefore set into operation. Because of a high rate of population growth 'industrialisation' is difficult to obtain. Because there is no 'industrialisation' the birth rate and the rate of population growth remains high."(44)

However Baran's account is concerned with the direct extraction of the Indian economic surplus by the European countries rather than its reduction through population growth. For him the former is the more important and direct cause of the lack of development and the destruction of India's once rich culture. Baran notes that between £500 million and £1000 million worth of treasure was taken by the British from India between 1757 and 1815. In the early decades of this century Britain appropriated something over 10% of India's gross national income, a figure which probably represented its total economic surplus. This process was effected by the collusion between British companies and the government here. Quoting an Indian author(45), Baran writes:

> "It is, unfortunately, a fact, that in many ways the sources of national wealth in India have been narrowed under the British rule (for example) . . . the East India Company and the British Parliament . . . discouraged the Indian manufacturers in the early years of British rule in order to encourage the rising manufacturers of England . . . to make India subservient to the industries of Great Britain, and to make the Indian people grow raw produce only, in order to supply material for the looms and manufactories of Great Britain . . . orders were sent out to force Indian artisans to work in the company's factories; commercial residents were legally vested with extensive powers over villages and communities of Indian weavers; prohibitive tariffs excluded Indian silk and cotton goods from England; English goods were admitted to India free of duty."

Baran speculates that had the wealth of India not been taken, its industry not been strangled by decree and by duties, its levels and geographical disposition of population not been disrupted by medical and commercial policies, it might have become a better and richer society, though a bourgeois revolution (either peaceful or violent) would have been necessary for that country too. In the most recent stage of capitalism (monopoly capitalism), the direction of flow of capital has changed. Here the problem for the First World is not capital accumulation but the search for profitable investment outlets and the increasingly avaricious search for markets.

Andre Gunder Frank

The exposition given by Frank, of the situation under monopoly capitalism is clearer, more developed and more radical than that of Baran. Frank notes that historians and others (including Marx) tend to concentrate their studies on the developed parts of the world. They take their concepts from these areas and only develop theories around these areas. It is noted by such theorists that many under-developed countries tend to have the urban part in the Western mould, and another, geographically much larger part, in the under-developed or pre-modern mould. The cause of this *dualism* is assumed to be that the trade and contact with the West has caused change in some parts, whereas the other parts have not been touched by Western influence and have remained unchanged. This view is challenged by Frank. He maintains that the under-developed part is as much the product of Western presence as the developed part. Those areas that are poorest today were precisely the ones most exploited by the West in the past. He argues that after the direct expropriation of wealth by the 'cosmopolitan' countries from their 'satellites' (as he terms the developed and under-developed countries and areas) described by Baran, an international network of exploitation was set up which would maintain the economic dominance of the cosmopolitan nation. The indigenous populations of conquered territories were put in a situation of economic dependency, producing raw materials for and consuming the finished products of the cosmopolitan countries while at the same time being kept in poverty, slavery or semi-slavery. This system of exploitation was, and still is according to Frank, organised in a tier system with local metropolises exploiting their satellites and themselves being exploited by metropolises in the developed world:

> "The metropolis-satellite contradiction exists not only between the world capitalist metropolis (eg the USA) and peripheral satellite countries (eg Mexico, El Salvador): it is also found within these countries among their regions (eg Sao Paolo as a metropolis for surrounding satellites, London as a central metropolis for the country, Milan and Turin as metropolises for Southern Italy) . . . (it) runs through the entire world capitalist system in chain-like fashion from its uppermost metropolitan world centre through each of the various national, regional and local enterprise centres."(46)

Each connection between a satellite and a metropolis is a *channel* through which the centre appropriates part of the economic surplus of the satellites.

Clearly, in Frank's model of systematic exploitation there is no hope of autonomous general social and economic development for the poor regions of the world. On the contrary there is an active process of under-development, where the First World is a parasite on the Third. The only prospect of development is through an act of withdrawal from the metropolitan/satellite relationship, and indeed, Frank points to the success of those countries which did just that; the independence achieved by the USA (post-War of Independence), Japan (post-Imperial Restoration) and the USSR (post-1917). During the World Wars, according to Frank, local industries arose in under-developed areas when industrialised countries were unable to supply manufactured goods. Even newly independent states find it difficult to achieve this withdrawal because they are already dependent on foreign companies for much of their income and the local capitalist class are too weak to compete with the multinationals in the hope of replacing them. Independent states are forced to allow foreign companies to operate within their borders but not keep their profits there. However they can sometimes exact concessions in the form of limited local reinvestment. This is usually designed to create more jobs in new foreign built and owned factories, a situation which suits the multinationals very well. They get lower cost labour than is possible at home and the local government has a stake in making sure that investment remains attractive by keeping the general level of wages low and ensuring that there are no industrial relations problems. To hope that the presence of these firms, (combined with the diffusion of the goods and techniques of the developed world) will result in the development of the Third World through exposure alone is naïve in the extreme according to Frank. Diffusion of this nature has been occurring for 400 years in Latin America with no real indigenous development – such development has been actively destroyed by North American interests, while native merchants and middlemen have been orientated to *foreign* companies and investment.

Frank's analysis of this process of underdevelopment is given support by two economists, R J Barnet and R E Müller in their well documented study of the multinational corporations' activities throughout the world. The managers of corporations such as ITT and General Motors argue that their companies have a beneficial effect on the Third World in that they spread technology and capital which can be utilised for the indigenous industrialisation of presently under-developed countries. This is an argument which is strikingly similar to that of Marx, even though it comes from the captains of industry of whom he was so critical.

Barnet and Müller point out that multinational corporations predominantly use local capital for operations rather than importing it from America or Europe. Indeed, multinational corporations find it much easier to obtain capital from banks and individual investors in the Third World than local entrepreneurs because the multinationals represent a safer and more profitable investment(47).

Despite the local origins of the investment, the profits are largely repatriated by the multinational, ie sent back to its home country(48). This may be done in an overt way or, especially if there are legal limits on the extent of profit repatriation, through the technique of transfer pricing. Here, the subsidiaries of a multinational deal with each other across national boundaries and are able to fix the price of goods that they buy and sell in such a way as to transfer capital to the home country. Thus the exports which the subsidiary in the Third World sends to, say, the USA are undervalued while its imports from there are overvalued. Not only does this have the effect of sending money to the home country, but it cuts the profits made by the Third World subsidiary. This avoids taxes, and increases apparent local investment, which is good for the image of the company. For the Third World country concerned, the effects include the loss of valuable foreign currency earnings, and income from taxation as well as highly priced imports. The presence of the multinational corporation has deprived local businessmen of investment capital and potential profits as well as stealing the local market from them. Profit making and reinvestment in the country to form the basis of nationwide industrialisation is prevented and funds are instead channelled to the already-rich countries. The authors echo Frank when they write:

> "The unfortunate role of the global corporation in maintaining and increasing poverty around the world is due primarily to the dismal reality that global corporations and poor countries have different, indeed conflicting, interests, priorities and needs."(49)

Theresa Hayter

Frank's thesis has many attractions, primarily in its forceful, if often overstated, analysis of the non-development of a large part of the world. This perspective has found many supporters who have contributed by clarifying and expanding various points. One such contribution is Theresa Hayter's study of the aid relationship(50), originally commissioned by the World Bank but disowned by them when they became aware of her criticisms of their liberal perspective and policies. Aid has many critics (those who argue that it is misspent, inefficient, creates dualism, is unnecessary or is needed more by us) but in general it is viewed as a form of charity, designed to help the Third World countries to develop through the provision of sufficient capital, combined with advanced techniques and up-to-the-minute knowledge. This development is seen as an indirect but long-term solution to the problems of poverty, disease and over-population which exist in the Third World. Modernisation theorists see it as a vital tool in the North's efforts to help the South.

If this view of aid were correct it would clearly contradict the Frankian thesis of the active under-development of the Third World. Hayter, however, suggests that aid is one of the techniques by which the North exploits the South and retains its dominant position. She points out that most aid comes from official government or multilateral institutions and is not usually a gift but a loan with lower than commercial interest rates attached. Only a fraction of aid comes from independent voluntary organisations such as Oxfam or Christian Aid. Aid from governmental institutions usually comes with some form of string attached. For example, it is given on condition that goods and services are bought from the provider, it is not available to those countries which nationalise foreign owned companies without generous and speedy compensation, aid is only available for desirable political regimes and even there is used as a form of leverage to influence the policies of developing countries. Aid is often given so that governing elites will tolerate the outflow of profits and interest on past debts, and it supports those elites who would otherwise be overthrown due to popular reaction to corruption and exploitation.

According to Hayter, aid has the function of a bribe to those in power to allow the continued exploitation of their country by foreign interests. At the same time it increases the dependence of that country and bolsters the capitalist outposts against communism. It is not particularly efficient in fulfilling these functions, which is why the net flow of aid has recently declined (foreign aid is now lower than in 1975 and more than two-thirds of it goes to richer countries anyway, eg USA to Egypt and Israel).

These views are not confined to radicals: American presidents of both parties have recognised the functionality of aid. Kennedy in 1961 said "Foreign aid is a method by which the US maintains a position of influence and control around the world". In 1968 Nixon said "Let us remember that the main purpose of American aid is not to help other nations but to help ourselves."(51)

In a more recent book(52) Hayter criticises some of the early theories of development we have already reviewed. After examining a number of examples of the kind of idealist approach exemplified by McLelland which blame lack of development in the Third World on lack of drive and initiative among its inhabitants she comments that:

> "... hard-headed, coldly calculating, ruthlessly profit-maximising people are to be found in all parts of the world. The materials with which they work, and the social and economic framework in which they operate differ."(53)

She then criticises the lack of capital theory which we have already referred to, concurring with Barnet and Müller's contention that foreign businesses raise most of their capital in the Third World and export it in the form of profits to the First World. She maintains it is not the capital which is lacking in the Third World but access to and control over it.

Her most detailed comments are reserved for those theories which blame lack of development on the Third World's population problem. This is an explanation often given by many people in Britain. This theory suggests that the demographic balance that used to exist in the Third World has been upset by the introduction of Western medical science. Now the death rate has been cut while the birth rate remains at its previous high level. The inevitable consequence is very rapid population expansion which means that capital cannot be accumulated, assets are thinly spread among a high population simply to keep them alive. Famine and poverty can only be eradicated and development initiated when population levels stabilise. Such theories, Hayter writes, have led to some drastic measures, such as the use of the dangerous contraceptive drug Depo Provera (discussed on page 188) as well as the highly contentious sterilisation programme introduced in India.

Hayter responds to the population problem theory by pointing out that despite increasing population levels in the Third World *overall* food supplies have been increasing faster, both within many Third World countries and in the world as a whole. She further suggests that it may be the population of the developed countries that needs controlling. According to some estimates, they and their animals consume over half of the available world supply of food grains, much of which is used to feed animals. This is a highly wasteful way of producing proteins for humans to eat. She quotes from Rene Dumont on this point:

> "The rich white man, with his overconsumption of meat and his lack of generosity for poor people, behaves like a veritable cannibal – an indirect cannibal. By consuming meat, which wastes the grain that could have saved them, last year we ate the children of the Sahel, Ethiopia and Bangladesh. And we continue to eat them this year with undiminished appetite."(54)

While not denying that rapid population increase does create its own problems in particular places at particular times, Hayter sees this as part of a wider problem. Allowed to develop, the Third World's demographic characteristics would stabilise through a drop in the birth rate as occurred in the West. Large families would no longer be necessary to the farmers who see them as social insurance in a society where no welfare state exists. The structural relationship between the poor and the rich nations of the world prevents such development and keeps the Third World in its misery. Like other exponents of this view, Hayter sees European development as founded on the imperialist, then colonialist and finally neo-colonialist plunder and loot of India, Africa and South America. Countries in these areas find their economies distorted towards the production of just a few agricultural products or raw materials instead of the diversified economies which would have kept the population fed but would have posed a threat of competition to the First World if allowed to expand. The products that are produced today are sold at highly unfavourable rates:

> "In 1960 the earnings from 25 tonnes of natural rubber exports from Sri Lanka would buy 6 tractors; by 1975 they would buy only two. And in their desperate search for foreign exchange, underdeveloped countries produce more and more, thus setting up a vicious circle of overproduction and declining prices."(55)

Furthermore, speculation on the commodity markets in London and New York leads to fluctuations in the price of the Third World's products which are largely outside their control. Hayter says that in the mid 1970's the price paid for sugar dropped from 64 cents a pound to 6 cents a pound in 18 months, while similar changes occurred to the price of sisal, cocoa and copper. Such price changes have drastic effects on economies which depend on only one or two commodities. This dependence is shown by the Brandt report's estimate that in the early 1970's Zambia got 94% of its export earnings from copper, Mauritius 90% from sugar, and Cuba 84%, while Gambia got 85% from groundnuts and related products.

The dedication of so much land to cash crops means famine for the landless with no money to buy food:

> "Ho Kwan Ping in the Far Eastern Review describes how the commercial exploitation of pineapples, bananas and other tropical fruits for export has displaced local farmers, giving employment for some of the new landless at $1 or $2 a day and in grim conditions, and how Thai exports of seafood doubled in recent years, while production has remained stable, so that local consumption of fish has declined."(56)

Given this context of exploitative international structures, attempts to solve the population/food problem are doomed to failure according to Hayter. The so called Green Revolution, which sought to solve the problem through the introduction of new high-yielding varieties of seeds and high technology methods of agricultural production in the Third World benefitted only the rich. Those with the capital to buy the seeds, fertiliser, pesticides and tractors found it immensely helpful in increasing their production, destined for export mainly. For the landless or the peasant farmer it may as well not have happened.

In *The Creation of World Poverty* Hayter goes on to catalogue other elements of the rich countries' exploitation of the poor. She documents a history of low wages paid by multinational companies to Third World workers. Capital is transferred to the USA and the UK, possible sources of competition are crushed, markets are monopolised. Meanwhile repressive political systems which permit this to go on are propped up by the Western powers. For Hayter the solution to these problems is resistence and, eventually, socialist revolution. She quotes China's escape from famine, overpopulation, poverty and backwardness (the latter being in fact only a recent characteristic – China's pre-imperialist culture was immensely rich) as proof of her point. We need, she writes:

> "societies in which what is produced is determined by need, rather than by the profit calculations of individual business people."(57)

Ivan Illich

Illich, perhaps most famous as a 'deschooler', is also an outspoken critic of the dualism which the diffusion of Western culture propogates. He argues(58) that the North imposes the worst features of its own culture on the South. Its harmful and unnecessary technology creates traffic jams, imposes too-complicated and quickly obsolescent machinery, creates pollution and at the same time exaggerates class inequalities by creating over-qualified professionals who are orientated only to cater for the rich while ignoring the poor. In medicine, for example, specialist doctors are trained to attend the rich rather than be paramedics for the poor. According to a recent World Health Organization study, India has lost

$144 million through training doctors who emigrated after qualifying. India itself can afford to employ less than one-third of the doctors it trains. In education, money is devoted to research and producing Ph.D's rather than providing elementary education for all. Similarly, luxury Western-style goods are imported or produced at home which are totally unsuitable for an under-developed country – vehicles need to be cheap, sturdy, easily repairable and all-purpose rather than the expensive ones of short life designed for well-maintained roads. Thus while:

> "Traffic jams develop in Sao Paulo . . . almost a million North Eastern Brazilians flee the drought by walking 500 miles".(59)

For Illich under-development is not just the social and economic condition suffered by those sections of the South who are disadvantaged, it is also a state of mind which:

> "occurs when mass media are converted to the demand for new brands of packaged solutions which are forever beyond the reach of the majority. Under-development in this sense is rising rapidly even in countries where the supply of classrooms, calories, cars and clinics is also rising."(60)

Needs are translated into the demand for manufactured products, ones designed for a more affluent culture, for example:

> "the translation of thirst into the need for a Coke. This kind of reification occurs in the manipulation of primary human needs by vast bureaucratic organisations which have succeeded in dominating the imagination of potential consumers."(61)

For Illich, under-development is the 'Coca-colonisation' of the mind, a form of colonisation which applies not only to goods but also services; the demand for health becomes the desire for hospitals and education for schooling. What is necessary is a profound revolution of existing medical, educational, production and political institutions to replace the ill-fitting and counter-productive ones of the developed world with ones which respond to the basic needs of the under-developed world. Only in this way could each *individual* 'develop' at the same time as the society as a whole. To do this it would be necessary to break what Paolo Freire calls "the culture of silence"(62), wherein the satellite society receives from the metropolis society a pre-processed version of reality which is mainly transmitted by the education system. Freire wonders how illiteracy in the Third World can be eradicated without at the same time inflicting upon its population the ideological imperialism of the developed world, which effectively preserves the present system.

Illich and Freire's position on these matters is supported by the work of the two economists Barnet and Müller quoted above. They counter the claims made by managers of multinational corporations by making the following points:

1. The technology that is exported to the Third World is designed for profit maximisation and not to fulfil the needs of the country to which it is going. It requires technicians, spare parts and expensive fuel, non of which can be afforded by Third World countries.
2. The technology that was exported was often out of date and therefore did not allow the Third World country to compete on equal terms with the First World, whose technology was many years in advance.
There are interesting similarities here to Gans' theory of the functions of poverty within nations, one of which is to provide a market for outmoded or secondhand items not wanted by the rest of society.
3. The importation of technology to the Third World is actually of benefit to the First and to the multinational corporations. This is because it is usually overpriced, thanks to the practice of transfer pricing, and the fact that it is usually imported under a contract which specifies that it shall not be used to create exports which would compete with the multinationals.

Barnet and Müller also provide evidence which supports Illich's point about the 'Coca-colonisation' of the Third World. Advertising by the multinational corporations encourages the poor to spend what little money they have on their artificially created psychological needs such as radios and lipstick, rather than on their physical ones, such as food. They argue that the self esteem of, for example, the Latin American peasant, has come to depend on what he or she buys rather than being judged by the criteria which were part of the national culture. Dietary habits have also changed. Peasants prefer imitation milk, sweets and white bread to the more nutritious locally produced fresh foods.

The liberal reply to structural theory

Radical views of the relationship between the rich and poor countries of the world are rejected by those who adopt a liberal approach to development studies. The liberal approach, as we have seen, believes that the Third World is in its current condition because it has been slower than the First and Second Worlds to industrialise. The process of industrialisation is underway and is being helped by the efforts of the rich countries. Aid and the activities of the multinational corporations have a beneficial effect on Third World countries. All countries and companies have a shared interest in the rapid development of the Third World, not only to eliminate poverty and suffering but because the future stability of the international system depends on it.

John Goldthorpe, accepting this view, rejects Baran's analysis of the colonial relationship and argues that the presence of the colonial powers was often of benefit to countries, giving employment and making land use more efficient(63). He points to the fact that Britain, Holland and Belgium did not prosper noticeably more than Sweden, Norway and Denmark, and that Germany, deprived of colonies after the First World War, seems to be doing well, as does Japan, which industrialised after losing an empire. Similarly, countries which escaped long periods of colonisation such as Afghanistan and Ethiopia have fared no better than colonised countries:

> "There seems" . . . he suggests "no warrant whatever for the assertion that the prosperity of the present day industrial societies is founded on colonial exploitation, and on the contrary industrial nations have been better off without colonies than with them."(64)

The recent Brandt report on International Development Issues which reported its findings in 1980 also takes a liberal perspective on the current international situation:

> "In this Report we stick to the thesis that there *are* growing mutual interests (between North and South). These require a change in the character of cooperation. We are becoming more aware that a quickened pace of development in the South also serves the people in the North. The mutuality of interests can be spelled out clearly in the areas of energy, commodities and trade, food and agriculture, monetary solutions and inflation control . . ."(65)

The report goes on to argue that the multinational corporations have aided the development of the Third World in the past through the spread of technology and capital and, if kept under sufficient control, will continue in this work. All that is needed is legislation to make the behaviour of these corporations more ethical, changes in the system of taxation of profits to the advantage of the Third World and the setting up of a framework for negotiations on how the poor countries can benefit more than they do at present from the activities of the multinationals. Interestingly, in their final chapter the authors of the report point out that:

> "The industrial capacity of the North is under-used, causing unemployment unprecedented in recent years, while the South is in urgent need of goods that the North could produce. Rapid inflation, erratic exchange rates, and unpredictable interventions by governments are seriously disrupting the trade and investment on which an immediate return to world prosperity depends."(66)

In proposing the reallocation of the financial resources of the world in favour of the Third World, the authors of the Brandt report are putting forward a solution to a problem identified by Marx at the national level in the 19th century; namely the overproduction of goods. As the means of production of capitalism develop, Marx argued, it becomes possible to produce more and more. The only problem is that there are fewer and fewer people with any money to afford all these goods because of the unemployment caused by the very technology which produces them. Thus cyclical crises occur in the national economy as some firms, unable to sell their produce, go out of business and create more unemployment. At least up to a few years ago it had seemed that this problem had been solved, that national governments had learned the "tricks of the trade", as Rostow puts it. The Brandt report shows that even if this problem *has* been solved on the national level, it still exists on the international plane. The solution is international cooperation, legislation in favour of redistribution of assets to the South, increased aid to the South with the eventual aim of enabling them to stand on their own feet financially, and an improved and increased system of lending to the South by the North.

All this is far removed from the structuralist perspective. From the liberal point of view the structuralists have misunderstood the role of international aid, of the multinational corporations and the developed world as a whole towards the Third World. Far from creating poverty, disease, over-population and one-sided economies, the First and Second Worlds have been material in bringing about what little progress there has been, and need to put more effort into this in the future if the interests of all are going to be served. Liberals believe that the world's rich and poor nations have common, not conflicting interests and the rapid development of the latter will be to the benefit of both.

The convergence debate

Evolutionism, like that of Rostow, Parsons or Marx, suggests that all societies follow the same path of progression from their earliest form to their final one. Thus all societies start with the primitive version of communism (Marx) or Traditional Society (Parsons and Rostow), and all move through the same stages of development to communism proper or the Age of High Mass Consumption or modern society. Convergence theory is more limited in its claims as it allows the possibility of different paths of cultural, political and economic change in early social history. It argues that once any society undergoes an industrial revolution it must then move towards a pattern common to all industrial societies.

This convergence is brought about by the necessities which industrialism imposes on the cultural and political system. In addition to this economic determinism, there is usually found in convergence theories the notion that the features of industrial society are diffused around the world in an undetermined way. The material products of industrial society carry with them part of the culture of the country of their origin and help to spread it. Furthermore, the attractions of industrial culture lead many countries to seek to copy it in a deliberate and conscious way.

Perhaps the clearest example of a theory of convergence is that put forward by Clark Kerr et al in *Industrialism and Industrial Man*(67).

Despite qualifications, the thesis is presented in a very strong form. It argues that the following factors are the main causes and consequences of convergence:

1 *Cause* A complex industrial system based on high technology. High levels of investment are necessary to purchase and modernise plant.
Effect There must be a large scale industrial workforce which is highly disciplined and has high levels of skill and competence. White collar jobs replace blue collar ones so that the industrial structure changes from a pyramid to a light-bulb shape.
2 *Cause* Rapidly changing technology, quick growth of new industries, the need for new investment and the selection of the right people for jobs.
Effect There is a high level of geographic and social mobility. The extended family declines because it "tends to dilute individual incentives to save and invest" (p 94). The importance of ascriptive criteria such as race and sex in placing people in the stratification system declines because talent would be lost. The individual's aptitudes and level of achievement become the only criteria for placement.
3 *Cause* Complexity of tasks in industrial society. The importance of numeracy, literacy and high skill of knowledge levels.
Effect There is a high level of educational provision. This is mainly vocational but provides adaptable skills in readiness for technological change. There is universal literacy and numeracy.
4 *Cause* Complexity of industrial organisation with a highly developed division of labour in industry. Large scale industry is predominant because of its efficiency. There are mass communications and ease of national and international transport.
Effect Society becomes largely urban to service the large industrial sector. Urban norms and values therefore predominate and subcultures are replaced by a common culture.
5 *Cause* Difficulty of administering highly complex and diversified industries and society as a whole.
Effect National government and industrial management is centralised and strong. Firm decisions are handed downwards and acted upon by citizens and workers. Management and government is able to take swift and correct decisions.
6 *Cause* The material and intellectual rewards of industrial society are great. Medicine, science and other benefits to humanity progress quickly in this form of society.
Effect There is universal support for the status quo. Materialism and the work ethic are unchallenged values. Thus the political system described in **5** above is not dictatorial because it operates on the basis of both consensus and, thanks to the high level of education, universal political literacy. Politics becomes merely administration as extremes of viewpoint, both on the right and the left, decline in support.

7 *Cause* The availability and relatively low cost of international transport. International mass communications by satellite. Mass production of goods and services for export all over the globe.
Effect The nations of the world develop close links of all kinds. Cultural differences begin to disappear and there is a common material culture.

Kerr's industrial society, then, is *always* large scale, state managed, urban, socially and geographically open. The population is highly educated and highly skilled and the rewards they receive in terms of income status and power derive from their ability to succeed. People can move quickly up or down the stratification system. Norms and values are universally accepted and a common culture, even down to dress and language, begins to spread among all industrial societies.

At first sight the convergence thesis would appear to have a good deal of truth in it. For example **1** and **5** seem to be confirmed by M D Morris' study of the Bombay cotton mills between 1854 and 1947(68) in which he notes that the Indian mills of the last century were characterised by the following features:

no rigorous set of regulations governing the conduct of workers;
no stable work relations between employees, caused by
  high labour turnover
  high levels of absenteeism
  the taking of informal breaks.

The situation was the result of the cheapness of labour in Bombay, the low skill content of the job, the high cost of supervision, the lack of competition from abroad and the fact that the Indian workers were unused to industrial discipline as they came largely from rural backgrounds. However Morris found that by about 1924:

> "The necessities imposed by industrial technology and markets required employers to select different systems of discipline and these determined the way labour would work."(69)

As far as **2** is concerned, there does seem to be high level of upward social mobility in industrial society. One study(70) found a common level of about 30% mobility across the manual/non-manual divide. The expansion of the service sector and the involvement of women in the economy seem the main causes of this. Clearly education has expanded during the course of industrialisation in all countries, especially in terms of its extension to the working class and the expansion of higher education (**3**). **4**, too, seems largely true, though a Marxist would talk in terms of monopolisation and the expansion of the state bureaucracy. **6**, the increasing degree of support for industrial society's values, is difficult to assess. On one level there does seem to be a degree of consensus, sustained by the education system and the mass media, but on another the spread of youth cultures as well as large-scale dissenting movements such as CND seem to contradict this view. As for **7**, clearly there are closer links between countries now. American English is a common form of communication for peoples across the world, and even in the Third World the material culture of the First and Second is known of, even if it cannot be afforded. Some degree of convergence has occurred between the First and Second Worlds in that state ownership and large scale bureaucracy have become more common in the West while in the East there has been some decentralisation and privatisation in the economic and political systems.

However, this acceptance of Kerr's thesis must be a qualified one. The theory can be criticised. Firstly, it paints an inaccurate portrait of what industrial society is like 'inside'. We will call this the internal critique. Secondly, there are industrial societies that are *not* converging to this type of society. We will call this the external critique. Finally, where there has been convergence, this has not been due to the causes which Kerr et al identify, but rather to far less mechanically deterministic ones.

1 The internal critique

One major criticism here is that Kerr's claim that "consensus develops wherever industrialism is successful" is empirically inaccurate. Looking at American, British or even German society, consensus appears hard to find and it is very debatable whether it is increasing. From a Marxist point of view any consensus that does exist is the result of the hegemony of ruling class ideas *imposed* on the rest of society.

Secondly, the importance attached to ascribed characteristics such as race, sex and family still persists. Racism can hardly be said to have died away in Britain or America, while class background and one's sex still have a very important role in determining success in education and one's life chances in general, as even a superficial study of the sociological literature in these areas will show.

Thirdly, while it is true that there has been an increase in upward social mobility in Britain during the course of this century due to the increase in clerical and middle management/professional jobs especially, one study of more recent trends concludes that:

> "relative mobility and rates, which we take as our indicator of the degree of openness (of society), have remained generally unaltered."(71)

Furthermore, this and other studies point out that there is very little downward mobility form the upper strata of society, at least among the sons of the rich and powerful. Those born into these strata find it easy to remain there, they merely have their numbers swelled by the upwardly mobile. The vast majority of those who are upwardly mobile find their 'journey' ends in the middle range of society's stratification system, as yet the uppermost reaches remain almost closed.

Finally, the argument which is potentially most damaging to Kerr's view of the future path of industrial society is the fact that new microchip technology threatens to create even larger scale unemployment than exists already. It is hard to see much future for the work ethic or materialism when for a large proportion of the population there is no meaningful work available and no potential for material consumption.

2 The external critique

As a country which leads the world in many areas of industrial production, Japan must be considered an advanced industrial society and should therefore display the features that Kerr argues are found in all such societies. In many areas of Japanese society, such features are not found, and this is especially the case in the industrial sector, the part of society which is supposed by Kerr to be the 'motor' of convergence and therefore where it should be found most clearly. If convergence can be shown not to have occurred here, then it is highly unlikely that it will by necessity happen anywhere else.

The industrial system in Japan is clearly divided into two. On the one hand are the very large firms, often in the field of automobile manufacture, hi-fi and television production. These firms possess the quite distinct characteristics discussed below. On the other hand there is a much larger number of smaller firms, many of which supply components to the larger ones. This second section of the Japanese economy has characteristics similar to those found in the USA and Great Britain, and are excluded from the following description.

The characteristics of Japanese industry which diverge from Kerr's model

1 *Recruitment to jobs in industry*, even at the shop floor level, is based on achievement. The Japanese educational system is famous for the arduous nature of its selection procedures. From kindergarten to university the student undergoes 'shiken jigoku' ('examination hell') because he, or much less often she, knows that:

> "if successful he will be able to join a large successful firm where he can remain for life. To be admitted to such a firm, one must attend a good university, and to attend a good university, one must pass the entrance examination. To pass the entrance examination for a good university one must have good training, and to acquire good training one must pass the entrance examination for good high school."(72)

So far this is in accord with Kerr's model. However, the Japanese firm begins to deviate from the model once selection of workers and management has been done. As the quote suggests, once in the large corporation the individual has a job for life, regardless of personal efficiency (or lack of it) or of downturns in the economy which lead to overmanning. Leaving the company is virtually unthinkable, as other employers would be doubtful about employing a renegade. As well as this security, the individual knows that wages and career advancement will progress in even and regular steps, regardless of his/her performance. As the worker's family grows, so the wages will increase to cover the extra responsibilities. Incompetence is not rewarded by the "sack", for which there is no single equivalent word in Japanese, but merely by relegation to a harmless job. Now ascriptive criteria such as length of service or size of family, rather than achievement are important.

The difference between Japan and Great Britain, then, could be summed up in the following table:

	Recruitment	Reward
Great Britain	Ascription	Achievement
Japan	Achievement	Ascription

Although recruitment to positions in British society is in theory based on achievement, as mentioned above, ascriptive criteria are important, although subsequent promotion (or sacking) is based on performance at the job. As Anthony Heath writes after careful analysis of the available data:

> "Education has come to play an increasing role in the transmission of status (loosely defined) from father to son (in Britain); the *direct* influence of social origins – whether through patronage, nepotism, inheritance or some other mechanism – on occupational attainment has declined, but simultaneously its *indirect* influence via the educational system has increased as family background has become more closely linked to educational success and failure."(73)

2 *The firm in Japan takes a much wider responsibility for its workers* than British firms do. It looks after the workers' needs in the areas of housing, education, holidays, medical care, recreation, physical fitness and even marriage. This degree of commitment is reciprocated by the worker who has complete identification with the firm. Singing the company song in the morning is an example of this. Though not specifically mentioned by Kerr, this is clearly a major difference between the British and the Japanese economy. Some writers have gone so far as to suggest that the company plays the role of an extended family and is a modern derivation of it. If so this does contradict Kerr's second point.

3 *Workers identify with the collectivity*, seeing the company as their own. In fact this is not totally an illusion on their part as they have a much greater degree of control over it than British workers do over their companies. Even shop floor workers are involved in the improvement of the production system which they operate and are expected to discuss the problems facing the company and recommend solutions. Decisions are ideally arrived at by discussion among all involved at all levels, and are implemented only after a consensus has been reached. These decisions are then binding on all who took part in them.

Participation and consultation of this sort clearly contradictcs Kerr's point **5** concerning administration from above in the workplace.

The experience of Japan clearly illustrates a divergence from Kerr's model. It could be argued that these divergent features are merely the result of peculiarities of Japanese culture and are likely to disappear in the near future as they are replaced by the Western model of industrial organisation. The traditional features of Japanese culture often pointed to in this argument are the traditional small paternalistic firm of the last century and before, the importance of the extended family and the generally solidaristic and group-orientated nature of Japanese culture, as opposed to the individualism of the West. According to those who hold this view the necessities of industrialism will gradually predominate over this anachronistic cultural pattern and Japanese industry will move toward the features of the West.

While it is true that traces of traditional Japanese culture are found in the organisation of the modern Japanese factory, the view that modern industry developed naturally from it is innaccurate. Up to 1920 Japan was following the Western pattern entirely, simply copying the methods of industrial production in a very deliberate way. However, from the early 1920s managers consciously moved away from the Western model and towards the present Japanese one because of the increasingly evident failures of the former. Firms found it difficult to persuade skilled workers to stay with them in times of boom. The cost of giving these skills to new workers was, and is, high. During times of slump there was labour unrest over threatened redundancy and drops in pay. Furthermore because Japan's industrial expansion was very rapid and based on an infrastructure which, pre-1868, had been geared to a rural, feudal society, there was inadequate provision for the health, housing and education of the new urban proletariat. These problems could be solved at a stroke by the firm taking responsibility for all the needs of the workers and by employing the worker for life. The apparent classlessness of the new system helped to neutralise potential union opposition to it and enabled managers to get union agreement to company-based unions rather than the national unions providing for certain categories of workers which we have in Britain.

Other, broader, aspects of Japanese society were also consciously changed to strengthen and unify the nation. There was deliberate shaping of the beliefs of the people by the ruling groups. Shinto, the ancient faith of Japan, had lost its once-strong following by the mid 19th century. But, in the 1880s, it was "taken out and dusted" by the ruling elite. They changed aspects of it and added elements from the beliefs of Bushido (the Samurai code of ethics), Confucianism and even Christianity. This new religion, or perhaps more properly it should be called a code of national ethics and rituals, was called State Shinto and was deliberately diffused throughout society via the schools. The aim was to create a strong unified and independent Japan and to create a powerful system of social control, and in this it was clearly successful.

The Japanese case supports the voluntarists' argument that individual decisions and unique events can play an important role in social development. Change is not necessarily directed by the necessities of industrialisation but is open to alterations by deliberate decisions and unique circumstances. There seems to be no reason to believe either, that Japan will move to the Western model in the future. Even the small Japanese firms which have followed the Western pattern in the past are now beginning to copy the larger corporations, while within the large corporations workers who were previously excluded from these distinctive patterns (women and people who have not come directly from full time education) are being included. The Japanese model is therefore spreading and, if anything, British firms seem to be moving in the Japanese direction. This movement is limited to the introduction of 'human relations' measures rather than a whole-hearted move which British workers would find difficult to accept. We can agree with Bendix, then, when he writes:

> "the point is that countries which come late to the process of development possess social structures which must be understood in their own terms rather than merely as 'transitional stages' to the type of industrialised society exemplified by the English or, better still, the American case."(74)

We can add, though, that these social structures are amenable to shaping by the human will, as was the case in the early stages of Japanese industrialisation. Thus it would appear that the Japanese case refutes both the determinist argument *and* that of modernisation theory, which maintains that a particular stage of development necessitates specific socio-cultural characteristics.

3 Non-determined causes for the convergence of industrialised societies

The idea that certain social features become common to all industrial societies can be disproved empirically both in relation to the first countries to develop and among those which developed later and from different cultural bases. Even where such features *can* be identified, their presence is not necessarily the result of some logic of industrialisation which generates them but may be the result of a process which is much less deterministic. Common features across industrialised countries (and even some in non-industrialised countries) may be the result of a simple process of spreading or diffusion over time. The words spreading and diffusion are misleading, because they imply peaceful and gradual change. This may be the case in some instances, but often the spread of one culture to another is rapid and enforced by military or economic power. Diffusion can occur in a number of ways, not all of which are peaceful. They include the following(75):

1 migration
2 elite missionary activity abroad
3 invasionism, including conquest and extermination
4 trade and technological exchange
5 the spread of ideas and institutions.

It is easy to forget or underplay the importance of diffusion through these means. It is easy, also, to forget that cultural diffusion is violent in many cases. In Parsons' work, for example:

> "one gets the impression that the history of mankind has been one happy, relaxed and peaceful exchange of ideas, stimulating progress here, there and everywhere where contact between societies was made. Cultural diffusion appears as a friendly merchant traveller, a timeless Marco Polo innocently roaming the world, gently picking up a few ideas in one place and harmlessly depositing them in another . . . (the words) 'domination', 'exploitation', 'imperialism' and 'colonialism' are *not* discussed in any of Parsons' works on evolution."(76)

We can usefully imagine a spectrum of ways in which cultural diffusion can occur:

Voluntary	Accidental	Involuntary
Pursued	Accepted	Often resisted

From being a society deliberately kept in a state of suspended animation during the Tokugawa period (1600–1868), Japan suddenly embarked on a course of industrial development after the Meiji Restoration in 1868. In these early years of industrialisation there was a conscious copying of the West's military and economic patterns of organisation and technology, a copying which in some ways continues today. In 1871 a contingent set out to report on industry and society in Europe and America and to use their experiences and observations there as the basis for recommendations for Japanese industrialisation. Their findings are reported in *The Journal of the Envoy Extraordinary Ambassador Plenipotentiary's Travels Through Europe and America*, in 5 volumes(77). Clearly these beginnings can be placed on the extreme left hand side of the above spectrum. But, just as the beginnings of the industrialisation of Japan were moulded by the conscious copying of the West, so its later stages had the Western imprint *forced* upon it by the American occupation of Japan after the second world war. The Americans deliberately set out to destroy traditional loyalties and values such as Emperor worship, nationalism and militarism which all seemed perfectly compatible with a society industrialising with remarkable speed. In place of these values America tried to install those of the West and to replace a non-representative political system with a democratic one. In this case the diffusion can be placed well to the right of the spectrum, though in both cases we should note that no *internal* dynamic was involved, rather the spread, in one way or another, of particular social patterns from abroad.

As we saw earlier, structuralist writers like Frank also take the view that any similarities with the developed world found in the industrialised parts of the underdeveloped ones are not the result of the incipient development of the whole of the latter. They are, rather, the result of the implantation of the structure of underdevelopment by the already developed countries. The purpose of this implantation is to set up local metropolises for the efficient exploitation of the heartland of the underdeveloped country. The similarities between these and the cities from which industrialisation spread in Britain such as Manchester and Birmingham are purely superficial. The former are artificial creations for the benefit of other countries, the latter were the genuine beginnings of industrialisation and development.

Ivan Illich occupies a position somewhere between the centre and that of Frank on the spectrum of diffusion. The culture of the North, both material and normative, spreads to the South and is accepted, often eagerly, by it. This acceptance is misplaced, because the adoption of the characteristics of an industrialised country by a non-industrialised one has unfortunate consequences. Far from aiding the process of industrialisation, the products and practices of the North bring poverty, disease and stagnation to the South.

To sum up, then, Kerr argues that industrialisation necessitates development, by which he means social and political change which is basically towards the Western pattern or, rather, some idealised version of it. In this Kerr is very close to the deterministic theories of social evolution which were examined earlier. This view also places him close to, if not in, the modernisation school, though he makes no claims (as they often do) about pre-industrial social evolution. Having said this it is true that while Kerr limits his discussion to the already industrialised countries, it is very clear that their example will speedily be followed by those countries which are currently non-industrialised.

To many countries in the Third World, the First and Second Worlds do not offer acceptable models and they are not prepared to accept that form of modernism without qualifications. Some are aware that 'over-development' is as much a problem as under-development. They wish to avoid alienation, isolation, production and consumption for their own sakes and the use of technical capacity for aims other than the fulfilment of basic human needs. A consciousness of the problem of over-development may persuade some Third World leaders to find a new direction for social change and their purposive actions may direct their nations away from the arrogantly ethnocentric paths of evolution or convergence described by First and Second World theorists. The example of Japan, as well as other countries not mentioned here, suggests that this is possible. As C Wright Mills suggests:

> "When we think about the 'under-developed society' we must also think about the 'over-developed society'. There are two reasons for this: first, if we do not do so, we tend to think of everything as moving towards the developed. It is the old notion of nineteenth century evolutionism. And this is no longer a very fruitful idea. Second, to think of the polar types (over- and under-developed) leads us to think about a third type – an ideal which we should always keep in mind; the properly developing society. We need all three types, not just the two."(78)

Chapter review

We have seen that development is not an easy word to define as it includes not only economic changes, which are relatively easy to classify and search for, but also social and political changes, which are not. The sociology of development is a field where it is very easy to be ethnocentric, ie to view other societies through the conceptual spectacles of one's own. Many of the writers we have examined have been guilty of this: viewing other societies as simply less developed forms of their own; classifying many non-industrial societies as the traditional form, despite enormous differences between them; viewing modern society as necessarily better and therefore more desirable than these other, so-called traditional ones. Ethnocentrism, then, is yet another form of bias to which the sociologist is prone, and the sociologist of development is particularly susceptible to it.

In this chapter we have examined some of the main areas of contention within the sociology of development. These can be summarised as follows:

The debate between materialism and idealism. Here the main issue revolves around the respective importance of *ideas* in determining social change. Idealists hold that change in beliefs and ways of thought can produce material changes in the structure of society. Thus the Protestant ethic can at least help to bring about the emergence of capitalism. Materialists argue that ideas and culture are merely the *result* of more concrete forces in society, and that changes in ideas in society are only the secondary consequence of changes in these material forces.

Linked to this debate is the one between determinism and voluntarism. Here the subject is whether societies *necessarily* change in any particular way. The strong form of determinism says that all societies of a particular type move in the same direction through a pre-ordained set of stages which eventually culminate in a predictable end state. The weak form says that there are possibilities of false starts, diversions, U Turns and stops, but that in the end societies *tend* to move one way. Voluntarism, on the other hand, argues that social change is not pre-determined and that paths of change in different societies are very different and may be altered by an act of will, by a social movement or a strong leader with forceful ideas. Broadly speaking materialists tend to be determinists and idealists voluntarists, mainly because material changes are said to be more predictable and to follow a more identifiable path than do ideas. The notion of development itself is full of determinist overtones and even idealists sometimes have a development theory of social change.

The third main area of contention is the issue of whether there is one critical variable which causes development (such as technological change or psychological motivation) or whether development is the result of numerous causes. There is the possibility of mono-causal or multi-causal explanations of development. Modernisation theory and the liberal perspective on development tend to take the multi-causal approach, one recent study(79) for example argues that India's failure to develop was not a result of British Imperialism but rather the lack of a number of factors which are all necessary if development is to occur. These include a strong modernising government, large scale internal markets and the opportunity to centralise production in suitable economic centres.

A fourth area of contention surrounds the issue of whether explanations of development and lack of it should focus their attention on the internal characteristics of the country concerned or on the international system and that country's position within it. An analogy could be made with the sociological study of poverty. Some studies of poverty stress the features of the environment – the structure of society around the poor which creates them (structural unemployment or the persistence of very low paid jobs). Others examine the characteristics of the individuals and groups who are in poverty to discover why they are in that condition (too many children, physical disability, factors creating a cycle of deprivation or a culture of poverty.) Sociologists of development take similar positions in their explanations of international poverty. On the one hand there are those who stress the structural characteristics of the international system which positively inhibit development and destroy it. Others seek the reasons for the non-development of some countries in their internal characteristics. Lack of achievement motivation, insufficient investment in technological development, lack of natural resources, overpopulation and conservative elite groups may be to blame according to this group of theorists.

Table 1 Perspective

	Materialist	Idealist	Structuralist	Modernisation Theory
Reasons for non-development in the Third World	Lack of capital investment in technology to date	Lack of progressive ideology or sufficiently motivated elite group	First developers have exploited the Third World and halted its development	Mixture of factors including lack of capital, markets, suitable political climate, suitable family structures, stratification systems etc
Prospects for the future development of Third World countries	Good. Technological progress in Third World will bring economic, social and political development	Good. Development ideology easy to spread through mass media and education systems now. Benefits of development clear so elite groups motivated to achieve it	Bad. Resources already taken by First and Second Worlds. Economies distorted to primary production only. No prospect of change as present system operates in the interests of those who control it	Good because necessary. International system under threat of collapse unless Third World quickly develops. Rich should be motivated to change present international economic structure
Influence of the First and Second Worlds on the Third	Good. Technology, capital and knowledge from rich countries will speed the development of the Third World	Good. Development ideology spread through contact with multinational companies and by radios and TVs imported from rich countries	Bad. Past and present exploitation of the Third World by rich countries	Generally good due to spread of capital, technology and knowledge to Third World. Bad effects are correctable
Best development strategy	Capital investment in technology either by indigenous or foreign entrepreneurs. Heavy investment by state may be desirable	Suitable education programmes both for elite and the general population	Withdrawal from the international system of trade and aid	Seek an increase of aid from the rich countries. Abolish retrogressive socio-cultural patterns. Diversify economies

Finally, we could point to the difference between theorists who maintain that it is enough to let developing societies get on with their own development, and those who argue that a fundamental change in the international system is necessary if the current problems of the poor countries are to be solved. Tinkering and waiting will only make matters worse according to the second group. Furthermore they accuse theorists of the first type of fulfilling an ideological function by suggesting that development is possible for the Third World and that it is desired by the First and Second. The accusations of ulterior motivations do not come only from one side; the exaggerations and over-statements of radical theorists are seen by the liberals as proof of their political bias. Cases where development has occurred or could be said to be occurring at the moment such as in Taiwan and Brazil are held up as proof that development within the present international system *is* possible, and is in fact desirable to it.

The final part of the chapter examined the convergence theory put forward by Clerk Kerr and criticisms were made of it. The example of Japanese development was used as a case study to see whether convergence could be identified there. The conclusion was that Japanese industrialism remains distinctively Japanese, at least in the large firms. Signs of convergence in some supposedly developed societies may be the result of factors other than the 'logic of industrialism'. The Japanese case also served to indicate that industrialisation and development can come about as the result of definite decisions by the ruling group, or at least can be shaped by their decisions. This case seemed to give at least partial support to the voluntarists' argument that social change is subject to human will.

The table on p. 48 summarises the approaches of the main perspectives we have examined.

Bibliography

(1) W Brandt *North and South* Pan 1980 p. 48

(2) P Donaldson *Worlds Apart* p. 80

(3) *A Dictionary of the Social Sciences* eds. J Gould and W Kolb, Tavistock 1959

(4) K Marx *Poverty of Philosophy* Lawrence and Wishart, p. 122

(5) K Marx *The Holy Family* Foreign Language Publishing House, Moscow 1956 p. 125

(6) K Marx *The Communist Manifesto* p. 41 Progress Publishers, Moscow 1969

(7) Radcliffe Brown The *Andaman Islanders* Cambridge University Press 1922

(8) M Sahlins *Stone Age Economics* Cambridge University Press 1974

(9) C Meillassoux *Economy and Society* Vol. 1 No. 1 1972 *From Reproduction to Production*

(10) For example Clark Kerr in *Industrialism and Industrial Man* Penguin 1973 and H Marcuse *One Dimensional Man* Routledge and Kegan Paul 1964

(11) A Halsey ed. in *Trends in British Society Since 1900* Macmillan 1972 notes that the spending power of the average Briton has tripled since 1900 and that the size of the white collar sector of the economy has increased from 18.7% of the total in 1911 to 38.3% in 1966 with a corresponding decline in the manual sector between those dates from 74.6% to 58.3%

(12) Marcuse op. cit.

(13) See for example R Hamilton *The Liberation of Women* Allen and Unwin 1978 London

(14) See for example S Firestone *The Dialectic of Sex* Paladin 1972

(15) W W Rostow *The Stages of Economic Growth* C.U.P. 1971 p. 4

(16) D Meadows *The Limits to Growth* Pan 1974 p. 192

(17) A G Frank *The Sociology of Development and the Underdevelopment of Sociology* Pluto 1973

(18) Rostow op. cit. p. 155

(19) *A Dictionary of the Social Sciences* op. cit.

(20) D McClelland *The Achieving Society* Van Nostrand Toronto 1961

(21) M Morishima *Why Has Japan "Succeeded"*? C.U.P. 1982

(22) M Weber *The Protestant Ethic and the Spirit of Capitalism* Unwin University Books 1968 p. 60

(23) Quoted in Weber ibid. p. 48 and 50

(24) Quoted in Gerth and Mills *From Max Weber* RKP 1970 p. 413

(25) M D Morris *The Emergence of an Industrial Labour Force in India* in H Bernstein ed. *Underdevelopment and Development* Penguin 1973 pp. 177–190

(26) K Marx *Capital* Lawrence and Wishart Vol. 1 p. 150

(27) Weber op. cit. p. 181

(28) R Aron *Main Currents of Sociological Thought* Vol. II Penguin 1971 p. 217

(29) Gerth and Mills op. cit. p. 139 and 155

(30) Figures quoted by J Goldthorpe *Sociology of the Third World* C.U.P. 1975

(31) N J Smelser *Towards a Theory of Modernisation* in A and E Etzioni *Social Change*, S N Eisenstadt *Social Change and Development* in *Readings in Social Evolution and Development* by the same author Pergamon Press 1970, see also his *Modernisation, Protest and Change* Prentice Hall 1966. E

E Hagen *The Theory of Social Change* Dorsey 1962, Talcott Parsons *Societies: Evolutionary and Comparative Perspectives* 1966 and its companion volume *The System of Modern Societies* 1971, both Prentice Hall. Other modernisation theorists include B Hoselitz *Tradition and Economic Growth* in *Tradition, Values and Socio-Economic Development* eds Braibranti and Spengler Duke University Press 1961, as well as McLelland op. cit. and W Rostow *How it All Began* Methuen 1975 and op. cit.

(32) G Myrdal *Economic Theory and Underdeveloped Regions* Methuen 1957 reprinted 1965

(33) Ibid. p. 16

(34) Ibid. p. 16

(35) Myrdal writes on the question of Western-style democratic institutions . . . "the poorer nations have [because of their general social and economic backwardness] and because of the very fact of existing internal inequalities often been less democratic and, in any case, have, because they are poorer, been up against narrow financial and, at bottom, psychological limitations on policies seeking to equalise opportunities". Ibid. p. 51

(36) Ankie M Hoogvelt *The Sociology of Developing Societies* Macmillan 1976 p. 61

(37) For examples of this see, for instance, C Stevens *Food Aid and the Developing World* Overseas Development Institute 1979, especially chapter 6

(38) Hoogvelt op. cit. p. 61

(39) Ibid. p. 62

(40) Ibid. p. 51

(41) W E Moore *Social Change* Prentice Hall 1963

(42) E Gellner *Thought and Change* Weidenfeld and Nicolson 1964

(43) *New Society* 16th July 1981 pp. 108–9

(44) C Cipolla *The Economic History of World Population* Penguin 1962 Harmondsworth p. 89

(45) R Dutt *The Economic History of India* London 1901 quoted in P Baran *The Political Economy of Growth* Penguin 1973 pp. 280–81

(46) A Gunder Frank *Capitalism and Under-development in Latin America* quoted in Turner *Industrialism* Longman 1975

(47) During Argentina's 1971 credit squeeze, when the availability of credit in the domestic economy was reduced by 20%, local firms were forced to cut their borrowing by 42% but global firms in Argentina *increased* their borrowing by 20% over the prior period. Firgures from F J Barnet and R E Müller *Global Reach* Jonathan Cape 1975 London p. 141

(48) In the mining, smelting and petroleum industries, the capital outflow result-

ing from the operations of global corporations is 79%, which is particularly surprising when one considers that the investment for these operations was 83% financed from local savings. Ibid. p. 154

(49) Barnet and Müller ibid. p. 151

(50) T Hayter *Aid as Imperialism* Penguin 1974

(51) Quoted by R B Sutcliffe in the introduction to *The Political Economy of Growth* P Baran op. cit. p. 81

(52) T Hayter *The Creation of World Poverty* Pluto Press 1981

(53) Ibid. p. 22

(54) Ibid. p. 27 quoting R Dumount – no source attributed

(55) Ibid. p. 67

(56) Ibid. p. 56

(57) Ibid. p. 121

(58) I Illich *Outwitting the Developed Countries* in H Bernstein op. cit. pp. 357–368

(59) Ibid. p. 359

(60) Ibid. p. 362

(61) Ibid.

(62) P Freire *Cultural Action for Freedom* Penguin 1972

(63) J Goldthorpe op. cit.

(64) Ibid. p. 69

(65) Brandt op. cit. p. 20

(66) Ibid. p. 267

(67) Kerr op. cit.

(68) M D Morris op. cit.

(69) Ibid.

(70) S M Lipset and R Bendix *Social Mobility in Industrial Society* University of California Press 1959 Berkeley

(71) J Goldthorpe et al *Social Mobility and Class Structure in Modern Britain* Clarendon Press Oxford 1980 p. 252

(72) E F Vogel *Japan's New Middle Class* University of California Press Berkeley 1968 p. 41

(73) A Heath *Social Mobility* Fontana Glasgow 1981 p. 191

(74) R Bendix *Nation Building and Citizenship* John Wiley and Son New York 1964 pp. 212–3

(75) A Smith *The Concept of Social Change* R.K.P. 1978 p. 163

(76) A Hoogvelt op. cit.

(77) Quoted in D Shively ed. *Tradition and Modernisation in Japanese Culture* Princetown University Press 1971

(78) C Wright Mills *The Problems of Industrial Development* in *Power, Politics and People* ed. I L Horowitz Oxford Unveristy Press 1963, quoted in I L Horowitz *Three Worlds of Development* 2nd. edition 1972 Oxford University Press p. 60

(79) N Charlesworth *British Rule and the Indian Economy 1800–1914* Macmillan 1982. Charlesworth considers that the impact of British Imperialism on the Indian economy was not that great. While British exports of textiles to India did deprive local producers of a section of the internal market, there was still a substantial market left for them in this area of the economy. Many imports from Britain complemented rather than competed with the Indian production. While British taxation of Indian land may have had a draining effect on her capital resources in the early part of the colonial period it is still possible to conclude that . . . "the scale of any expropriating force arising out of external forces must have been relatively small" p. 69

2 The social construction of race relations

Introduction

The discussion of the sociology of development has shown how complex it can be to try to unravel the competing interpretations of this topic. The same difficulty occurs when we examine the issue of 'race' relations. There is equally powerful disagreement about the origin and continuance of 'racial' antipathy. This chapter will discuss the explanations that have been offered to account for 'racial' conflict. It is a controversial area, but we will draw the main outline of this argument taking into account the historical aspects at issue as well as the attempts by social and natural scientists to understand the processes underlying 'race'.

We began this introduction with the term 'race' in inverted commas, which itself is an important part of the discussion. The common-sense, or folk-lore view of races is that they exist as biological and physiologically distinct categories. Races are supposedly 'born from nature', they are invariable, genetic populations according to the general view and not socially constructed, variable groupings. In short, an unquestioned view has generally been *received* that there are a variety of distinct races to which we all belong. Races are popularly seen to be based on our skin colour (black, yellow or pink) or possibly our nose-size (semitic 'Jewish' nose versus the chiseled Anglo-Saxon equivalent).

Sociology rejects the coarser aspects of common-sense, beginning instead from the assumption that most socially organised knowledge is not what it seems. Race, like gender is in the eye of the beholder. It is blended together as folk-lore from a cocktail of objective observation, and social expectation, then stirred with a twist of learned behaviour. Beliefs are socially constructed and quickly become part of the cultural norm, a portion of the social heritage absorbed by people through the language, and reinforced by the family and mass media.

One result of this complex process is to reduce the perception of social behaviour to easily understandable ideas; we develop beliefs about how people ought to act and views about how they live which may bear little relation to reality. For example, citizens of the UK generally believe that the agents of social control (such as the police) are, by and large, fair in their treatment of people, and that Parliament broadly abides by democratic principles. Yet, when we examine evidence relating to the circumstances of those we define as racial minorities in Britain, we find substance in their complaints of police indifference to their plight, indeed of some harassment(1). Parliamentarians too, have displayed little sympathy to the problems of those minorities in the inner cities of Bradford, Wolverhampton and Liverpool.

If we add the view that most biologists, anthropologists and sociologists hold – that races do not exist, the contradiction is apparent. Two opposing views co-exist. Popular discussion assumes the world is inhabited by distinct racial groupings; whereas the academic world insists all belong to a varied, but essentially biologically identical human race. The topic is inevitably a polemical one. It involves much controversy and can produce fierce argument because any investigation of its complexities reveals much that is relevant to social inequality. The question of race does seem to be problematic. We will be as objective as we can, – bearing in mind Paul Barker's comment that "to see and to listen are very different skills"(2).

The chapter begins with a sociological definition of race and then examines the biological and psychological explanations. The topic has essential historical antecedents and we present a migration analysis of 'races' and the attendant legislative and cultural results such population movements have engendered. Classical sociologists like Marx and Weber have influenced the contemporary views of sociologists like John Rex and Stuart Hall, so we consider the broad differences that exist between the various schools of thought and finally endeavour to perceive racism from the point of view of ethnic minorities themselves. The ethnic minorities have often been visible on the streets because of their supposed alien characteristics, but invisible to sociology courses because their experiences have not been particularly accessible. The chapter will hopefully remedy a part of this problem.

A definition

We begin our argument from the assumption that most societies have different groups, classes, generations, gender categories and ethnic groups. None are necessarily treated equally, most are presented and perceived in quite specific ways. The young are ascribed with immature values, the old with wisdom and experience; women are seen as child-minders and rearers of the next generation. Racial and ethnic inter-relationships are part of this general social network, one aspect of all the *subordinate* (inferior) or *superordinate* (superior) links in a complex chain of social behaviour; perhaps at times it is the weakest junction. This is, therefore, not simply a question of inherited characteristics of colour and appearance, or of different cultures making minorities undesirable neighbours. It is the *presentation* of these groups within Britain's political, economic and social system that is the relevant fact. The dark 'strangers' within our midst tell us much that is sociologically relevant about the covert processes of social behaviour in our own society.

There is enormous diversity in methods of social classification that try to establish criteria as to why one category of people should be treated in a different manner to another. Race, is a label that has emerged in numerous cultures to construct meaning to the way society is ordered. It is a term with many qualities fixing the recipient with supposed sexual, biological and psychological attributes. Its pejorative (insulting) quality is self-evident; the terms 'nigger', 'boy', 'jew' have tense significance when used in a racial context. Whole communities have been exploited or exterminated on the basis of scientifically dubious but socially powerful racial labels(3). This is true in the slave economy of 18th and 19th century America, or the concentration camps of Nazi conquered Europe during the 1940s.

The term race has no universal quality or definition. Its interpretation is variable, very much culture-bound and it is quite regularly confused by its users within the same society. In common usage it usually provides a stereotypical frame of reference by which people make sense of their world; and it varies as historical and material circumstances change. In the present situation of Irish political instability many British people have an image of the 'Celtic races' with fiery temperaments as being *naturally* derived. The red-haired, aggressive Celt, fond of alcohol and prone to mystical, religious devotion using primitive methods of birth-control and irrational to the point of political extremism, is much expressed at the stereotypical level. The Irish Joke, indicating the stupidity of the average manual worker from Ireland belies the fact that constant political struggle has raised the general level of political literacy in that country to impressive levels. During the 19th century, Charles Kingsley, the writer and Christian Socialist was horrified by the primate features and body structure of the white 'race' he saw in Ireland. His revulsion was quite consistent with his egalitarian views at this time(4). The Victorian profile of race differences is not too different from the modern Elizabethan view; social construction has reworked the criteria but to similar effect.

When we talk of races, what do we mean? From a common-sense view we might discuss the yellow or black races so that *skin-colour/tone* is one means of classification. Or, as above, we may refer to the English and Irish races (Anglo-Saxon and Celtic respectively) where supposed *blood-lines* and *geographical nationality* offers some significance to racial status. Alternatively, we could speak of the Jewish or Indian races, mingling geographical origin with supposed *cultural* indicators of difference (diet, religion, dress variations) adding a dash of *psychological* and *physical perceptions.* The Jew, supposedly having an acquisitive instinct, is clever at organising money or has a semitic nose. The Pakistani is efficient at running a small business despite unsociable eating habits. It is common to find these views used in an interchangeable way in any social situation:

folk-lore has a resilience and internal logic of its own. After all, it is common knowledge that 'races' exist, is it not?

Any sociological definition of race that tries to provide understandable criteria to account for these overlapping criteria of physical appearance, skin-tone, culture, nation, as well as explaining the social construction and perception of racial difference is facing a serious task.

Confronted with the diversity of the human world it is understandable that social investigators have attempted to classify groups whose physical and cultural profusion exhibits similarities. Scientists have tried to make some order by devising rigorous, conceptual-categories that appear to be common and patterned according to some determining factor. Anthropologists, biologists, psychologists and sociologists offer rather contrasting race explanations. As Michael Banton has argued, it is essential that we try to be precise in our use of definitions to indicate how any discussion or analysis of this topic should proceed(5).

We take race therefore, *to be a social concept that is held by groups and individuals to differentiate other groups as being distinct from themselves; physical appearance and cultural indicators are the key criteria of such labelling processes.* The use of the term race is *purposive*, it has an objective, that is to distinguish a power relationship of superiority and inferiority. This socially constructed concept is dynamic. It is a perceived difference, a social definition, and skin colour is often the most commonly used mechanism of reference. So the white Anglo-Saxon may view the dark skin of the West Indian as the significant factor in race relationships. The Fascists in Germany during the 1940s sub-divided white Europeans into a finer series of categories, a racial hierarchy, with Aryans (blondes, blue-eyed, whites) at the apex, and the Mediterranean peoples counted for much less (derk hair, brown eyes, olive) so their racial status was lowly. At the base of the pyramid were peoples of the Battic, the Somiet Un on, Jezish races and itinerants such as gypsies. The racial label had enormous social significence; the gas chambers of Dachau and other concentration camps was a probable destination if successfully applied. The fact that yellow stars, special uniforms, and inner-city ghetto locations were forced upon these supposed inferiors to make them visible is pertinent to our discussion. Jezs and gypsies do not automatically present convenient physical appearances. The power relationship of physical segregation and its attendant genocidal impact omitted these niceties of definition.

Sociologists have recognised the weaknesses of using physical appearance and skin colour to create racial typologies and in recent years the idea of *ethnic group* has become fashionable. This term is rather more a generic concept; it covers a socially defined group on the basis of their *cultural traits* and less so on their physical differences, although they are both points of reference. Again, ethnic group involves a process of social perception that enables such a group to be stigmatised as distinctive. Cultural factors such as dress, diet, family structure or religion rather than black, brown, yellow or white skin are points of demarcation. Of course, in everyday use, race and ethnicity are often used interchangeably, but the social importance of both terms has been profound. Educationalists, politicians and social workers, who 'man the moral barricades' (to use a phrase borrowed from Stanley Cohen), have been active in their construction of policies directly related to this perception of ethnic minorities. Depending upon the mood of the nation, programmes of assimilation (say through language training) or anti-discrimination legislation, or redefinitions of who is entitled to claim British nationality, all relate to this topic. It is no simple debate on semantics.

Ethnicity(6) has anthropological antecedents, it brings to the study of race relations ideas derived from the study of small-scale, minority cultures and places them within the social processes of more complex industrial societies. It may help us understand the reception of white Yugoslavs arriving here after their civil war during the 1940s, or Italians during the early 1950s and to compare this with the perception of Pakistani or Indian migrants during the economic boom up to the mid 1960s. Each ethnic group may present itself as culturally distinct from the majority and these *dietary* or dress differences may combine with their phenotypical characteristics. The word *phenotype* is a biological concept which in this case refers to the effect of natural, genetic evolution on humans as it modifies their body structure. So, the skin colour of people is related to climatic changes and the body attempts to combat excessive ultra violet light and heat by producing a natural substance called melanin which is present in greater amounts among darker skinned peoples. When physical characteristics (part social, part biological) combine to create a distinct ethnic group the visual differences of dress style as with an Indian sari, or Jewish cap are reference symbols of importance. The treatment given to minorities by host populations is very significant. White ethnic groups such as Yugoslavs, with their Greek Orthodox religion and tendency towards extended families might escape attention, whereas the Punjabi may become visible if economic problems worsen. Rising unemployment in the UK has often been blamed on the latter but not on the former.

We now begin to move into the realm of ideologies (these will be discussed more fully later in the chapter.) It is important to re-affirm that terms of reference help us to comprehend the framework of this complex debate. For example, as Banton has argued *racism* is a belief, held by some groups, that inherited psychological and physical factors influence the behaviour and culture of that group. It is a dogma asserted rather than one that is capable of demonstration. When this dogma manifests itself in social practice the consequences may be profound for the stigmatised group and this is termed *racialism* ie the implementation of a racist dogma. It involves practised discrimination which may be illegal, as in the UK. It can be deliberate and institutionalised as in South Africa, with its legal sanctions on racial mixing, inter-racial marriage, and patterns of residence that coerce blacks into particular relationships of subordination to whites.

Classical and contemporary sociologists have noted that social behaviour tends to be conformist. Strangers are often ill-received even if they comply with the host groups conventions. Credibility and acceptance is part of this process of social construction. It depends on a power relationship, on other people's views of our behaviour and appearance and their ability to exclude or accept us. Societies that display internal divisions and carefully ranked inequalities tend to cohere when they meet diverse, external cultures; we may absolutely reject and feel antipathy towards those societies we see as foreign. Remember the wave of patriotic fervour generated by the Falklands dispute and the way the 'Argies' were often presented. As the Marxist, Stuart Hall, has noted, "Going to war for a scatter of islands 8000 miles away, so integral a part of the British Imperium, so fixed in our hearts, that we have not managed to build a decent road across the place or to provide it with a continuous supply of power"(7) – makes perfect sense in the context of this ethnic debate. Togetherness was the fixed reference point of social rhetoric, and this form of emotional populism is not only powerful but constantly appears capable of being aroused. Sociologists refer to such views as *ethnocentric*. They express a consciousness of similarity of a host group that may lead to social distancing taking place against those perceived as alien. We must not confuse this with the concept of racism because, as we have already noted, that partly depends upon the perception of skin colour as part of the process of judgement. Ethnocentricity is different as it focuses attention upon the foreigner without necessarily making reference to phenotype. For example, white Americans and black Americans may have felt the brunt of ethnocentricity expressed in a mildly antagonistic form during the Second World War when these allies were commonly said to be, "Over-paid, over-sexed and over-here." Racial prejudice involves the perception of colour and culture as the key variables; the linguistic significance of the argot terms (this means common words of slang) 'kraut' or 'frog' have quite different social meaning or virulence to those of 'nigger' or 'paki'.

To summarise, we have to carefully consider the origins of those concepts that we associate with race and ethnic relations. Race is a socially constructed category and we shall try to demonstrate that it has little scientific validity because there are no biological rules that clearly demarcate boundaries between the black 'races' (negroid), the yellow 'races' (mongoloid) and the white 'races' (caucasoid). To draw the implications of this introduction together a number of themes will need to be developed in this discussion:

1 We need to understand how classical and contemporary sociologists interpreted the origins and social significance of race relations. There are substantial differences for example between Max Weber and Karl Marx, and those who have synthesised their perspectives.

2 A second theme that has to be studied is the reason why the terms race and ethnic group carry such enormous social significance.

3 The long-standing debate as to whether racial prejudice is innate or learned will require consideration. It is perhaps worth pausing here to indicate that the concepts of socialisation and negotiation of social roles may help us understand the behaviour patterns in question.

4 We need to consider how such racist ideas and practices relate to social institutions and structures. It may be possible to argue that they have a function to play in a social system by re-inforcing traditional values of social organisations such as the family or religion. Additionally as Chapter 1 has indicated, this must take into account the possible importance of racial categories for international socio-economic relationships too. Putting it simply, we may perceive people in racial terms to justify our expropriation of their talents eg using their cheap labour as inexpensive raw materials like tea and sugar.

We must decide, too, whether racism (the dogmatic belief in the importance of physical difference) is the cause of racial antagonism or the consequence. This again raises the debate between idealism and materialism. Do socio-economic circumstances, such as a desire for cheap labour, produce racist ideas to legitimise this exploitative practice or does the belief create the conditions for the circumstance to exist? Finally, during the post 1960 period race-ethnic relations have become crucial issues in British society, they have taken on an inflated and polemical quality. We need to look at the sociological significance of inequality, colour and culture in order that this topic can be placed into a context carrying equal validity in our studies to, say, that of youth culture, education or the family.

From the point of view of understanding the intricacies of this topic we begin first by looking at the interdisciplinary context of the race debate. The evasive and complex themes do overlap and we can therefore only touch upon the main boundaries of the discussion. However, the sociology student must acquire some basic guidance from biological and psychological principles if a reasoned consideration of the debate is to be developed. It is worth reflecting upon a curriculum that parcels up investigation in such a manner, through its division of learning, so as to inhibit our perception of underlying relationships.

Physical anthropology, human biology, and the scientific construction of race

In the 18th and 19th centuries the positivist social and natural scientific trend was to note the variation of physical appearance. Both investigated laws regulating the distribution of mankind. The Biblical interpretation, termed *monogenist*, was that the human race evolved from Adam and Eve, ie came from single stock. Their offspring wandered the earth and adapted physically to varying conditions of temperature, water supply and food, and so their appearance differed. *Polygenists* in the 19th century disagreed; they suggested the origins were from distinctly different human groups scattered across the world. A classification process began to occur: women and men were to be measured according to their physically observable characteristics. For example, woolly hair or straight hair, light or dark skin, or different stature as with the African pygmy or tall European. Physiologically based groups were identified by early anthropologists and termed races; the positivist belief emerged that one race could be distinguished in physical characteristics from another (8).

The populations of the world were categorised by scientists according to their physical variation. It was believed that this determined the psychological character of the races, ie physical traits were inherent, and transmitted from parents to children. A permanent breeding cycle influenced by say, the size of one's skull and therefore one's cranial capacity (almost literally the weight of brains) gave us an explanation based on rigid biological determinism. In short, the negroid race was physically less sound than the caucasoid, had less actual intelligence, and therefore no potential for improvement. The phenotypical-racial factor 'explained' why the former was ignorant and the latter economically and socially advanced. Many scientists put forward such ideas throughout Europe and America; Robert Knox's, *The Races of Man* (1850) and Gobineau's, *Essai sur l'inegalite des Races Humaines* (1853) are two famous examples.

In the 20th century we believe that scientifically proven laws control some of the biological processes of mankind. In the Victorian period the principles of human variation were by no means agreed, there was no biological *paradigm* (no agreed set of scientific rules which we call protocols). It was believed that observable physical features provided the basis for racial observations. In practice, each race was a *species* on its own (a species being particular categories of humans sharing common inheritable qualities). Each species could reproduce within its own group, but not outside without physically corrupting, and weakening both species members: *miscegenation* being the result. Mixed race was viewed as probably leading to infertility of future offspring of such a union of opposites. The term *miscegenation* in the 19th century was used to argue that if a white man married a black woman their different biological characteristics would not combine at all well. The children were thought to be weak (adulterated) specimens of the human race. At the very least, physical degeneracy would be the short term effect. As the 19th century advanced special instruments were devised to make the classification process more factually precise, and the empirical accuracy was believed to lend more scientific validity to the case. Broca, a scientist, devised a craniometer to measure the variations in cephalic index (differences in head size), so long headed races (dolicho) and round headed races (the brachy) were isolated.

The basic problem, however, was unresolved. Whose classification scheme was to be used? Linnaeus (1758) had distinguished four varieties: Europeoeus Albus, Americanus Rufus, Afar Nigus, and Asiaticus Luridicus. Other scientist talked of many more species. The principle weakness of the analysis was in maintaining that colour should be the key variable for classifying different physical populations. The degree of colour could be so variable that any shade or tone from white, to pink, to yellow, brown, beige, or black might define a separate species. How was this overlapping racial mosaic to be properly co-ordinated; even using a Broca? The general principles of species-race difference were accepted. Physical appearance, behaviour, biology, culture and differential endowment in intelligence were chained together into a doctrine of human difference. Hence, almost any belief was valid. As the sociologist R Miles has suggested:

> "Now it was already clear that the various phenotypical features did not co-vary with each other in a consistent way eg not all people with dark skins had black tightly curled hair and flattened noses"(9).

It became impossible to suggest which classification system was superior. Scientists meticulously tried to discover all kinds of differences of physical appearance.

With the development of biology and the publication of Charles Darwin's '*On the Origins of Species*' (1859) the debate moved into higher gear. It refuted the earlier explanations of rigid races, separated by deterministic inherited qualities. The theory of natural selection was much more dynamic. Darwin argued that nature preserved the favourable variations of a species and tended to filter out weaker members of plant or animal populations: a constant process of adapting to the environment, surviving, evolving and adjusting to the prevailing conditions. The crucial relevance of natural selection was that any species would adapt to its environment as best it could, this explains varieties within the same species. There could therefore be *no permanent static races* as distinct species such as the mongoloid and caucasoid, instead humans adapted and changed. Essentially black men, white men and yellow men were phenotypically varied; but all belonged to the same species – the human race. As John Gabriel has concluded:

> "If 'man' is not fixed, then attempts to sub-divide on the basis of further typological varieties or sub-species becomes absurd"(10).

Biology was coming to accept that it was impossible to use the idea of race in any meaningful way. The black could inter-breed with the pink, or yellow with the olive and each human group could produce perfect biological offspring. The social perception and presentation of these arguments was a very different matter as we shall see later. Race, in the social sense still had enormous importance.

To the present day biologists, the concept of race means a population that makes up a sub-division of the overall species. Individuals in such sub-divided groups hold some genetic characteristics (ie their biochemical make-up) in common that are somewhat different to those of other sub-groups. All the various sub-divisions when totalled make up the species as a whole, ie they could reproduce with each other. Major migrations of population, famines, wars and alliances throughout history have blended such genetic races, making it impossible to biologically distinguish between them. In other words, biologists argue that the observable characteristics of the organism (*the phenotype*) and the genetic, internal, constitution of an individual (*genotype*) are not congruent. To sociologists, modern science confirms that we construct social races. Societies choose to identify particular biological characteristics as the ones they consider to be relevant. These choices are the result of power relationships, of social inequality and economic circumstances. Social races vary in their socially constructed forms; they are not universal groups.

This is not to say that we do not inherit biological characteristics, we do. The Hapsburg Kings passed on their famous protruding lower lip from the 14th century. We also know that certain dominant inherited genes can be responsible for particular conditions. Blood types too are inherited, and conditions associated with it regularly re-appear.

As the modern geneticist W F Bodmer(11) has argued, the constituent parts of our biochemical composition is so little understood. The total genetic endowment of each individual (the internal genotype) is made up of more than 100 000 genes, often existing in complex chains called alleles. If we could isolate particular alleles in particular groups, ie if they occured more frequently than was normal in certain societies, we could talk of a biological race. The problem is that this does not occur. When we measure allele frequencies and try to link them to the distribution of skin colour and physical appearance (the phenotype) we find little variation. Sociologists are saying, along with biologists, that we may talk of the human race as a general category but there is very little difference in our biological make-up across the world. Skin colour, lip shape, or nose size is accounted for by a very small percentage of the genetic code of the body – well over 90% of genetic endowment is similar for all humans. The concept of racial purity in the skin colour sense is therefore meaningless biologically; its significance is sociological, social races have locked onto particular biological variables and interpreted them to be the crucial sources of prestige or stigma. Instead of belonging to the human race, we learn to see ourselves from the point of view of race, gender, class and nation. Each category has profound consequences for our life chances.

In conclusion, from a genetic point of view the white South African shares much similarity to the black South African; the English Jew has as much genetic similarity with his protestant neighbour as any Israeli. The chapter on development has shown that the First, Second and Third Worlds owe more to the international structures of economic inequality than to any factors that might emerge from inborn genetic characteristics. Races do not exist in a biological sense. The question still remains as to why appearance (phenotypical variety) takes on such social significance. Nineteenth century anthropologists and biologists believed we could quantify the differences between human societies using physical characteristics as the basis of measurement. This is now considered incorrect. The fact remains that we still tend to think of people around the world using scientifically discarded racial concepts which is interesting in itself. It indicates a continuing social need to divide the world's populations in such a manner. In the next section we will look at the views put forward by psychologists as to why race is still a durable idea. The next section tries to suggest one answer as to why race takes on such social importance.

The psychological construction of race

In the 18th century the Bible was widely used to explain the subordinate quality of inferior races. In the 19th century, prejudice, it was argued, followed from the discoveries of physical anthropology and biology that mongoloids were physically inferior to whites. In the 20th century the analysis began to pivot on a new axis – psycho-analytical theory. The work of Sigmund Freud found widespread support. This new theory suggested that disguised impulses in the personality, perhaps primitive instincts of the inner-self were related to prejudice. It became common to argue that such prejudice was inevitably irrational (the logic of biological arguments were therefore irrelevant) and could be explained by references to the individual's experience. Perhaps, even, such prejudice was instinctive. The racial antipathy found in German society, among others, during the mid 1930s that resulted in attempts to exterminate millions of the Jewish race during the Second World War (a process termed *genocide*) led social scientists to examine the causes of this behaviour. The dominant argument that emerged was that racialism was linked to personality abnormality.

The prevailing theme of psychology is to explore the *individual* basis of racial attitudes and beliefs, how they originate and how they link to social behaviour. Sociologists accept a rather different perspective, instead of concentrating on the origins of these characteristics that make up a prejudiced personality it moves towards an exploration of those factors creating attitudes on a *social* basis. John Rex for example has linked racial prejudice to the struggle for scarce resources in the inner cities as we shall see later(12).

A famous example of the psychological perspective is provided by the work of T W Adorno and his colleagues in the late 1940s. As we have seen, the economic and political tensions of the inter-war period sharpened the social perception of race and led some commentators to suggest that racialism was a consequence of abnormality. The question was, could normal people send millions to the gas chambers or was it more likely that their particular personality qualities could be dissected into specific, analytical constituents that would help us understand their behaviour. The study began in 1943 taking the Jewish atrocities as a starting point, and more than 2000 people were examined as part of the investigation(13). In many ways the conclusions have the classic characteristics of Durkheim's 'Suicide', their effect upon psychology was very important.

In summary, the research concluded that the deep emotional and sexual needs of the individual which often conflicted, could be even more imperfectly amplified by rigidity and conventionalism in the child rearing patterns of parents. Status anxiety, barely controlled tension and the way races are perceived meshed to reproduce measurable attitudes that were termed 'authoritarian'. For example *conventionalism*, a firm loyalty to specific values such as 'decency' was often found; as was *authoritarian submission*, a rigid acceptance of deference to moral superiors in an unquestioning way. Another characteristic was *authoritarian aggression*, whereby any perceived deviants would receive punishment. A final illustration of the values found was *anti-intraception*, which is defined as a kind of taboo on tenderness so that the person would insist on a resolute attitude to depression or problems. Adorno argued that these characteristics were primitive and often contradictory impulses that were poorly controlled, but nevertheless they helped the individual cope with his anxieties. Attitudes and beliefs are not necessarily logical in any universal sense, the important factor is that they make the authoritarian person make sense of the conflicts in his world. So the key to understanding the implications of psycho-analytical theory is in its view of the subtle interplay between parent and child. The disciplined, authoritarian father whose role was ascribed (father is correct because he is father) as opposed to being achieved (father makes decisions for the family because he is its most experienced member) tends to recreate these characteristics of emotional privation in his children. Adorno believes that such repression, anxiety and controlled aggression required release, therefore the scapegoat for hostility became those perceived to be deviant from conventional norms either by colour or by culture. It is interesting to reflect on how this theory could be applied to certain youth cultural forms. The skinheads of the 1960s, referred to in the chapter on youth culture, apparently fulfill many of the requirements of Adorno's authoritarian personality (see page 146).

Psychologists therefore have tended to talk about racial prejudice by suggesting that aggression has to be displaced away from parent figures and projected from the inner authoritarian personality to the convenient target group. It did not matter that the initial belief was stereotypical, the label had such power.

Sociologists have mixed feelings about these findings. The authoritarian personality is a useful concept for examining race but it tends to take individuals out of the context of social and economic circumstances. Modern neo-Marxists like Castles and Kosack point out that racism often follows capitalism's need to exploit labour (see pp 112–117). To talk of racism coming from strained parental relationships seems to neglect social pressures. Additionally Adorno found that those of lower socio-economic status tended to be more rigidly authoritarian. He argued that working class status anxieties were inevitably projected from parents to children through excessive discipline and dominance; there was an absence of democratic persuasion and tenderness. Considerable sociological research has demonstrated the existence of racial antipathy spread widely across the social structure. See for example Stuart Hall's work '*Policing the Crisis*'(14). Additionally, prejudice may be disguised rather than openly projected in an aggressive manner on minorities as W W Daniel and D J Smith have demonstrated; perhaps a necessary process of disguise when any discrimination is illegal. Yet other critics wonder whether the deterministic views of Adorno are entirely valid; could it not be equally correct to argue that authoritarian tendencies can be acquired in later life rather than in the early years of personality formation? Paul Willis has demonstrated the importance of racial attitudes learned at school in his study of Hammer Town Comprehensive(15).

Racial prejudice therefore may not simply arise from the crucible of personality formation. Instead, it could emerge from situational constraints where a desire to conform to group views may temporarily produce racism which could be abandoned if the context changes, such as a reluctance to articulate prejudice at home. This is more a process of drift and withdrawal than of fixed attitudes. This is not to dismiss such views as Adorno's with faint praise. The social psychologist David Milner, in his study of children and their acquisition of racial values, has shown that the psychological stress of racist labels can often lead to ethnic minorities rejecting their own self images and their own cultures. The *subliminal* (hidden deep in the personality) effect of prejudice has profound consequences. Milner's study was based on experience of working with Asian, West Indian and English children; he tended to find that far from prejudice being normal, it stemmed from general experience and was:

"The almost inevitable result of the socialisation of the child within an environment in which prejudiced attitudes are commonly held, rather than solely a consequence of individual personality disparities"(16).

In short, prejudice is a white problem that ethnic minorities are forced cope with. Modern social psychology tries to locate racism in a broader context than that of 'imperfect socialisation' by authoritarian parents. Perhaps whole societies can exhibit such prejudiced attitudes, and if racism is so institutionalised positive attempts to eradicate it need very careful attention.

Sociologists find the social-psychological frame of reference a useful starting point for their research, rather than a concluding position in itself. It is learned behaviour, as such research suggests, and if there are historical explanations to indicate an extensive pre-history of race-relations the question now presents itself as to why this is the case. Social theorists have moved onto a consideration of the purpose of race in terms of its socio-economic and structural importance. We now, therefore, move on to consider the social, economic and political aspects of this topic as classical and contemporary sociologists have interpreted it.

Max Weber, race and ethnicity

It is revealing to compare the psychological perspective developed by Adorno (which has had widespread research application, for example with E J B Rose's '*Colour and Citizenship*' (1969), with similar explanations concerning the origins of deviance put forward by Hans Eysenck. The location of racism, or criminality within the context of personality (such as the inability of certain people such as delinquents to be 'conditioned') carries the basic argument that deviance and prejudice are disorders, the consequence of pathological factors (by this term sociologists mean socially diseased factors) distorting the supposed 'normal' development of individuals. The racist, like the borstal boy is temperamentally unsound and this diagnosis lends itself to particular policy recommendations. The central objective may be to cure the disordered criminal (or to rehabilitate him in a total institution); at the very least he is constrained by the social control process so he can do little harm. Similarly the prejudices of the racist can be kept within legal limits if their freedom to discriminate against coloured peoples is subject to the rule of law. The *Race Relations Acts* of 1965, 1968 and 1976 attempted to encourage racial harmony by punishing discrimination. Sociologists offer a rather different diagnosis; they tend to argue that focusing upon the individual abstracts him out of social and economic relationships which are taken by psychologists to be 'given'. In short, perception of racial significance may not be fixed by social training experienced in childhood, instead individuals are part of a social system that generates particular responses to ethnic groups in a patterned manner – which may be covert, overt or absent depending on the social pressures that exert themselves at specific times.

Max Weber has already been examined in terms of his contribution to patterns of development and mechanisms of economic growth. His comments on race relations are less systematic but they are fundamentally different to Adorno in their significance for ethnic relations. Weber has attempted to locate race within the context of his theory of classes in the market situation. Essentially, he slants his explanation of the social perception of race towards the social actors involved in group relationships. He argues that one of the crucial factors to comprehend is the intentions and consciousness of people as they interpret their social world. Weber moves away from the structural views of sociologists like Marx (where black races are labelled as inferior by determining economic forces that shape their class position and result in the creation of an easily exploited proletariat) towards the argument that physical and cultural differences (ie ethnic relations) are important if actors attach relevance or meaning to them.

Ethnic groups are understood in terms of the struggles in the market-place between classes, status-groups and parties. The migrant is subject to pressure from the already existing and entrenched host populations that consist (in terms of their social organisation) of a proliferation of finely tuned strata groups, already competing for scarce resources. The following example shows this point more clearly. When West Indians came to Britain during the late 1940s white workers tended to shun them, despite their contribution to the war effort. In the post-war period inequality still existed and despite the drive for full employment, work could be difficult to find. Any immigrant newcomer could be seen as a potential rival, whether at work or in the housing market where state built housing was still scarce. Racial tension is essentially about the competition for scarce resources.

To understand the relevance of this we need to refer to Weber's more general theory of social behaviour, as it was his ambition to show that motivation, attitudes and action relate to how people interpret their complex societies. Any action towards an ethnic minority by the ethnic majority depends upon how each group is perceived by the other. To illustrate this, Weber links his view of race to that of culture, first arguing that races are "common inherited and inheritable traits that actually derive from common descent"(17). This shapes the response of one group to the other. Secondly, Weber maintains that social factors such as kinship patterns, language, dress, religion and food differences may also provide a basis for inter-ethnic hostility. Individuals within the *host ethnic group* recognise the cultural and physical differences of the *ethnic migrants* and attach subjective meaning to these differences. In this sense, it does not really matter whether any genetic differences exist in a biologically scientific sense: the crucial factor is whether social actors think they are of consequence.

If we accept Weber's argument – if some act, or visual display is relevant to another person of different ethnic origin – it may help us to understand the importance of ethnic identity, and explain how such socially constructed meanings function in so divisive a manner. Ethnic antipathy is therefore linked to Weber's theory of power. He offers an explanation of how some groups retain the rights and privileges of domination, and others accept (actively or passively) their subordination. To Weber, power is the way some groups or classes get their own way despite the resistance of others. It may be that the losers in this struggle accept the victor's asserted dominance (Weber calls such consent 'authority') or that the subordinate refuse the claims of the victor (power is then perceived as coercive, it is enforced against their preference). A power relationship between, say, white society and black members can begin to be understood: those with common life chances, with specific access to goods, or high income and disposable wealth (a class), struggle to retain their authority or coercive rights. Stratification systems are the arena of struggle, they locate ethnic and social rivalry in a socio-economic context. We can again look at the inner-cities of Britain during the 1950s and 1960s. In Birmingham, as J Rex and R Moore argued, the existing middle classes used their financial power to maintain exclusive white dominated suburbs; the working classes through the local Labour Party tended to encourage a manual suburbia of working class housing estates. The immigrants from Asia and Jamaica, having no political influence and modest financial influence, tended to be funnelled into the undesirable, inner-city slums of Sparkbrook and Handsworth (see pages 94–98).

The competitive struggle for social prestige and ethnic honour are very similar as far as Weber is concerned. Low ethnic status, prejudice, discrimination are all reflections of this – ethnicity is one of the indices of differentiation. It is a social device to separate the already diverse strata into their most appropriate places. The tendency in Weber's writings is to suggest that obedience comes more from dominant pressures by powerful groups rather than it being more of a struggle between finely balanced equals. In other words, to secure compliance the inferior ethnic group tend to be constantly immersed in a powerful host culture that seeks to actively negotiate its docility. Weber therefore reduces race relations to ethnic relations, and in turn this fits into his theory of stratification whereby social class corresponds to those who share a common economic niche which influences their life chances. Inevitably the first generation immigrant finds it hard to cope with such pressures.

The subjective aspect of these ethnic relationships is equally vital to fully comprehend Weber's intention here; race is one of many cultural attributes which individuals label, or perceive, as significant. Meaning is given to the colour of a person, or religion, or clothing style; they are real in their social messages to the host and in turn help to explain how they are ranked. Once specific ethnic groups are perceived as significantly different in a hierarchical society, they are fitted into the system of stratification, and they may initially be allocated low status and differential treatment can be accorded to them.

So, to Weber, the ethnic group is one additional variable that is active in the market place. Resources are allocated partly according to noticeable social origin, and the visible signs of ethnicity mark people out for certain ascriptive treatment. The way one's 'race' is presented or defined is more important than what it actually is; ethnicity is in the eye of the beholder. The implications of this for 20th century race-relations are most important. If we argue that there is a proliferation of status groups, and a finely tuned status hierarchy, this implies that socio-ethnic relations can be regraded. Weber believed that political parties were an independent dimension of stratification, not simply an extension of economic group privileges. Once an ethnic group secured the franchise or the rights of citizenship improved socio-economic circumstances could be secured. If domination and racial discrimination are the two sides of the same coin, and if the former is politically altered then it follows so will the latter. Ethnic groups who are second and third generation will eventually enter local politics and try to balance their unequal political situation.

These changes can work to the advantage of the ethnic minority as in the case of the impact of civil rights campaigns like those of Martin Luther King during the 1960s and 1970s. Alternatively, it could entrench low prestige as in the case of emancipated black slaves after the American Civil War (1861–5). Then the prejudiced venom of economically poor, low-status whites was turned more savagely against the politically liberated negroes. In effect the blacks retained their *pariah* (outcast) characteristics by focusing the hostilities of those whites whose only (relative) status was based on the ascribed inferiority of blacks. Although their objective political rights advanced, their subjectively (perceived) esteem was still qualitatively inferior. The fact remains that Weber holds out scope for improvement; possibly the assimilation of the ethnic minority (whereby the second generation is absorbed into, and accepts the language or culture of the host) or perhaps integration occurs (whereby the host tolerates the immigrants differences.)

The concept of ethnic struggle in the context of the market place has been adopted, in part, by J Rex and R Moore in their study of racial conflict in the inner-city areas of Birmingham arguing that ". . . we follow Max Weber who saw that class struggle was apt to emerge wherever people in a market situation enjoyed differential access to property"(18). The twilight zones of inner-cities partly reflect local government policies but are also influenced by the scarcity of housing in general. Ethnic minorities were stigmatised as undesirable neighbours and this enabled more powerful political and economic lobbies to direct them into decaying urban districts.

To summarise, the key implications of Weber's work are that status and ethnic groups can overlap, cutting across class boundaries: society is constituted of many diverse ethnic and prestige groups often interpreting social life in a variety of ways. A plural set of socially constructed circumstances of race/ethnic reality can emerge where similar economic classes may also sub-divide into Hindus or Protestants and Catholics, Blacks or Whites (ie status groupings) or into a multiplicity of occupational categories. The ethnic status groups may cut a line into other strata vertically, or create horizontal rivalries or loyalties. But ethnic integration is a possibility; a rather different view to that of Marx which is discussed in the next section.

Engels, Marx and race in a capitalist society

The 19th century Marxist views on the development of capitalism never provided a systematic exposition of the relations of those socio-economic groups defined as races; a vacuum that modern neo-Marxism has attempted to fill. Like Weber, the writings on this subject are fragmentary asides rather than complete, lucid statements. Contemporary Marxists, such as Castles and Kosack or G Miles have tried to piece the essential detail together clarifying the main emphasis of the classical arguments and applying them to the modern world. As we shall see later on in this chapter, their conclusions have significant differences in style and analysis.

It was Marx's academic partner, F Engels who first related the theme of race to the needs of capitalism in his famous study of the English working class published in 1845. Engels linked the appetite of British capital investment to a determined recruitment drive for labour; he suggested that the industrial revolution was polarising society, reshaping the socio-economic relations then in existence. He described a growing proletarian class located in Lancashire and centralised on Manchester and demonstrated that the feudal peasantry living on the geographical fringes of Britain were inevitably affected by the periodic bursts of economic growth and slump that occured in a cyclical manner. Rural labour was pulled into the new urban environment that was rapidly built between 1780 and 1850; factory, workshop and casual employment were sufficiently attractive to Irish labourers to merit large scale migration to these new areas of concentrated industrial production.

The consequence, Engels argued, was that rural migrants were sucked into a capitalist system of low-wages, coercive work-relations and periodic unemployment. If destitution threatened as it did from time-to-time during the 1830s and 1840s then the options available to the unemployed labourer were unpalatable – either return migration to their original subsistence lifestyles, or perhaps remain and face the rigours of the poor law workhouse. Either respite was exceedingly harsh but if destitution threatened as it did in 1837, 1842 and 1847, few other alternatives were possible. Slum life in Manchester or Liverpool, early death, long hours of non-union labour were quite normal conditions of life experienced by town labourers. This fulfilled a need with the expanding capitalist system of production – that of providing a pool of cheap labour to draw upon periodically, and of acting as an appropriate scapegoat group for the frustrations of indigenous workers, themselves already having their wages driven down by female and child labour.

> "English manufacture must have . . . an unemployed reserve army of workers. . . . This reserve army, which embraces an immense multitude during the crisis, and a large number during the period which may be regarded as the average between the highest prosperity and the crisis, is the 'surplus population' of England, which keeps body and soul together by begging, stealing, street-sweeping, collecting manure, pushing hand-carts, driving donkeys, peddling, or performing small jobs"(19).

Engels believed that the Irish migrant workers, already brutalised by their impoverished rural existence were further degraded by their exploitation in a capitalist system that used their labour-power in a ruthless manner. Indeed the Irish were additionally treated as an outcaste group, subject to much prejudice and treated as a race apart. He went on to suggest that the repression 'criminalised' many of them who even sought illegal means to escape pauperism and its attendant hunger. Engels and Marx saw social inequality and racial antipathy as being linked together; unlike Weber they saw racial conflict as an inherent part of the economic relations of ownership and control in a capitalist society. Instead of viewing race as another element in the prestige struggles of ethnic minorities and host majorities, or being a function of competition in the market-place Marxism suggests that racism is one further aspect of class exploitation.

The proletariat, according to Marx, was split into two antagonistic groups in all of Britain's industrial centres by the middle of the 19th century. The English proletarian "cherishes religious, social and national prejudices against the Irish worker. His attitude is much the same as that of the 'poor whites' towards the 'niggers' in the former slave states of the American Union,"(20) Marx argued in 1870. The consequence was to deflect the attention of each fraction of the proletariat from the real cause of such conflict, and the antagonism was fanned by the newspapers, the clergy (Protestants against Catholics) indeed "by all the means at the disposal of the ruling classes"(21).

Racism, to Engels and Marx, was a product of capitalist relations, which suggests that in Ancient or Feudal (pre-capitalist) societies the ideologies of division, the means of legitimising exploitation operated in a rather different manner. The Romans perceived their conquered peoples as barbarians not as genetic inferiors. So the famous phrase, "It is not the consciousness of men that determines their existence, but, on the contrary, their social existence determines their consciousness" also links to Marx's view of race relations. Racism is part and parcel of the ideas surrounding the methods of production and distribution existing in a complex capitalist society. In short he meant that operating machines, or working in mines, or manipulating the efficiency of industry through white-collar employment, places people alongside the forces of production (the physical-material elements of an economy). In such socially active work people are linked together in specific patterns. This has significant influence on the relations of production, that is the class system that results from the way work is organised.

In a capitalist society, social production becomes highly differentiated. Labour is divided in the sense that workers take on specific occupations which are manual or non-manual, professional, skilled or unskilled and all are arranged in rank order. The whole system of relationships at work and at home are perched on this industrial mode of production; the benefits however are distributed in an unequal manner. The conflict of interest is essentially between owners and non-owners of capital: the former class, the *bourgeoisie*, require the latter, the *proletariat*, to be exploitable at work in order to extract as much profit as possible from their labour-power. The economic surpluses of unequal wealth and suppressive political power controlled by the bourgeoisie flows from this process. The subordinated need to be convinced in the inevitability of such an inegalitarian system of selfish accumulation by a minority who live from, and enjoy most of the benefits of, collective work effort. Here, we may return to Marx's view of the role of racist ideologies; the ruling class tends to strive to legitimise its domination as being natural or necessary and establish this in the consciousness of the proletariat. So just as religion was viewed as a means of social control, so racism was part of the ideological apparatus of capitalism, a new and potent opiate. Religion might dull the worker into a brooding suffering on earth in order to inherit the next world after life, but racism was a rather more immediate social divider. Such ideas became an ideological mechanism that located responsibility for socio-economic distress in the immediate, common-sense life chances of the workers. Unemployment, or under-employment, poor housing or overcrowding, low wages or casual hours of work in 19th century capitalism could be easily explained. The perceived, obvious cause was the immigrant; the Irishman who could live at a relatively lower level than the indigenous English or Scottish labourer who reciprocated with a venomous hatred of this alien, Celtic 'race'.

According to Marx, the immigrant was in an impossible position. As a part of a surplus pool of labour he was liable to be disposed of in recession and exploited as vigorously as possible in periods of economic growth, as indigenous workers resented their presence and therefore tended to keep them out of the trade union movement. Marx believed that these class tensions could be resolved if the landed aristocracy in Ireland were overthrown (the weakest link in the chain of ruling class control); this would then lead to alliance between the two proletarian fractions and the ultimate overthrow of the English ruling classes. The eradication of racism was possible only when the conditions for its creation were abolished; Marx in fact argued in the 1870s that the Irish National struggle was a primary determinant of the liberation of the English working class. So in the 20th century the rise of the National Front in Britain, with its working class support is more understandable if we link it to Marx's explanation. The fact that the system of capitalism itself regularly undergoes crises that create mass unemployment is less understood by Front supporters; instead they grasp the immediate – immigration is the great evil, and the solution similarly appears obvious, immigrants should be sent back to their homelands. To the Marxist this is simply another example of the success of the ruling class in its policy of divide and rule: the working class (immigrant and host worker) are the losers.

We must now consider how such classical theorists as Weber and Marx helped to shape the views of contemporary theorists, and with what consequences for sociology.

Migration, race and ethnicity – an historical perspective, 1596 to 1945

The perspectives outlined so far are immersed in an historical context of population movements. The biological and psychological explanations with their positivist desire to quantify differences between races have established a trend that has been very much an empirical one. Each has measured or itemised certain criteria to draw similarities or differences between races. Similarly, the sociologies of Marx and Weber sought to locate their analyses in a quantitative framework; population and racial migrations were rooted in the economic and cultural changes taking place as part of an historical process. It is therefore useful to chart the impact of racial migration and population movements to detect any patterns that may emerge.

In 1596 Queen Elizabeth I issued a directive commanding that black people should be sent out of the realm; this early attempt at repatriation was reinforced when a Royal Proclamation was issued in 1601 asking for her subjects co-operation in locating "the great number of Negroes and blackamoors which are crept into this realm"(22). This was one of the earliest recorded panics about immigration. The reshaping of the old Poor Laws of Tudor and Stuart England and the cyclical economic growth patterns of that era are related to the contrived social perception that blacks were undesirable; the poor and unemployed needed no African competitors. Similarly when the erratic but sustained growth of industrialisation began in the late 18th century periodic slumps brought similar calls for aliens and blacks to be exported abroad. The cost of poor relief and the prevalent obsession with the belief that paupers were often undeserving and rebellious, led to the American blacks who had fought for the British against the Americans in the War of Independence being ungraciously treated when their services were no longer required. The Morning Post lobbied the government for immigration legislation(23). Resettlement rather than repatriation was the order of the day in 1786 when a Committee for the Relief of the Black Poor planned to move those blacks receiving poor relief to settlements in Sierre Leone. A modest number of volunteers came forward, so in 1787 the Mayor of London gave his consent to a programme of forced rounding up of black 'beggars' and eventually 441 people were sent to Africa.

Organised black opposition to such practices accentuated the racial conflict and led to the Morning Post suggesting that the French policy of expelling all black people be adopted remarking:

> "Are we to be told what articles in a treaty should be adopted or rejected, by a crew of reptiles, manifestly only a single link in the great chain of existence above the monkey? Should a sooty tribe of Negroes be permitted to arraign, with impunity, the measures of Government?"(24)

It should be pointed out immediately that resettlement, or deportation practices, were not unusual, nor was it simply blacks who felt the wrath of 18th and 19th century justice. West Africa, the Americas and Australia were all areas for transportation of the casual poor, the vagrants, and those who had resorted to stealing food or illegally hunting game when their wages were insufficient to feed themselves and their families. Punishment was swift for those who were unlucky or inept thieves, particularly when the population explosion occurred during Britain's industrial revolution; much employment became casual rather than permanent. Labour power for industry, and agriculture plus all the essential but largely casually employed activities of heaving and carrying required in Victorian Britain necessitated an adequate pool of workers. The trade cycle depressions and the Governments' insistence that official relief be given only in Poor Law controlled institutions meant that deviant behaviour was manifest. White migration, or deportation to the colonies for criminal offences was as common as calls for controls over black immigration, and this had long been the case.

The pattern of migration in and out of the UK was extensive and complex; the Irish had moved into Scotland and England for centuries. Despite popular 1980s suspicions, immigration and its ensuing tension have not simply been of recent origin, nor is prejudice solely based on phenotypical difference and colour code. Irish people had arrived looking for seasonal work on the land in large numbers from the mid 18th century, often undercutting local labourer's wages. The decline of agricultural employment and the rise of industrial work meant that the era of the landless wage labourer was to become more common by the end of the century. The sociologist R Miles has argued that the seasonal migration of Irish workers was crucial to agricultural production at a time when industrialisation was pulling rural labour into the factories. The move from conditions of rural peasantry to those of industrial employment, dire as they were to English workers, was a qualitative improvement for many Irish workers and therefore there was a tendency for the migrant to become a permanent resident.

R Miles, using a Marxist perspective, maintains that the Irish were subjected to intense racism during the 19th century.

> "So, conceived of as a 'race', as s separate physical type, the Irish were also attributed with a range of negative social and cultural characteristics . . . these included the claims that the Irish were particularly prone to violence, drunkenness and theft . . . Irish immigrants were held responsible for overcrowding, inadequate sanitation and the spread of disease . . ."(25)

'Paddy' bashing in the 1840s was as widespread as 'Paki' bashing in the 1960s. The social construction of race relations once again emerges from this historical comparison.

The parallels between the living and working conditions of the 19th century migrant Irish and those present today recruited from the Indian and West Indian nations are revealing. In the last century, semi-skilled employment in decaying handloom weaving, or as diggers and cutters on the canals and railways, living in segregated inner-city districts and distanced socially was the lot of the Irish. In 1841 there were over 400 000 Irish residents in England, Scotland and Wales. Ten years later the census revealed nearly three quarters of a million such inhabitants – about 3% of the total population, a figure *strikingly* similar to the Asian and African immigrants in the UK in 1983. Ireland's wages were usually half those in England and Scotland, which created much conflict between English and Irish workers; the latter were regarded as wage-cutters, and often used as strike-breaking, black legs. As Terry Coleman has shown, the savage battles between Scottish and Irish, or English and Irish railway navigators was a regular feature of the 1840s railway building period(26).

The comparisons are not entirely valid, and we must be careful not to exaggerate the similarities but there are factors that we can see here. The significance of a Punch cartoon in 1846 portraying an Irishman as both "comic peasant ('Paddy') or as an ape-like animal"(27) helps to support Miles' argument that the migrant tends to be subjected to racist practices. The location of such attitudes of ethnic hostility in the context of class and the material poverty found amongst manual labourers under capitalism gives some support to the Marxist argument that disposable pools of labour and racial antipathy manifest themselves to the advantage of the ruling class. Similarly, the actual social perception of difference, the desperate competition in the market-place for scarce income and marginal but crucial status differences lends support to the Weberian argument that ethnicity is a complex derivation of finely tuned rivalries. The fact is that the Irish in the 20th century are not perceived as they were in the 1850s; it is worth considering the view that they have been replaced by a new parish group, perhaps a new underclass.

Whatever we may decide later, the historical dimension of migration and racial images has long been part of our culture and economic relations expressed at various levels within the stratification system, and have a resilience in popular folk-lore imagery that is intense. Moving from the apex of the socio-economic pyramid with Queen Elizabeth's repatriation programme in 1601 to its base in the early 20th century, Robert Roberts experiences of slum poverty in Salford during the lead up to the First World War expressed the enduring proletarian view that "you couldn't trust foreigners of any sort. Taking our cue from adult canon, we lived by the belief that all 'niggers' were congenitally stupid and funny, all 'sheenies' (Jews) dirty and ridiculous."(28)

The migrating Jewish populations of the world have been examined by many social commentators interested in constructing theories of race and cultural difference. Their British experience has been similar in certain ways to that of the Irish, although in significant aspects it was rather different. It can be argued that sheer volume of movement from Ireland combined with a reasonable similarity of culture eased their passage into the mainstream culture. The destitute Jews fleeing Russia and central Europe had a rather different reception, their rites of passage into British society were more problematic. The lean years of the 'Great Depression' during the last quarter of the 19th century saw Jewish migration accelerate from 60 000 resident here in 1880 to about 250 000 in 1920(29). Many settled to the sweated textile trades, competing with machine production by using the cheapest labour possible, thus undercutting many indigenous workers. A new urban 'Irish' labouring in the tailoring trade, cobbling shoes, small shopkeepers in furs and tobacco and so on, all keen to preserve their cultural traditions and religious beliefs. In this late Victorian climate of recession and unemployment the stigma of socially constructed racism grew amongst manual workers in particular; when this underemployed indigenous labour mass was 'a captive labour market'(30), and very resentful of any competition.

The erratic economy of the Edwardian era saw the introduction of *The Aliens Act* of 1905 which reflected the growing concern of Parliament to the perceived 'new' threat of immigration. It established a legislative principle that 'undesirable aliens' were liable to be deported (in practice it was little used). The world of the 20th century was to rapidly enter a period of intense industrial competition and international trade rivalries, inhibiting the free flow of manufactured goods and inevitably undermining the mobility of labour. The collapse of international trade between 1919 and 1939; the resulting mass unemployment and the demise of immigration into the UK went virtually hand in hand. The 1914 and 1919 *Aliens Restriction Acts* reflect precisely these pressures; this early legislation qualified the right of entry to those seeking residence and work.

This presented significant obstacles to persecuted groups, such as Jews fleeing fascist discrimination. Only an estimated 16 000 refugees entered the UK between 1933 and 1938 out of approximately one million seeking to escape the horrors of forced labour and the concentration camps. Paul Foot argues that British politicians during the 1930s bear some responsibility for the fate of many who were refused entry(31). That is a complex topic. What is well known is that there was much incitement to race hatred and overt discrimination against the 'Jewish race' during the inter-war period. Various right-wing groups, not dissimilar to the National Front, known as the Blackshirts supporting Oswald Mosley, regularly held marches in urban areas dominated by established Jewish residents. The 1970s assaults on Pakistanis and Asians had its parallel in the earlier 19th century assaults on the Irish, and the street attacks on Jews in the 1930s. Two banner headlines in the tabloids reflect the continuity of immigration fears, 'Aliens pouring into Britain' from The Daily Mail, and 'Smuggling of exiles alarms Britain' from The Daily Mirror were both to be found in 1938(32). It could equally have been 1601 or 1968.

Post 1945 migration, the law and racial denationalisation

The push-pull mechanisms of population migration are related to a range of variables, often operating simultaneously. This in turn often gives rise to entry *closure* procedures that operate in a social-political and economic climate.

One important aspect for students of race to comprehend is that the post-war immigration problem in the UK was a European phenomenon in the sense that the broad economic scene was the context of migration. The post-war affluence of Western Europe embourgeoisement was fuelled on the basis of recruiting labour from Eastern Europe, the Southern fringes of the Mediterranean and North Africa, as well as the West Indies and the Indian subcontinent. In Britain's case, Poles, Ukranians and Yugoslavs arrived in large numbers after 1945. An estimated 200 000 Eastern Europeans came looking for work in this era of labour shortages(33), many were dispersed into specifically regulated occupations such as mining, agriculture and building. (This policy provoked strong United Nation's criticism for not allowing such immigrants free occupational choice.)

From 1948, as Britain's formal territorial holdings overseas began to reduce, the right to hold British citizenship had to be re-examined. Under the 1914 *Imperial Act* at the zenith of empire, those born under the control of Crown administration anywhere in the empire became a British subject. As territories established their independence from Britain these ex-colonial nations tended to join the Commonwealth and were entitled to claim the status of being a British subject with all its privileges. If they migrated to the UK they could qualify for citizenship with all its attendant rights. At this time migrants from the Caribbean and the newly partitioned Indian subcontinent were actively encouraged by politicians and employers. The contribution of such migrants to the war effort had been considerable, Jamaica alone sent 10 000 volunteers to the UK between 1940 to 1945 to work in munitions factories or as recruits to the armed forces.

The *British Nationality Act* of 1948 attempted to rationalise the citizenship regulations relating to the Commonwealth, colonial and ex-colonial territories. Two types of British citizenship were established, that of Commonwealth citizens, and those of the United Kingdom and Colonies. For immigration purposes both groups could come to Britain, they were entitled to enter freely to look for work and bring their dependents, and to enjoy full rights of citizenship. At this time this was considered perfectly reasonable. Our allies from the colonies and Commonwealth had been socialised into a British empire culture believing themselves to be part of the motherland and were therefore loyal to its traditions, many speaking English. They were quite ill-prepared for the social closure and isolation that emerged rapidly in the later 1950s. Indeed, in 1955 the Conservative government rejected the idea of immigration control as a matter of principle. It is important to recognise the core dilemma of the 1950s which underlay the 'race' panic in-the-making; the constitutional idea of the Commonwealth with all its reverential implications for many politicians encompassed an ideal, that of a generic, internationalist citizenship based upon an ideology of the reciprocal benefits of Empire. Prior to 1948 *all* were subjects of the Monarch, the Empire sentiments of paternalism in return for filial devotion for all colonial and Commonwealth subjects encompassed the essence of Britain's colonial past.

In short, during the post-war period it was politically difficult to frame laws that encompassed all the prior responsibilities of Empire and yet took into account the changing economic and political circumstances of de-colonialisation. In effect two stratas of migrants were created, the first were from the independent 'old' Commonwealth (essentially the whites of Canada, South Africa, Australia and New Zealand) and the second were Her Majesty's colonial subjects (the blacks of Africa, Asia and the Caribbean) who were political dependents, later to become the 'new' Commonwealth. The respective white-black division was a cultural and racial one, pivoting on the axis of Britain's labour *shortages* during the 1950s, and then complicated when periodic recession choked off demand for foreign workers. Indeed this was then reflected within sociological research of the 1960s when the immigrant problem was presented and analysed – the tendency was to deflect attention away from the context of the reception of recruited foreign workers back onto the migrants themselves. The language of hosts (in practice singularly discourteous) and dark strangers carried clear code messages of a chilly, rather formal tolerance of the immigrants presence.

The post-war period was discussed in terms of the 'immigrant problem' through a colour spectrum based upon an excess of black-brown immigrants. In fact the majority of 1970s migrants to Britain are now from the *old* Commonwealth or the EEC, but it is still usually discussed in the context of blacks. The early 1960s saw many of these contradictory pressures manifest themselves when the foundation of the embourgeoisement hypothesis was slowly undermined by poverty studies. The Balance of Payments crises of 1952 and 1957 demonstrated the recurrence of 1930s anxieties; post-capitalist aspirations for social equality and constant economic growth were proving to be erratic even then. Stuart Hall has suggested that thc latent fears about these emerging economic weaknesses had to be soothed or displaced elsewhere and therefore '*symbols of dislocation*' had to be identified. By this he means scapegoats had to be found to distract attention away from the more complex economic problems that were proving very difficult to resolve. Assumptions reappeared in the folk-lore of the late 1950s that the British had carried the burden of civilising the Commonwealth only to see the dire consequences of reverse migration into the Motherland. Under the twin pressures of low economic growth and 'stop-go' financial policies the control of immigration was to be presented as the logical step in maintaining the material benefits of social democracy.

Assaults on blacks in Nottingham, and Notting Hill in 1958 followed by political and media comments that immigration entry should be more rigorously controlled led the Conservatives to introduce the 1962 *Commonwealth Immigrants Act.* The process of retreating from 'laissez faire' principles of population movement formally begun in 1905 was now fully confirmed. The main clauses of the Act were:

1 A voucher system was established. 'A' vouchers could be issued to those who had employment arranged in Britain such as nurses recruited to the National Health Service. 'B' vouchers were to be issued to those whose skills were scarce, such as doctors or dentists needed here. 'C' vouchers were to be allocated to the remainder, essentially semi and unskilled workers.

2 Dependents were able to join a voucher holder eg they might be wives, or children under 18 or elderly parents. The emphasis of the legislation was still to encourage family mobility, not viewing the worker as a migrant being forced to return to his kin at home.

One of the significant factors is that the Act controlled the incidence of Commonwealth migration but not that of the second category, that of the UK and Colonies passport holders (basically now people of Indian origin living in Uganda and Kenya). A queue had been established and the tenuous post-war consensus image of politics had begun to fragment; the Labour Party viewed the 1962 Act as racist. This is what we mean by '*denationalisation*' of race, the right of entry was gradually whittled away; as unemployment steadily rose and runs on the pound sterling became everyday news items the discretionary powers of immigration closure were tightened. In 1965, the year a Ku-Klux-Klan group was propagandising about race in the Midlands, the Labour Government limited 'A' and 'B' vouchers to 8500 per year (of which 1000 were for Malta) and the 'C' vouchers were phased out. The fact that more people left the UK in that year than entered it was politically irrelevant and 1966 saw immigration being limited essentially to the very skilled – of the 3976 vouchers allowed for Indians, 1511 were for doctors, 1391 were for science graduates and 667 for teachers(34). In 1972 the voucher scheme was terminated.

Towards the end of the 1960's Enoch Powell and his views on race relations were given much attention by the media; as the undercurrents of the economy began to erode much of the social democratic orderliness of the 1950s. The pound had been devalued in 1967 as a response to deep-seated economic pressures. Britain's export uncompetitiveness was incompatible with steady growth and the resulting inflation and unemployment increased the anxieties over immigration. Common-Market countries averaged annual growth rates of 5% between 1960 and 1968, in Britain the 3.5% average was inadequate to maintain full employment. Immigration became the central issue of the period. Many common-sense assumptions re-appeared, for example sections of the inner-cities were populated by new Commonwealth citizens – therefore urban deprivation (which had been a part of Britain's history since the earliest days of the industrial revolution) was now perceived in the context of black overcrowding. The Labour Home Secretary in 1968, James Callaghan announced in April that the Ministry of Social Security would repatriate immigrant families wishing to return home.

Earlier in 1968 a second *Commonwealth Immigrant's Act* had been passed in less than one week as the Labour government feared an influx of Kenyan Asians after Kenyan Africans had been given greater control of their economy in the previous year. The Kenyan Asians had retained British passports when Kenya was decolonised and the feared influx was attacked by the Conservatives, so their right of entry was withdrawn. This Act stated:

1 Holders of UK passports issued outside of the UK would now be faced with immigration control unless they, or their parents or grandparents had been born/naturalised/adopted in Britain or in a Commonwealth country that was self-governed by 1948.
2 A maximum of 1500 vouchers was to be issued each year. (The vouchers increased to 5000 in 1975.)

The politicians well remembered that the prolonged debate over immigration control between 1960 and 1962 was well reported abroad and thus accelerated the rate of migration to frantic proportions. Critics in 1968 attacked this legislative haste, others later arguing that 'The 'close connection' device was explicitly designed to ensure that white settlers in East Africa retained their right of entry to Britain by virtue of possession of a UK passport while black settlers despite holding the same passport, did not'(35). The result once again confirmed that rights of citizenship for blacks could be retrospectively defined, and hence taken away. Phenotype and culture were the criteria for exclusion, although in practice Kenya co-operated with Britain to phase this East African migration into Britain, so 83 000 were admitted between 1968 and 1975.

The 'racial' messages were quickly received by those abroad in the Commonwealth and ex-colonies, and within the UK the black Britishers felt this wind of change. However, as dependents could still arrive the numbers of black migrants continued to grow: the 1971 Census indicated that the total population of those born in the new Commonwealth now living in Britain was 1.2 million, in 1951 it had been 0.2 million. The numbers game had begun in earnest during this period and it tended to take on the context of 'managing' the problem of immigration. By 1979 it was estimated that over 1.9 million persons of New Commonwealth and Pakistani ethnic origin were resident in the UK – about 3.6% of the total population of about 55 million. We must be careful with oversimplifying our statistics but it is clear that 90% of the NCWP citizens who settled in Britain in 1979 were children, women and elderly people ie dependents. The fact that 157 000 German Nationals or 108 000 Italians and many other foreign whites were resident here in 1971 was notable by its absence from the immigration debate: this too was part of the ideological 'management' process.

A third Act limiting the freedom to migrate brought little real surprise, although its racial implications were attacked by many liberals, academics and the representatives of ethnic groups now resident in Britain. This 1971 *Immigration Act* was introduced to bring us into line with EEC principles as the UK joined the Common Market, it was to come into force in January 1973.

It had a number of highly significant clauses, and replaced the two earlier Acts of 1962 and 1968.

1 A *'patrial'* clause was established whereby 'right of abode' was granted to citizens of the UK and Colonies who had been born, naturalised or adopted – or who had grandparents in Britain, or who had been born of parents one of whom had UK citizenship. Patrials are free from immigration control; many Canadians, Australians, New Zealanders and white Zimbabwe citizens are patrial.
2 EEC citizens could enter the UK for six months without any work permit; upon finding employment a five year residence permit would be issued. These aliens are *non-patrial* but are better off than non-patrials from the new Commonwealth (some of whom, like people of Indian descent living in East Africa held British passports.)

The full implications of our retreat from Empire were now on view, although the Act did not actually destroy the notion of the Commonwealth citizen it stratified potential immigrants into carefully delineated legal castes. Workers from the new Commonwealth and Pakistan were now equivalent to any other overseas worker, controlled by work permits issued on a yearly basis with no right to stay in the UK. The white-black division between the old and new Commonwealth peoples meant that Asians and West Indians were unlikely to have close parentage or grandparentage links with Britain. The reluctance of the Conservative Party to accept 28 000 Ugandan Asians expelled by President Amin in 1972 was yet another example of Britain's political pragmatism: they were received but with bad grace amid much media ballyhoo only because they had retained their UK passports. White Commonwealth citizens enter and settle with few hindrances as Robert Moore and Tina Wallace demonstrated in their study of this topic(36), non-whites had been reduced to disposable migrant worker status. Gender discrimination was one part of a triple burden (the other two portions were class and race) as Asian, female passport holders who were widowed, deserted or who had divorced had to prove they were 'heads of households'.

Summary

Throughout Britain's history migrant workers have followed the trade cycle, they have been pulled in when it was possible to find employment, and excluded when the job market tightened up. The migrant, black or white, Asian or Celt has often been subjected to racial stereotyping – being portrayed as a *'folk devil'*, a sociological term that refers to their deviance. Such 'devils' distract social attention on to them as the cause of any problem of the period. In 1810 the Encyclopaedia Britannica said of negroes that they had:

> "Vices the most notorious seem to be the portion of this unhappy race; idleness, treachery, revenge, cruelty, impudence, stealing, lying, profanity, debauchery, nastiness and intemperance . . . They are strangers to every sentiment of compassion, and are an aweful example of the corruption of man left to himself."(37)

Shrill moral panics affect British society from time to time in her history; the immigrant from the New Commonwealth has been easier to identify and label as causing unemployment or overcrowding. Before she became Prime Minister, Mrs Thatcher lent her elbow to the debate when she argued in 1978 "it is not as if we have wide open spaces or great natural resources: we have not. So either you go on taking in 40 000 or 50 000 a year, which is far too many, or you hold out a clear end to immigration". She also pointed out that "people are really rather afraid that this country might be rather swamped by people with a different culture." Irish, Jewish, Asian or West Indian have been perceived as threatening 'races' at some time or other.

Yet between 1964 and 1975 about 2.5 million immigrants came to Britain, but 3.3 million emigrated; again in each year 1976/7 and 1977/8 about 40 000 more people left this country than arrived. The 'swamping' fear is, of course, quite correct, but the socially manufactured images of 'race' and the rhetoric of immigration require us to look for explanations of such anxieties outside of the views articulated by Mrs Thatcher. As we have seen, migration to and from Britain is, and always has been, a common feature of our historical experience. Our present immigration system "does *not* control immigration as a whole, since between 100 and 200 million non British people have the right to enter and take work (patrial Commonwealth citizens and EEC nationals.) It controls only non-patrial Commonwealth and non-EEC alien immigration and that so severely that civil liberties and family unity have often gone by the board."(38) In short it *largely* excludes those whose skin colour is brown to black.

N Deakin's summary of the consequence of the 1962 Commonwealth Immigration Act pointed to the central irony of this legislation – it slowly closed off entry into Britain but before it could be introduced it hastened the flow of migrants *thus ushering in permanent settlers, with their families*(39). If our historical perspective is relevant to the present discussion it is obvious that socio-economic change is continuous. Therefore, there is every probability that the legal definitions encompassing immigration will be equally dynamic, so further changes can occur. Indeed in 1981 the *British Nationality Act* was passed and has been seen as a further move away from the 1948 Act. The UK and Colonies citizenship has been abolished and a separate form of British citizenship will be held by those people who have a 'close connection' with the UK. Critics fear that birth in the UK will not be sufficient to denote citizenship as the 900 year principle of *ius soli* (right of citizenship by birth on British soil) has been altered. Salman Rushdie expressed this when he insisted that as the British have decolonialised their overseas territories so they have imported a new 'internal' empire of subject peoples. "This notorious piece of legislation, expressly designed to deprive the children of black and Asian Britons of their citizenship rights abolished the ius soli. From now on citizenship is in the gift of the government"(40). The Act came into force in January, 1983 and a new campaign has begun to have it repealed. The Action Group on Immigration first formed in 1976 now includes a broad range of pressure groups committed to altering the definitive clauses of this Act. The principal objection to this legislation is not to open the UK to all immigrants in an uncontrolled manner, but to establish criteria for entry that do not emphasise race and gender, and that provide for genuine, independent rights of appeal. The law is massively complex and places significant discretionary powers under the control of the Home Office. Confidence in the legitimacy of legislative measures at the very least re-assures those ethnic minorities resident as citizens of the UK. At present the evidence on poor 'race relations' is all too manifest. A lengthy report on the attitudes of many of London's policemen and women by the Policy Studies Institute published in 1983 found a good deal of 'racist' talk among the Metropolitan officers. One constable is quoted, referring to the disturbances in Southall of July 1981:

> "We went wanging down there, jumped out of the van and just started fighting . . . It was a great day out, fighting the Pakis."(41)

The next objective is to examine those sociological theories that offer credible explanations as to why socially constructed 'race' categories continue to have such resilience.

Contemporary sociological explanations of race relations

Introduction: the functionalist view

The recently published text, *The Empire Strikes Back*(42) highlights the concern that is felt not only for race relations, but for the future of 'pluralist democracies'. This neo-Marxist work is different in tone and analysis to the approaches taken by many sociologists in the 1960's when integration and assimilation were high on the agenda: S Patterson's, *Dark Strangers*(85) was liberal and optimistic for the future. The images and style of K Pryce's study of West Indians in the Bristol 'shanty-town' district of St Paul's reflects not only a conflict perspective but a grim tale of alienation and continuing discrimination(43). A distinct change of emphasis has appeared.

One aim of this section is to define a context for post-war 'race-relations' approaches and to provide guidelines to help the reader consider the implication of respective positions, and to develop an awareness of the essential arguments.

Dark Strangers was a part psychological, part sociological book. Its approach assumed racial problems could be analysed from the perspective of host and immigrant – cultural variables are the important factors. The initial conflict between the foreign immigrants and the settled host is temporary from an historical perspective. Patterson argued that the reception of such strangers has always been uncertain and problematic. The Flemish migrants, Irish, and Jews, provided material to support that those who entered British society were, at first, subject to the same chilly reception as Brixton West Indians, the subjects of Patterson's study. Colour was of incidental, or rather temporary significance in comparison with culture; the different ways of life provide the clues to the potential conflict of the late 1950s and early 1960s. This view of race relations stems from the *order* perspective in sociology whereby society is seen as a macro formation socialising its members within groups or institutions and therefore resolving social tensions in the medium term. It presents a consensual view of society deriving from Durkheim and leading through to the structural-functionalism of Talcott Parsons.

The argument used by Patterson is that the host society has a set of role expectations and values, that are understood (implicit) by most members of that society. British culture has evolved a *universalistic* set of values that the immigrant is not party to by virtue of being socialised in a different culture. People are measured and judged by these 'normal' standards of behaviour. Wearing Sunday best clothes, eating the traditional British Sunday lunch and attending church or chapel are defined as 'normal' activities. The immigrant by contrast has a 'strange' value structure, it is *particularistic* so the outcome of immigration is predictably one of a culture clash which takes a 'racial' and 'dark stranger' form. However the portrayal of race relations is an optimistic one, as competition and discord are believed to be temporary. Patterson suggests assimilation occurs when the host fully accepts the immigrant, with all their cultural differences; alternatively integration may result where the immigrant strangers accept many of the universal values of the new society but manage to retain certain essential culture traits. These are the beginnings of mutual tolerance; basically a process of role adaption and resocialisation has begun. Eventually the immigrants accept some, if not all of British society's behavioural patterns, and so lose their threatening differences. Alternatively, the host society accepts some of the behavioural characteristics of the immigrant and the tension eases. The emphasis and argument in the Patterson thesis is that the social system is based on the twin pillars of *order* and *consensus*.

In one sense the analysis seems valid. The variety of eating habits, and dress styles seen on British streets brought by Asians and West Indians have added a dash of variation and interest to our culture. The question is whether this signifies mutual tolerance between cultures or whether the symbols of difference are retained because the British are so distant. Retained cultural independence can be interpreted as a defence mechanism to give an isolated ethnic group some sense of identity.

The functionalist Talcott Parsons provides a similar analysis for the experience of Negro Americans within the structure of American society, again locating the sociological discussion within an historical framework. He argues that a comparison of the discrimination shown to other minority groups provides guidelines for the probable progression of Negros towards fuller acceptance into white society. Parsons suggests that by and large American society has a record of tolerance towards minority groups such as Jewish or Dutch migrants. As a decolonialised nation in the late 18th century it established its independence based on a Bill of Rights assuring the relative freedom of individuals and creating conditions for the emergence of a mature pluralistic democracy. Although the white, Anglo-Saxon Protestants established the strongest influence within this new state, the federation of republican states (creating universalistic boundaries to society) allowed individual states to cope with their internal preferences and individualities (particularistic groups were accommodated).

Parsons argues that the democratic traditions of freedom of individuals, and the right of each federated state to take its own path in the early years was healthy. It may, as in the case of Alabama and Georgia, have led to the short-term suppression of negro rights but in the longer term the general democratic traditions were re-established by the universalistic (the generally accepted) shared values of society as a whole. Particularistic options, such as repressing the blacks freedom to vote, or to move looking for work, treating them as commodities would be inevitably eradicated by the system as evolution towards democracy occurred. American society is seen from the functionalist view as a self-regulating mechanism getting rid of the exploitative use of negro minorities.

As industrialisation and urbanisation began to dominate American society in the 19th century, the structure of the whole system started to change the constituent social structures of the less integrated states to "the relatively open and pluralistic situation, although it provided opportunity for much obstruction"(44). Putting it simply, the Civil War 1861–65 was a power struggle for democracy where progressive forces for change created an acceptance of the principles of democracy for all Americans. The plight of enslaved negroes was a vital part of this struggle for a fairer society. Parsons recognises that the process was slow, and that much white prejudice was shown against impoverished immigrants from Eastern, and Southern Europe in the late 19th and early 20th century. Indeed, in 1882 the *Chinese Exclusion Act* specifically limited immigrants of Oriental extraction. This racism showed itself again in the 1920s when insulting names such as Kikes, Wops and Polacks were only too common, as was discrimination. Parsons repeats his belief that a pluralised social structure creates a context for 'the process of inclusion' where immigrants initially are perceived as a strange, alien community by the hosts but slowly demonstrate their economic usefulness and social reliability. The Jews are cited as an example of foreigners who faced discrimination in America for many decades, but eventually became successful in terms of social mobility and citizenship rights.

Parsons applies this optimistic prediction to the Negro American. He recognises uneven progress but points to the evidence of growing social inclusion, such as improving welfare and educational facilities and legislation against racial discrimination. These are resulting in the urban Negro being able to build a solid family structure and community life so that "sufficient ingredients for socially effective self-help"(45) can emerge. The basic rights of citizenship have been institutionalised, liberating many suppressed groups from exclusion. Parsons cites the changing role of Negro movements pressing for civil rights, which now mobilise to 'activate' white religious and moral sentiments, instead of retreating into a peasant fundamentalist religion, or singing their blues away. The Negro, says Parsons, has reached the front of the pluralistic queue, able to press for inclusion within American society while still preserving many necessary cultural traits. Integration is on the agenda. To Parsons once this occurs the colour issue will fade out of social awareness, as its central purpose has been symbolic, to stigmatise the oppressed. Once the conditions for the stigma disappear, blackness becomes irrelevant as a socially constructed issue.

To summarise, Patterson and Parsons see racial integration as simply a question of time. Since the system tends to strive for consensus and order, new arrivals such as blacks will eventually merge into the system and become as normal a part of it as any other identifiable group. Universalism balances with particularism in the long run; society responds to new arrivals by gradually changing to accommodate their uniqueness within the diverse host culture as a whole. Nothing changes, nothing stays the same.

The criticisms made of this functionalist approach are similar to the specific charges laid against this school of sociology: it is a view of society that is reassuring in its belief that social institutions and structures evolve towards consensual order. We must question whether this matches the experience of minority groups among others. There appears to be no inevitability that the immigrant will be resocialised, or that second-generation children will be accepted by the host culture. Such a reassuring, evolutionary model neglects such sub-cultural patterns as the rastafarian cult found amongst many black British youngsters of West Indian ethnic extraction. Rastas tend to be young, black males who have rejected much of what they view as corrupt white dominated society and they try to create an alternative dress style, religion, and world view that is largely anti-western. Also conflict theorists criticise Parsons for placing too much emphasis upon 'core American values' such as those emphasised by the Bill of Rights, which are supposedly guarded over by those having institutional authority. Inequality of wealth and income is given minimal attention in his work and the argument that those minorities could be kept in their lowly position by systems of domination never presents itself. Social conflict is minimised in Parson's work.

A further weakness emerges with the stress on cultural variables as the cause of racial tension as it tends to take the 'stranger' out of the social structure in which he is embedded. Adorno's psychological perspective saw racial prejudice stemming from the individual's belief system, but conflict theorists maintain it originates within a social context of stratification and inequality of life chances. Patterson and Parsons fail to pay sufficient attention to the unequal distribution of material rewards, of prestige or political power within which immigrants were received. To critics such as R Miles and A Phizaklea(46), the fact that many immigrants are working class suffering the general disadvantages of the dispossessed is more relevant than a culture clash. The functionalist view optimistically disregards the permanent problems that such immigrants face in the continuity of class systems that are inherited between generations, instead preferring to emphasise the long term assimilative process.

Robert Moore, reflecting on his earlier study with J Rex rejected the functionalist-order perspective precisely because of this point, ". . . order and consensus were treated as themselves problematic and as the outcome of domination and subordination or of truce in conflict. Order and consensus are not given, they have to be discovered and explained, not used as the basis for explanation."(47)

It is useful to examine the work situation of British immigrants in an attempt to assess the functionalist view. The evidence gathered in recent years on patterns of black employment may show whether this absorption process has taken place, or is likely to take place in the near future. The question of racial integration as a question of time is a most important consideration.

The employment pattern of immigrants in the United Kingdom

The productive social activities of work in an industrial society say a great deal about access to life chances, material rewards and general inequality. Power relations, whether exercised by management or unions at the workplace dominate broad areas of social activity. On the simple level it determines where any individuals can afford to live (by strictly controlling income), or leisure interests (by limiting the workers access to expensive holidays or items of consumption). In a more complex way, the productive relations of work may influence how an individual actually sees the society of which he is a part: it helps to define his construction of social reality. Immigrant groups are affected by these socio-economic relationships.

Certain social observations made by *New Society* contributors have partially reflected the links between ethnic groups at work, at play and at rest. *The Other Britain* attempted to represent the lifestyles of the underdogs of English society by collecting together some of the detailed, descriptive comments of Paul Barker, Paul Harrison and Ian Walker on the topic of ethnicity. The daily round of pressures and social influences surrounding ethnic minorities is reflected in Walker's sentence, "Tombstones and synagogues are daubed quite regularly" – a comment relating to the common experience of Jews in Cheetham Hill in Manchester. Harrison describes 'heavy concentrations' of the Irish "in one or two areas of Birmingham" (phrases so often associated with black immigrants). Barker refers to the conspicuous presence in Peel Square in Bradford of the Asian community in the remark that "the empire has come home". It is a journalistic style that harks back to the sympathetic investigative work of Charles Dickens, or Jack London in the 19th century. The poor, the dispossessed and the stigmatised have the same 'feel' about them.

The 1971 Census showed that about 6% of all economically active persons (about 1.5 million people) in the labour force were born outside the UK, or had parents born outside of Britain. Many of these were from the EEC or Eire; about 2.2% of the work force were black (about 0.5 million workers). After 1962 the voucher system and controls over immigration tried to steer newcomers into the more skilled areas of industry and the service sector. The Act also precipitated a panic abroad and speeded up those trying to enter before the law was enacted. This inevitably complicated the pull mechanisms of the British economy.

We can still note certain clear trends. For example, *Britain's Black Population* points out that black people are heavily concentrated in certain economic sectors, and in specific occupational groups defined by skills, or the lack of them. Their employment pattern differs in many respects from that of the British population as a whole:

1 Immigrant labour is a very large part of the textile industry of Yorkshire and Lancashire. This industry experienced recruiting difficulties because it has declined, working conditions are relatively poor and therefore the pay is low. Shift work is a common feature of this industry. In 1971 almost 12% of male workers were immigrants; the Courtaulds Northern Spinning Division in 1973 employed 47% male immigrant operatives for unskilled jobs. A very strong concentration of immigrants was found in Humberside and Yorkshire; nearly 21% of male workers were immigrants in the wool and worsted trades there. The stereotype that suggests many Asians are in distributive trades such as shop-keeping or restaurants was shown to be incorrect according to D J Smith's research. About 12% of white males were self-employed in the 1977 PEP survey; when we compare this with the ethnic minorities 8% of Asian working men and 6% of West Indians are so placed. The "self-employed shopkeepers account for only 5% of the total Asian working population"(48).

The argument that blacks take away work from whites is equally untrue. W W Daniel's research into immigrant employment in the 1960s found blacks recruited into unpleasant, dirty, heavy manual type work. Such jobs had been largely rejected by the white working classes or they had attracted those indigenous workers who subsequently did not react well to shift-work, low-pay and clocking on. Immigrants took the work few others wanted; jobs that in the relative prosperity of the Macmillan-Wilson boom were deserted by indigenous labour.

2 In the West Midlands, John Rex and Sally Tomlinson found a disproportionate representation of West Indians, Indians and Pakistanis in the forges, furnace works, foundries and rolling mills of the metal industry. "Between a third and a half of the immigrant workers . . . appear to be working in hot, dirty industries, marked by shift work"(49). We must remember that the car industry has dominated the Midlands and 1 in 8 West Indians and 1 in 20 Indians work there. David J Smith nevertheless found evidence that 18% of the ethnic minorities were in the Midlands car industry compared to only 7% of the general population. As far as the concentration of over 33% of New Commonwealth immigrants in the metal industries is concerned we can note that less than 10% of the general population works in these areas.

3 If we take a gender statistic, about 27% of the West Midlands indigenous female population are clerical (white collar) employees. Immigrant females tend to be factory hands, 27% are so employed. Only 16% of New Commonwealth females are in clerical work.

4 According to the 1971 Census, immigrant labour makes up 6% of all workers. A higher proportion of them work in manufacturing industry (47% of all employed immigrants compared with 33% of the indigenous work force). If we look at low-paid service work such as employment in snack bars, and restaurants, nearly 25% of all these

workers in Britain are immigrants. The figure is over 50% in Greater London.
5 In the NHS in England and Wales about 33% of the medical staff are born abroad according to 1979 figures. Over 20% of student nurses and 15% of General Practitioners are of similar origin.

These black, ethnic minority groups break down into specific occupational strata defined by their skills. D J Smith's research showed how heavily manual their work tends to be. Roughly 60% of white males undertake unskilled, semi-skilled or skilled work; but 80% of Indians, 91% of Pakistanis and 91% of West Indians are similarly employed. This broadly bands ethnic minorities into blue trouser and white collar categories. If we examine the lower levels of the job-skill structures of British industry (the semi and unskilled) the proportion of whites is 18% of all economically active whites. In the case of Indians 36% are so placed; 32% of West Indians and 58% of Pakistanis are on the lowest rungs of the occupational ladder.

At the same time many ethnic minorities have "penetrated into the better, skilled manual jobs on a very substantial scale" argues D J Smith. Here 42% of the white population are so employed but 59% of West Indians, 44% of Indians and 33% of Pakistanis.

When we come to the middle (non-manual) tiers of British society the proportion of ethnic minorities in such work rapidly diminishes. Approximately 40% of whites are in professional-managerial white collar work, but this falls to 20% of Indians, 8% of West Indians and 8% of Pakistanis. It is hazardous to interpret these statistics in any precise manner because a broad range of influences are at work. We can summarise most of them thus:

1 Many Indians and Pakistanis do not speak English as well as the indigenous population. This hampers their search for skilled work despite their qualifications.
2 The employment pattern reflects the demands of the UK economy for workers to fill low status jobs vacated by the white working class or for skilled manual workers in specific occupations such as building. This pulled black workers into particular industries, such as textiles or forge-foundry work.
3 A relatively younger New Commonwealth immigrant population came, willing to undertake work wherever it could be found. As immigrants became established they could also suffer disproportionate unemployment with diminishing work situations (as a consequence of their weak bargaining power and the "last in first out" rule.)
4 The role of the trade unions has been passive rather than active as far as ethnic minorities are concerned. While ethnic minorities are officially supported by the TUC, local resistance to black advancement has been very influential. N Hedges and H Benyon's, *Born To Work* comments

upon job selection at the Bilston steel works, where a black worker argues:

"The colour bar operates from the Personnel Office. If you go to some departments here you will see only Englishmen or white men in that job. They've already laid down that policy that if a black man comes onto that section they'll walk out . . . look how many Indians and Jamaicans are on the yard doing the dirty jobs."(50)

In a society constructed upon a variety of social influences, the working class tend to be disadvantaged in the struggle for desirable scarce resources, whether they be income, occupational status, leisure or housing. Clearly to be black and working class, and to face discrimination from both management and unions alike (as the PEP reports have consistently reported) means that the New Commonwealth minorities encounter a variety of intersecting *structures of domination.* By this sociologists mean that layers of socially constructed inequality are superimposed on one another to hedge in the black immigrant.

This is not passively received. Such concentrated social pressure has produced its own immigrant defence and attack. In 1975, 60% of Ford workers at Dagenham (14 000 from 23 000 manual workers) were black. This is an industry that has encountered many production difficulties since it began in the 1920s, one of the main areas of dispute being a struggle between speeding up the assembly line, another involves company policy to lay men off when car demand falls. The conflicts over these issues were actively supported by blacks during the 1970s. If we reverse the *New Society* tradition of reporting about 'them', the underdogs, and look at British society from within, the comments take on a very different style. As Clifton a 25 year old Rastafarian stated in the 1983 *Policy Studies* report seeing the police as the immediate control agent holding the domination process together:

". . . me nah a tek dat no more from dem people. If dem holds me again me would do one a dem an injury . . . But the next time dem stop me, me hope is ina de tube because me will just push one a dem under the train and gone."(51)

Very frightening, violent words indeed but a view stated in the context of much low status employment and rising black unemployment. The continuing disproportionate trend in black youths inability to obtain work is evident. Between November 1973 and February 1981 total unemployment doubled, but the number of blacks on the official unemployment registers quadrupled. Justice Scarman found that in the Brixton Employment Office "the rate of registered unemployed among black males under 19 has been estimated at 55%". Racial stratification with all its attendant disadvantageous life chances seems a fixture of black society whether at work, or out of employment, particularly when young blacks are on the streets. According to the Policy Studies report six out of ten black youths are stopped on average five times each year by the Metropolitan police. With rapidly rising black unemployment and significant police scrutiny of young men of West Indian origin the possibility of conflict is always present. The functionalist – order perspective with its emphasis on minorities being gradually absorbed into the social system does not seem to fit too well with the empirical evidence about black peoples' experience of work in British society.

J Rex and R Moore – race and the inner city

Many modern sociologists like John Rex and Robert Moore have turned to the Weberian analysis of class and race in an attempt to see whether a conflict theory of stratification is more useful in explaining the persistence of racial segregation practices. From this point of view race relations are a form of social relations which arise between groups.

Weber believed different strata within a system of inequality had different access to property, status and political power. Instead of two great classes (the proletariat and the bourgeoise) as Marx had claimed, there were a *variety* of classes and status groups constantly struggling with each other for relative superiority. Each stratum has a lot in common with its own distinct life styles and different influence in the political system. This view of social inequality sees a complicated, wide variety of conflict between different groups at work, in the housing market or over access to leisure resources. Immigrants, therefore, form part of this general struggle for resources, for status and political power. To Marx, the immigrant's exploited role at work largely *determined* his lifestyle, including his ability to live in particular parts of a city. The analysis given by Weber argued that immigrants could be exploited at work but they could use other areas of struggle to obtain a foothold in the housing market. From this position the immigrant could establish a basis of influence and improve his position in the struggle for relative prestige.

The Rex and Moore research programme assumed a plurality of competing groups and classes in any society, and that complexities of this interaction of host and immigrant within a system of stratification provides a more realistic sociological model of race. Conflict rather than consensus is the basis of race in society to these authors. Their study of the Sparkbrook district of Birmingham is durable and applauded by many sociologists. When the research began in 1964 Rex and Moore were caught up in the wider body politic of disintegrating race relations. 'Nigger for a Neighbour' leaflets emerged in local constituency politics and in this atmosphere Parsons seemed much less relevant than Weber. The study, attempted to explain how conflict over access to scarce urban resources could be related to the stratification system within the city. Marxism was rejected, in part because Rex and Moore believed there was no simple or clear relationship between the ownership of the means of production, and the social race relations of production. City politics were not seen as a basic reflection of those found at work, ". . . the contenders are not labour and capital"(52). The researchers drew upon the work of the Chicago School or urban sociologists of the 1920s and Weberian conflict theory.

In summary the study concludes that:

1 Birmingham's physical and spatial shape was controlled by the forces of the industrial revolution. In the very early phase of economic growth worker's homes were built near the production centres of small workshops. This was an extension of rural production where labourers had lived near or on the farms they worked.

2 In the maturing phase of capitalism during the late 19th century, industrial concentration in urban centres became less intense. The earlier pattern of Victorian back-to-back terraced houses for the workers began to diversify into less and more desirable residences. The growth of relatively cheap urban transport (trams/railways) meant that the skilled labour aristocracy and white-collar workers could separate their residence from their workplace so they moved towards green-belt suburbia.

3 By the 20th century a housing market was well established, but in an era when housing was essentially privately built (before 1945) there was an inevitable struggle for the prized possession of desirable homes. Residents clustered into housing classes. The housing pattern was partly a consequence of the distribution of income but it is seen by Rex and Moore as a process of neighbourhood segregation that had a conflict base *of its own*.

4 A number of housing classes were in evidence by the mid-century when the state had established a responsibility for building houses after the Second World War. The working classes tended to live in State-rented property congregated close to the inner-city, hoping to move to their own council estate suburbia. The rich controlled their own access to privileged property markets, and by virtue of vastly superior purchasing power could segregate themselves into exclusive districts – closing off entry to inferiors. Medium placed salaried groups, and affluent workers could save and obtain mortgages through private agencies such as Building Societies and become owner occupiers in the suburbia that they could afford. The lesser white collar and semi-skilled manual workers lived in modest areas (often council-owned), or perhaps rented private accommodation near the city centre.

5 The immigrants from the New Commonwealth had similar problems to any new arrival: to break into a scarce housing market with its own housing class-structure when the waiting lists for council homes were lengthy. The problem was compounded by the deteriorating race relations. This is not the culture clash of Patterson's '*Dark Strangers*', instead the city is the fulcrum upon which the stresses of resource shortages pivot. As the white hosts with their young families were removed to suburbia, immigrants were funnelled into the inner-city of Sparkbrook.

Rex and Moore found evidence to support their thesis that a combination of low-paid employment and the discrimination processes of the housing system run by the privileged middle classes of white suburbia, or influenced by the power of the local Labour Party machine kept immigrants in specified neighbourhoods. Those of low status and modest income were ill-equipped to match this 'racialist' socio-economic system of housing closure. As Estate Agents discouraged immigrants purchasing in the more desirable districts, and because the local council was prepared to provide mortgages to blacks who moved into the dilapidated inner-city, Birmingham manufactured its own 'race ghettos'. The immigrants who purchased slum clearance property and the tatty but preservable larger houses created a viable lodging district. A mixture of inner-city council property, lodging house zones and flatland formed a new housing class of property-owning immigrants. A secondary housing system resulted. The flotsam and jetsam, the social deviants, students, ex-prisoners and other transients could now obtain accommodation alongside the Birmingham born white English who 'lived' this process of change with a mixture of fear and bewilderment.

The hosts now saw immigrants as creating the slums and overcrowding their living facilities despite the fact (as Rex and Moore demonstrated), that in practice the immigrant landlords were a *de facto* housing department.

> "In a strict sense this does not produce a ghetto. A ghetto would appear to imply a segregated ethnic community . . . the zone of transition includes various ethnic communities, transitional people awaiting rehousing and isolates and deviants of all sorts . . . Clearly the situation demands the existence of a parish group who do not themselves feel bound by welfare state standards and are culturally distinct enough to be blamed for their departure from such standards."(53)

Immigrants were scapegoats to the more dominant political-housing classes, but they reacted by building their own communities. These were often hostile to what they perceived as white attempts to colonise their history and traditions. The solid Pakistani community with its own film centres, urdu papers, and shops stressed that their traditions placed a great responsibility to house their relatives, even more so in the climate of discrimination. The real paradox is that in this study racism flourished because of the complexities of a scarce housing market, but both the white host slum dwellers and the immigrants where victims of very similar circumstances. Each of the antagonists saw poverty, underemployment, modest political influence and their residence in the inner-city as somehow the fault of the other; this was the real dilemma.

Rex and Moore have been criticised for suggesting that the housing class structure is somewhat independent of the broader class-structure. Neo-Marxists have pointed out that the ownership of the means of production manufactures the urban setting housing as much as it sets the scene for industrial relations, or gender stereotyping. In short, the immigrant is a member of the working class, suffering virtually identical disadvantages. The Sparkbrook author's retort that it was Max Weber's theory of finely tuned strata that had the finesse in empirical research to explain and account for the urban housing classes of mature industrial society rather than the coarser theories of Marx. The five classes produced by the system of house ownership and allocation in Birmingham were identified by Rex and Moore as:

1 Outright owner-occupiers (having higher income; capital for mortgage deposits and secure employment; immigrants tended to be excluded as they were vulnerable to redundancy.)
2 Council house tenants (provided on the criteria of long residence and not expected to take lodgers. Some immigrants, of course, were given poorer council houses.)
3 Tenants of whole private houses (the indigenous landlords usually did not rent to immigrants.)
4 Lodging house proprietors (immigrants worked hard or borrowed from friends and family.)
5 Tenants of lodging houses (immigrants and social deviants were highly represented but with all the disadvantages of overcrowding, minimal privacy and expensive rent.)

As Rex and Moore point out, "Being a member of one or other of these classes is of first importance in determining a man's associations, his interests, his life-style, and his position in the urban social structure; moreover each class has its own qualifications for entry"(54). In this explanation the Weberian argument is that the worker's relation to the means of production might be less important than his differential access to scarce housing; conflict can as easily be the product of competition over accommodation shortages as industrial exploitation. Any individual's income clearly influences his ability to manipulate his house purchase potential, but there are other factors, such as the Weberian variables of access to political influence and the negotiated status (low in the case of blacks).

It is a question of which emphasis we take that has been at issue since this study was published. How valid is it to see 'housing classes' as a relatively independent category of the wider stratification system? A Giddens has certainly endorsed the specific emphasis of this argument regarding urban conflict but concludes that such disagreement contributes "to the overall character of the class structure of a given society"(55). So the way urban neighbourhoods cohere, or the styles of life that emerge in a mixed cultural-ethnic environment often reinforces the class structure, or it may fragment it. The fact that the skilled working class are likely to be more favoured in the mortgage market place over the semi-skilled might lead to segregation within the working class pattern of residence, or ethnic discrimination might isolate 'objective' working class groups into a white housing area and a black one. Perhaps the essential theme that the city is both part of, and a modifier of the overall social system; the urban structure and character may well express the complexities of the broader society of which it is a key part. Welfare-capitalist urban policies and the location of the work-place tend to be reciprocally linked but it may be more helpful to understand that living space is determined more by the pressures of industrial production than of any individual status group's house consumption. This is an easier judgment to make with the benefit of hindsight. R Moore states that if he were examining the inner-city today he would begin by looking at ethnic minorities in the context of European labour migration as a whole, and the contribution of accommodation scarcities in dominating this labour mobility(56).

The housing pattern of black immigrants in the United Kingdom

The housing market has changed significantly since the Second World War as successive governments have been committed to easing access to the housing stock. In 1947 only 13% of British households rented accommodation from their local authority, whereas by 1971, 31% did so. The state has promoted council housing as part of its social service committment to minimise overcrowding, homelessness and insanitary conditions. Local authorities have been encouraged to lend mortgages to allow people access to the independence of the private owner-occupier sector. A comprehensive 'social need' programme covering all aspects of the housing market (private rented, council rented or owner-occupier) has been subscribed to by all political parties.

If we look back to privately rented housing we find that in 1947, over 60% of British households were so accommodated compared to 18% in 1972. By and large, the private sector is now seen as 'last resort' housing for the most needy. Today over 50% of Britons live in owner-occupied housing.

Despite the attempt to improve the housing supply, we have not solved the housing supply in terms of numbers of available dwellings and the quality of their amenities. Britain's inner-cities have a long history of urban deprivation. In an attempt to compensate for this inadequate housing stock which constantly deteriorates two particular policies have been followed. First, the state encourages private purchase by providing tax incentives for people to take out mortgages; and secondly the council rent system is subsidised to help those whose incomes are relatively lower to maintain their living standards.

In theory, the objective of Britain's housing policy (public and private) is to stimulate the supply but at the same time to ensure that the disadvantaged are provided with good housing. It is a mechanism of redressing social inequality.

The sad fact is that the supply of housing, particularly in the council sector is inadequate to keep up with demand so access to local authority rented accommodation is problematic. This housing has to be rationed so the needs of competing applicants have to be constantly re-assessed. It comes as no surprise to find from the detailed research of D J Smith and other groups like the Runnymede Trust, that black people have been caught up in this matrix of disadvantage to a greater extent than the general population.

The figures regarding housing for black people look good in the first instance. D J Smith found 26% of West Indians lived in council properties, whereas the text *Britain's Black Population* which is more recent discovered 45% were in local authority rented accommodation. This compares favourably with the 31% of the average population who live in such properties. Now, in addition if we look at the owner-occupiers we find that few Asians are in the public rented sector (4% only) whereas most are buying their own homes (over 50%).

From these statistics we could draw the broad conclusions that black people have succeeded quite well in purchasing their own homes, or in obtaining council properties, and that by and large the practices of discrimination in housing (banned by the 1968 *Race Relations Act*) have been eradicated. It would be an error to do so, given the general sociological criticism against official statistics which often mask a variety of social processes at work.

For example, when we look at factors such as the *quality* of housing available to whites and blacks very clear differences show themselves. D J Smith set out to measure quality by taking into account four factors.

1 The basic *structure* of accommodation (whether the home was detached, semi-detached, terraced, flats or rooms.) Blacks in general have access to old, rather inferior properties as the table over indicates.
We can see that 86% of minority ethnic groups have pre-1940 properties compared to 48% of whites.

2 The question of *shared dwellings* was measured (indicating a lack of privacy, or shared amenities.) According to the 1971 census less than 4% of general households in England and Wales were in this category; yet 30% of West Indians and 22% of Asians were in this position.

3 Deprivation related to the *density* of occupation. Again, Smith found

	Minorities %	Whites %
Type of dwelling:		
Detached	1	21
Semi-Detached	15	36
Terraced	66	30
Flat/Rooms/Maisonette	15	12
Not Stated	3	1
Age of dwelling:		
Built before 1914	46	24
Built before 1940*	86	48
External condition of dwelling:		
Very good	28	55
Very good or average	58	89

*Includes previous category D J Smith, op. cit. p 230

four times as many Asian, and three times as many West Indian households compared with whites lived in high density accommodation (for example 2 or more people sharing bedrooms).

4 *Amenities* available in accommodation were measured. Facilities like cookers, baths, hot water supply and inside or outside toilets were quantified. All the minority ethnic groups were consistently worse off than the white population for amenity provision. When it comes to the quality and distribution of amenities it is better to be a white labourer than a black professional. Ethnic origin dominated over social class in this situation.

If we move on from these circumstances we can see that rationing of council housing has also worked to the disadvantage of black people in comparison with whites. People without homes can find themselves housed relatively quickly but often their desperation has meant the quality of council accommodation offered has been inferior. One example publicised by the Runnymede Trust in 1975 is that black people in the Greater London Council area tend to be living in pre-1940 flats in central London, whereas whites are found more often on the newer, outer estates. This was not necessarily discrimination; the GLC maintained that as the problem of housing disadvantage was more acute among blacks so they tended to take the first, often worst, property made available to them. The question of 'funnelling' into districts that Rex and Moore found was not at play here, nor was it a question of blacks choosing to 'congregate' – many had their first choice of the poorer properties down. It was more a question of the underdog in the complex market system faring worst.

This is not to say that discrimination of a subjective, prejudicial kind does not take place because clearly it does. Rex and Tomlinson found that in Handsworth one typical comment from a housing visitor was:

"We don't want to offend people. We try to put people in neighbourhoods where they won't conflict. Aftere all, some of the Asians may just be getting out of the stage where they made curry patties on the floor. It's like the English working class – they kept coal in the hall and donkeys in the kitchen when some of them were put in council houses in the twenties."(57)

At the same time the objective operation of the council housing market in a situation of general scarcity means that rationing works against blacks. The fact that ethnic minorities are generally manual workers, and that they are in relatively lower paid occupations indicates that a combination of subjective discrimination and objective scarcity works against their housing circumstances. The broad social policy of the state has failed. "A system which is intended to help the needy and deserving has actually tended to perpetuate previously existing disadvantages"(58). *More* black people should be in council housing *not less*, and its quality should be superior to the average household not the reverse if public housing policy had succeeded.

When we look at the high owner-occupying found among Asians the preceding arguments partly explain why over 80% of manual working Asians are owner-occupiers (twice as high as the general population). Smith's research and that of Rex and Tomlinson are congruent on this point. It is not so much a question of blacks becoming part of Britain's 'property-owning democracy'; instead they have tended to buy the worst property available for owner-occupation. In Bradford, Liverpool or Birmingham, working class Asians get poor housing in the more dilapidated areas because "buying cheap, poor-quality and central properties has replaced private renting"(59). Although home improvement grants are available for private owner-occupiers it is found that 70% of white applicants are successful in acquiring them but only 35% of Asians and 26% of West Indians.

This suggests that the complexities of the housing market work around a cluster of factors of deprivation. Class, scarcity of dwellings, access to mortgages or council waiting lists, discrimination and the general economic recession of the late 1970s have all played their part. The evidence leaves little doubt that the social perceptions of the actors involved plays an important part in the social closure processes that operate around that most important variable, the social construction of race.

The pluralist view of race relations

It is worth re-emphasising the important feature of the research cited so far is that social significance is given to supposed physical (genotypical and phenotypical) and cultural differences, the migrants ethnicity is *transacted*, or given meaning by the importing stratification system. The supposed differences are then used to legitimate the behaviour of the dominant hosts. Racial antipathy is socially constructed, and structured by group interaction but in a political, economic and cultural context. The structural pressures of society including class, patterns of employment and political power are the broad context within which race relations are conducted.

There is room for a broad range of competing explanations of racial antipathy. One view that differs from that of Rex and Moore is a plural perspective which maintains that races do not dovetail neatly into the stratification theories of Marx and Weber. Placing less emphasis upon structures of society that shape social behaviour, pluralism tries to construct a theory of race whereby ethnic groups tend to cut across classes rather than conveniently slot into them. Plural society is much more elastic, it is composed of a wide range of varied groups. A multiplicity of social, political, cultural, religious, economic and ethnic groups highlight the complex range of social loyalties and possibilities for interaction. Both Marx and Weber recognised that certain classes constantly exercise their domination with varying degrees of enforced compliance being used to preserve a privileged position against immigrants. Pluralists view modern society as rather more democratic entities where political institutions balance competing interests, acting as mirror images of society, reflecting all its needs and aspirations as far as possible. Both conflict and consensus can exist, life is presented as a struggle, but a relatively fair one in the end because the governmental system regulates conflict to minimise the conditions that create it.

According to this view, race and strata do not necessarily coincide. Perceived 'racial' difference is not necessarily related to a class struggle for income, wealth or scarce housing resources. Different racial treatment may result because the minority ethnic groups are isolated, and therefore discriminated against because of their language, customs or appearance. Race presents itself as a convenient factor allowing social stigmas to be successfully applied. D Lockwood in particular has been keen to point out that each sub-section of any strata can be varied in a range of ways. Societies exist with a broad matrix of cultural, ethnic groups and class groups who might share certain general values of the broader culture but who do not necessarily form an integrated whole. A plurally complex racial society might have wide ranging, conflicting social groups who could live in distinct portions of an urban environment, but commonly support the wider values that link the social fabric as a whole. In other words a *segmental* society is indicated. So ethnic groups could work together, buying and selling from one another but then returning to their own secure enclaves. This is a kind of social kaleidoscope endlessly varying with many culturally distinct, if overlapping elements.

Lockwood suggests that ". . . it may be noted that no racial problem at all comparable to that of the present day presented itself in the historical situation in which the basic structure of sociological theory took shape"(60). He believes that as race problems were not as crucial to the investigation of the classical sociological theorists compared to class or political dominance, the habit has passed down that race is a secondary issue. It is a 'complicatory factor' of social inequality. The black immigrant is *status-disqualified*, or as worse off than the white worker, perhaps belonging to an underclass of dispossessed people. Race then becomes of secondary importance to stratification.

Instead Lockwood believes that we should begin by recognising that society may be segmental, with partially independent sub-systems and a whole range of sub-cultures existing each capable of having different ways of life. The 'fatalistic' unskilled working class sub-culture co-exists with a variety of other class cultures such as the middle-class 'rational' view of planning for the future. The repetoire of belief systems and behaviour meet but only touch; this is *cultural pluralism*.

In addition to this, social pluralism may exist where the actual structure of society is differentiated into an organisational setting of residence, employment and school. Race, therefore, has become an additional element, a new basis of plural society, another portion of this medley of differentiation. An example would be in colonial Uganda. Traditional African native cultures persisted alongside those of the moslem migrant Indian, middle class traders – but each dwelled in their own segment of the social system. Each group knew their appropriate social roles, worked in the economy at various levels but cultural pluralism was the order of the day. Conflict between such groups should not simply be presented as class conflict argues Lockwood. In British society the funnelling of blacks into inner-city districts may have occurred but the fact is that these deprived minorities often unite with white dominated political parties to improve their civil rights in a collective effort. Much depends upon the perception of the social actors involved in a matrix of cross-cutting loyalties so integration, assimilation or further tension could be the outcome of economic recession.

The theory of plural society has been criticised by many race sociologists for being too general and descriptive. S Zubaida, for example argues that it is more valid to rely upon the structural tradition of sociology rather than upon the more subjective perceptions of actors choosing to negotiate their own segments. The plural society is viewed as an aspect of an existing economic and social structure; certainly actors can interpret alternatives and select certain behaviour patterns (the rasta is an example) but the system constrains their options. Race relations and class relations operate within power systems and patterns of dominance to which migrants are usually subjected. A variety of discriminatory practices do occur but structural sociologists prefer to rely upon the specific features of inequality rather than general theory of segmental pluralism.

It is worthwhile considering how immigrants are part of an international labour market, between First and Third World societies and how they are part of systems of economic relations.

Education and race in Britain

One test of the reality of the existence of a plural society is to examine whether different social and cultural groups manage to preserve their individuality in a system where other values and power structures are dominant. In the case of ethnic minority groups we must see how they have fared in the education system to understand whether there is a significant degree of equality given to their minority circumstances. In short the question is whether they have preserved their cultural differences.

We have already seen that there is considerable evidence from both the housing market (public and private) and the pattern of employment and unemployment that suggests only modest concessions have been made to ethnic group needs. One reason for this is that the respective power of the indigenous white population, and those defined as racial minorities is unequal. This inequality is further reflected in the British educational system. The initial optimism of the 1950s was based on the view taken by many teachers and headmasters that black people could be *assimilated* into the culture without too much difficulty; such children would become 'English' in all but colour. This policy proved to be wrong, largely because there is no homogeneous culture to be absorbed into, all sorts of class, race, gender and regional differences existed. If you wish to test this argument try to define what you consider to be the British way of life: possibly it would be close to the culture of white, middle class people. In addition many immigrants resented the assumption that their own culture should be displaced to please their hosts.

The tensions this assimilation policy produced revolved around giving pupils from Pakistan pork or beef for school dinner, or treating Moslem girls refusals to change into PE kit as 'unco-operative' or as evidence of 'dissent'; as H Townsend and E Brittan showed in their research(61). Although many teachers were sympathetic to immigrant children, some insensitivity inevitably occurred as a consequence of not understanding, or in some cases of ignoring black cultural traditions. Assimilation tried to flatten ethnic minority culture into conforming with English as the mother tongue and British history, literature and social studies were the basis of a remodelled ethnic culture. To minority groups this denial of their history and culture comes perilously close to subtle racism.

This policy met with resistance from ethnic groups and partly as a result an alternative strategy was evolved using the principle of *integration*. Labour Home Secretary Roy Jenkins in 1966 argued for an atmosphere of 'mutual tolerance' and of an acceptance of 'cultural diversity' This was much closer to the pluralist perspective. Extra financial provision was part of the programme of integrating Asians and Caribbean peoples into wider society. Local Authorities began to provide extra financial resources for their special educational needs; Section II of the 1966 Local Government Act allowed the Home Office to give grants of 50% of the costs of staff appointed to help such children (later raised to 75%). In 1975 LEA's spent £20 million under Section II. Additionally an Urban Aid Programme began in 1966 to provide money to help those 'authorities dealing with the problems of multiple deprivation in the inner cities'.

Pluralists have argued that the integrationist policy stance was evidence of society's recognition that minorities would be given the opportunity to retain their own identity, and participate in the advantages of public education. The school was an important factor in constructing a successful plural society.

The reality of experiencing primary and secondary education from the point of view of black youth has been rather less satisfactory. It is important that some 40% of the black population in Britain are British born, so it is not a problem of 'immigrants and hosts'. The overall evidence is still rather uneven, but it does seem that children whose parents are Asian have coped with their educational experiences rather better than those children whose parents enjoy an Afro-Caribbean culture. Partly as a result of this B Coard(62) attacked the British educational system in 1971 alleging that schools interpreted the special *difficulties* of children from a broad West Indian culture as *deficiencies*. Coard argued that the construction of the school curriculum in its tendency to deny black cultural origins as being valid subordinated black children in an intellectual sense. He maintained that British history was presented as superior, as the unfolding of white superiority over primitive peoples they colonialised. It was highly ethnocentric. Black pupils who resented this (puzzled that authority figures like teachers could not lie) developed poor self images. Similarly the patois of the West Indies is a mixture of linguistic skills which did not fit the traditional elaborated code of white, middle-class society, its rural nuances were interpreted as errors from standard English, and criticised as an inferior form of expression. Coard suggested that teacher evaluations produced conflict in the minds of black children steeped in Caribbean traditions and periodic aggression or lack of co-operation, or straightforward confusion was perceived as evidence of their educational subnormality. A number were being labelled as mentally defective. "In 1972 West Indian children constituted 1.1% of all children in state schools and 4.9% of all children in ESN schools"(63).

It is interesting that also in 1971 the psychologist Hans Eysenck had published *Race, Intelligence and Education*, which supported the view that there was strong evidence that American negroes were genetically different from whites in terms of their IQ potential. Essentially they were biologically inferior, he claimed, possibly because centuries ago many of the more intelligent ones had avoided the slavers, or died trying to. Eysenck speculated that perhaps "If . . . the brightest members of the West African tribes . . . had managed to escape, so that it was mostly the duller ones who got caught, then the gene pools of the slaves brought to America would have been depleted of many high IQ genes"(64). The consequences of such arguments as Coard's and Eysencks was to provide a polemical structure around which the stark reality of ethnic group underachievement was to be discussed. Again it was a variation of the 'nature versus nurture' debate.

Many factors have been identified that demonstrate the relationship between social origin and a pupil's educational progress, from *material* circumstances (such as low income, overcrowding or the inability to support offspring after 16 years of age) to *cultural* variables (such as parental aspirations, teacher perceptions and so on). Halsey, Heath and Ridge in their relatively recent analysis of social mobility found that 75% of the working class respondents they studied left school at 16. Exactly the same proportion of their sample from the 'service class' (largely a middle class, professional-managerial strata) stayed on after 16. Ethnic underachievement has to be understood against this broad background of circumstances of material deprivation, parental aspirations and the skill to negotiate school culture and the organisation of the learning process in the school.

These classroom encounters between blacks and whites have had an uneven impact in the sense that codes of meanings transmitted through the curriculum, and the values brought by ethnic minorities have to some degree been antagonistic. In exam terms (a limited criterion for measuring success or failure in education) the statistics are nevertheless revealing. The Rampton Committee set up by the Labour Government in 1979 to examine the situation of ethnic minority education published an interim report in 1981 on 'West Indian' children's performance. 16% of white school leavers obtained GCE 'O' level grades 'C' or above, or CSE grades I compared with 3% of 'West Indian' children. At 'A' level GCE, 2% of West Indians gained passes compared with 12% of other school leavers(65). Rampton maintained there was some evidence to support the ethnic minority feeling that racism was a contributory factor; even if it was not a large problem the *belief* that it was prevalent could be as important as the fact. In other words the danger always present was that if black children were seen by the staff as a 'problematic' category, and suspicions were harboured by the students such a mutual prophecy could easily be fulfilled.

Material factors in schools, such as the lack of skilled staff, and of black staff were cited as contributing to the problem of underachievement. Additionally West Indian parents tended to see the school in the same way they reared their children. In other words, as an authoritarian institution and they often resented, or were confused by, the liberal-democratic attitudes of the staff. The potential for a culture clash was a further complication.

Inevitably most teachers are white; one estimate by the Caribbean Teachers Association put teachers of Caribbean origin at only 0.15% of the teaching staffs of British schools(66). The possibility of minimising the lack of symmetry between the school and the home is probably further eroded. The ILEA literacy survey carried out between 1968 and 1975 showed what this could mean. It concluded that there was a broad gap in reading skills between West Indian and other children, a performance difference that widened as the children grew older. Rex and Tomlinson's study of Handsworth lends further strength to the argument that ethnic minority group education is worsened by the cumulative result of such deprivation.

> "Most (black) children will go to immigrant majority schools ie they will not simply be a minority presenting unusual problems against a background of white British normality. Their problems will be *the* problems of the school. They will be what its educational processes are about."(67)

As Rex notes as early as 1967, 47 of the school's in Birmingham had more than 30% of immigrant pupils, and 14 schools had over 50%. The black school is a fact of life in Handsworth, and elsewhere as white parents attempt to escape the stigma of having their children educated in immigrant schools – a *de facto* system of racial segregation.

The overall drift of this kind of argument (still it must be emphasised based on rather limited research) is critical of cultural pluralism and the Lockwood view in the preceding section. Pluralism advocates a view of a society which can unite or divide into a range of distinctive categories. It is a kind of 'all things to all people argument.' Everybody can be accommodated in a civilised society if it is based upon reciprocal tolerance of cultural differences. The problem is that the evidence on race and employment, housing or educational experiences suggests that what separates society into its divisions is the ability to force a particular set of constraints upon those defined as different. In other words, it seems rather more relevant to look at the access to power in British society. Ethnic minorities have found it very difficult to maintain their cultural sovereignity in a society that still has not been able to comprehend their particular problems in schools, council housing or at work.

We will now look at a structural perspective of British society, to emphasise the point that the indigenous working class have disadvantages in a stratified society and that migrants will have to struggle not only with their racial stigmas but with their class disadvantages too. The French sociologist P Bourdieu argues that in a stratified society apart from material disadvantages, the subordinate strata are evaluated in the educational system according to their skills in mastering the dominant culture. The subtle pressures of the education system constantly divert the subordinate into less prestigious forms of education, low status and poor self-esteem. In the case of ethnic minorities they suffer material deprivation in the inner city, or at work but cultural dominance on two counts – their class position, and their racial origin. Multiple deprivation may well be the result.

It has been argued that black people, and those defined as 'races' (like the Turkish workers in Germany, or the North Africans employed in France) have a particular role to fulfill in the economic order of things. Some sociologists believe they are recruited because they are cheap to pay, stigmatised to divert indigenous workers attention onto 'them' as causing unemployment, or reduced wages and 'racialised' to minimise the social capital (housing, education and the social services) allocated to them. The argument believes such groups are an *underclass*, a tier of people below and outside the traditional class structure. This is a view we will now discuss.

The idea of the existence of an 'underclass' has been developed by Rex and Tomlinson who adopt a sociological perspective of conflict based on Weber rather than Marx. For our purposes the two schools overlap in their support for this argument; it is a development of Engel's concept of the sub-proletariat which we discussed earlier. The underclass theme maintains that the manual working class is now clearly divided along occupational and racial lines: in America, Western Europe or the UK there are white workers who participate in their unions, or belong to political parties or who have reasonable job security. On the other hand an underclass has been 'peeled off' the bottom of this manual strata, made up of blacks and other ethnic minorities (eg negroes, Mexicans, Puerto Ricans in the USA or Turks, Greeks and Tunisians in Germany). This underclass is stigmatised by 'race', lacks legal protection in employment, and is shunned by traditional labour organisation. Rex argues that the underclass encounters a structured 'tangle of pathologies', multiple socio-economic deprivation is their normal experience. Polarisation of the underclass into their own housing areas, jobs and schools has been the order of the day: they have become a marginal, sub-strata of the working class.

We will move on to look at work by two American neo-Marxists, Baran and Sweezy, who began to formulate their views of blacks in the United States economy from this perspective. Then we will examine the underclass arguments of Castles and Kosack on labour migration in Europe, before returning to consider how such arguments may apply to British society.

The neo-marxist view of race-relations: the recruitment and perpetuation of the underclass

The sociological agenda on race is now quite different to that of the consensus orientated 1960s. During the last decade conflict sociologists have developed Marx's outline ideas and attempted to apply them to the present day. *The Empire Strikes Back* draws heavily upon the argument that race and class disadvantage go hand in hand. The suggestion is that black people are a *fraction* (a sub-section) of the working class more easily exploited because they are identifiable as aliens by skin colour and culture. They are presented as disposable migrants, cheap-labour for capitalists and as dividers of the working class as a whole because racism sets people against each other rather than making them aware that their real problem is to overcome a socio-economic structure that exploits all workers. The race riots of 1981 in Toxteth and Brixton and other inner-city areas are seen in this neo-Marxist view. Exploited ethnic minorities resist the trend to discriminate against them, or to make them the equivalent of the Irish in the 19th century (blaming 'them' for 'causing' economic decline and unemployment) by fiercely expressing their frustration. To a neo-Marxist like S Hall in *Policing the Crisis* the popular media's attempts to link mugging with black youth is a symptom of these socio-economic pressures. The argument suggests that as a welfare-capitalist society encounters severe recession it drifts towards firmer control of potential deviance. Political power becomes more authoritarian and a minority group – like blacks – are scapegoated, and stereotyped as causing social problems.

This view explains racial distinctions in the context of social antagonisms and therefore attempts to relate conflict to social stratification. It is a *structural* view of social behaviour in the sense that ruling class domination and racist beliefs are linked together. The practices of discrimination in schools, or at work allow the disadvantaged immigrant – blacks little flexibility in the job market or in their search for social acceptance. The capitalist system has grown, according to this view, upon slavery and exploitation of the labour and raw materials of the colonised nations of the world. It has created a massive sub-proletariat, what the French writer Fanon called the 'Wretched of the Earth'. At the same time capitalist control sowed the seeds of race inferiority (on the principle of weakening opposition by divide and rule) which are still in flower in the late 20th century. Despite the collapse of formal empires, and the growth of political independence in the modern world, racism still has a purpose. Racial stereotypes are seen as functioning to fulfill the many needs of consumption lifestyles upon which capitalism is based. In the UK we see little clear relationship between spending £4.279 million on tobacco, or £525 million on cosmetics and toiletries, or £180 million on slimming foods(68). The DHSS estimates that 50% of the adult population of Britain are overweight, but to link this in any lasting way with the fact that 500 million people in the underdeveloped world suffer severe malnutrition often leads to criticisms that such statistics are taken out of context, or are no *real* basis for comparison.

The neo-Marxist argument maintains that these affairs are all part of international structural relationships, one group of societies directly effects how the others life style is to develop. From the point of view of races, blacks are part of the propertyless colonial poor, by and large, and many try to better themselves by migrating to the heartlands of urban-industrial centres to obtain greater purchasing power and an improved lifestyle. Their socially significant colour marks them out for special exploitation by the capitalist employers who wish to extract the cheapest wage labour they can. In the labour market the migrant is received with muted or overt hostility by the native (white) worker who fear his wages too might be driven down. The colonial mentality developed through many generations within the host culture functions to allow prejudices to operate, so generally blacks are excluded from organised unions, or their grievances at work are rarely taken up. Neo-Marxists argue that this hostility by the resident, established working class operates against themselves. The 'false ideas' about racial inferiority divides the proletariat into two sharply contrasting sections: the oppressed, largely white host proletariat and the super-exploited, essentially black migrant sub-proletariat at the bottom of the social pyramid. The latter are scapegoated, blamed for taking away jobs adding to housing shortages and accused of requiring greater support from the meagre resources of the welfare state. To neo-Marxists it is no coincidence that black dominated inner-cities are heavily policed. Any degraded group tends to respond by resorting to deviance and is likely to become 'criminalised' by the society that denies real participation. Conflict theorists have gone so far as to argue that a system of internalised colonies now exist in many capitalist nations. Immigrants are living in specific urban districts, working in migrant occupations when employed, and acting out the role of a reserve army of labour. Race is not seen as a legacy, a remnant from the past, but as having a necessary vital role in contemporary societies. Racism is a key aspect of welfare-capitalism. In recession the blacks can be disposed of back into their ghetto's without too much social concern being expressed. When the economy revives they can be absorbed into the workplace but often at low wages. This neo-Marxist view can perhaps be best illustrated by reference to specific examples of where it has been applied. We shall explore the American and European experience to assess the validity of this approach.

The American experience of race: a neo-Marxist account

Any examination of American race relations should compare Parson's views with those held by conflict theorists such as Oliver C Cox and P Baran. The thrust of emphasis away from consensus sociology towards seeing race in the context of dissent is clearly evident. In their text, *Monopoly Capital*, P Baran and P Sweezy attacked the liberal, integrationist views of the functionalists. They suggested that those who supported Parson's views had little historical or empirical appreciation of the negroes experience of the harsh life imposed upon them by American society(69). These authors argue that the black slaves were forcibly shipped to the Americas in the 17th century along with a code of ideas that allowed this brutal state of affairs to exist – racism was the means of legitimation, the way in which slavers justified their activities. Racial inferiority was 'common-sense', so slaves became objects of possession. This is not to say slaves were treated with ferocious brutality on a permanent basis. Indeed, the American historian and Marxist E Genovese has suggested in *Roll, Jordan, Roll* the mutual obligations between owner and slave were reciprocal(70). Slaves were valuable commodities, they often received paternal indulgences from their masters so tolerable conditions were quite normal.

Baran and Sweezy suggest that the American Civil War was fought under the banner of negro emancipation but that it was in reality a struggle between the Southern ruling class (the plantation elite) and the Northern ruling class (the industrial and finance capitalists.) Once the southerners were defeated and blacks emancipated they were only free in the sense that all wage-labourers under capitalism were free. Most of the negroes remained half-starved pauper, peasant class in the south until well into the 20th century. It is further argued that when America began its major phase of economic growth from the 1870s it absorbed huge amounts of labour from Europe, Asia, Canada and South America. Baran and Sweezy draw parallels between the way these newcomers were treated by their established hosts and the way in which blacks were destatused. In a sense each new wave of migrants were subjected to racial initiation rites similar to those of the Irish in England.

The First World War is seen as a turning point by Baran and Sweezy. The massive industrial demands feeding the war combined with the effect of the agricultural revolution pushed and pulled whites and blacks from the Southern states into the Northern industrial towns. Foreign migrants outside the shores of America were unnecessary when a large internal pool of labour existed to be drained. From 1924 a quota system was introduced in America which effectively closed off Eastern and Southern European migration. The neo-Marxists argue that the old Confederate states became the internal labour colonies of America and the negroes became "a substantial segment of the urban working class,"(71). Many were happy to leave behind the skimping and scraping of rural pauperism. However whereas whites by and large improved their income and living standards, particularly after 1945 the negro achieved little socio-economic mobility. Negroes were ghetto dwellers, segregated by residence and the first category to be unemployed in recession.

Baran and Sweezy believe that the circumstances within which blacks found themselves were shaped and used by American capitalism:

1 Private enterprise obtained cheap labour from blacks desperate for work. Landlords received higher rents than deserved from slum properties when little alternative housing was available and the affluent middle classes had a large pool of servant-domestics to draw upon.
2 The white proletariat tended to exclude blacks from skilled trades and unions and a two-tier system of occupations emerged – the lowest paid, unskilled work being doled out to the blacks. A precisely ranked, carefully differentiated labour force was moulded by the pressures of class, race and capitalist need. "Such a society becomes in time so thoroughly saturated with 'race' prejudice that it sinks below the level of consciousness and becomes part of the 'human nature' of its members"(72).
3 Baran and Sweezy maintain that as technology is under pressure to become ever more efficient the tendency is for less opportunities to be available to those poorly schooled and culturally disadvantaged. 'Deskilling' means that blacks become excluded from more and more occupations and although black militancy has meant more political concessions to exploited minorities (eg successful desegregation of the armed forces and civil rights legislation) it has had a marginal impact. Most blacks remain poor. A relative few, have become socially mobile but the conflict theorists see them as a *token group.* They are largely a black bourgeoisie or privileged by exceptional talents in entertainment, sporting activities or members of the service class like teachers, dentists and lawyers who may have a vested interest in maintaining the present unequal arrangements. In short a conservative, negro middle-class was sponsored and funded by white interests and co-opted into a system that is dependent upon the relative poverty of their black fellows. The result is to co-opt articulate, able blacks into white, privileged American society leaving the mass of blacks even worse off.

The implications of this overall argument are clear. Racist opinions, antipathy to others thought to be culturally and biologically different were socially constructed by the rise of capitalism. Basically the need to maximise profits shapes social attitudes, schooling, employment and residence. To talk of integration as simply a question of time or of any political programme aimed to create mutual ethnic tolerance neglects the unequal economic processes upon which racial relations are organised. The stratification system of urban capitalism is the starting point for a neo-Marxist interested in examining the persistence of racial antipathy.

The European experience of race: a neo-Marxist account

A very similar theoretical perspective has been adopted in recent years by European writers keen to develop the outline principles indicated by Marx and Engels. Again the analysis is macro-sociological in that it examines the role of immigration within capitalist societies and the role of racist ideas in the context of movements of labour. The most famous account was that outlined by Castles and Kosack. They put forward the classical Marxist arguments that capitalism demands a surplus pool of labourers(73). The reserve team of workers always hovers over the shoulders of their relatively fortunate fellows (employed but moderately paid) until the majority of the reserves are brought into play. Then the tendency is for unions to seek higher wages because their bargaining power increases as quickly as the reserve army shrivels. Higher wages tend to produce inflationary pressures, so profits diminish as shareholders get less of the cake and the economy enters recession. The cycle is almost complete when workers are laid off, ethnic minorities at the faster rate. The whole process is then ready to slowly begin once again.

Castles and Kosack looked at post-war migration into Europe, basing their research upon the United Kingdom, Switzerland, France and Germany. They concluded that the links between the migration of workers, racism and capitalist development are evident and overwhelming:

1 Migrants add to the pool of employable-disposable workers depending upon the state of economic development. Their primary role is an economic one, a latent surplus population.
2 The ability of some capitalist economies to transfer migrants back home is very important. Sending Turks from Germany in recession avoids any excessive costs of welfare benefits such as unemployment pay or rent subsidies. Unemployment is exported to the cost of the Third World type nations who have to bear the brunt of it.
3 The drawing-in of foreign workers from the fringes of industrial Europe, such as Spain, Portugal, Yugoslavia, Greece and North Africa helps to differentiate the host working class, almost into a series of castes. The immigrants tend to become 'untouchables' doing the lowest paid, arduous, essential manual work. Ford cars in Cologne employed 25 000 workers in 1972. Of these 10 000 were Turks, mostly working on the assembly lines; a further 5000 guest workers (gasterbeiter) were similarly employed. Again the indigenous worker's general response to migrants was similar: the migrant was seen as a potential threat to employment, and received with some aloofness even in times of economic growth. The relationship was rather like that of the skilled worker, a labour 'aristocrat' tolerating the lower status of the unskilled migrant.
4 Migrants tended to be segregated away from the work place in poor hostel accommodation, or in the worst housing districts of the cities. The echoes of Rex and Moore's research are evident here, because the clearly visible migrant workers were physically congregating as aliens in specific districts. The cause of their being there, and the consequence are easily confused by hosts and migrants alike.

Essentially, racism for Castles and Kosack stems from this competition between migrants and the indigenous working class, themselves prone to struggle for a decent standard of living in a social structure that is unequal. The neo-Marxists view class relations and racist opinions as having very similar causes. Critics of this whole argument reply that if the economic factors of ownership of the means of production cause class position – why does the white worker not recognise his fundamental interests lie with the migrant workers, not in denying them entry into trade unions or by turning a blind eye to the low wages they obtain? This argument has not been satisfactorily resolved. Castles and Kosack believe that political and ideological factors cause this dissent within the proletarian ranks; that the newcomer is presented in the media, and other areas of the superstructure as a migrant in order to preserve race and class antagonisms. This process is called *fractionalisation*, meaning that the ruling class divide the potential unity of the subordinate by setting them against each other. Also as work tends to be a signifier of social esteem (or social dishonour) the fact that many migrants from the New Commonwealth (in the case of Britain) entered poorer paid, unsociable jobs further confirmed their inferiority. Colour was underpinned by class.

Other comments have been made about this argument. The migrants

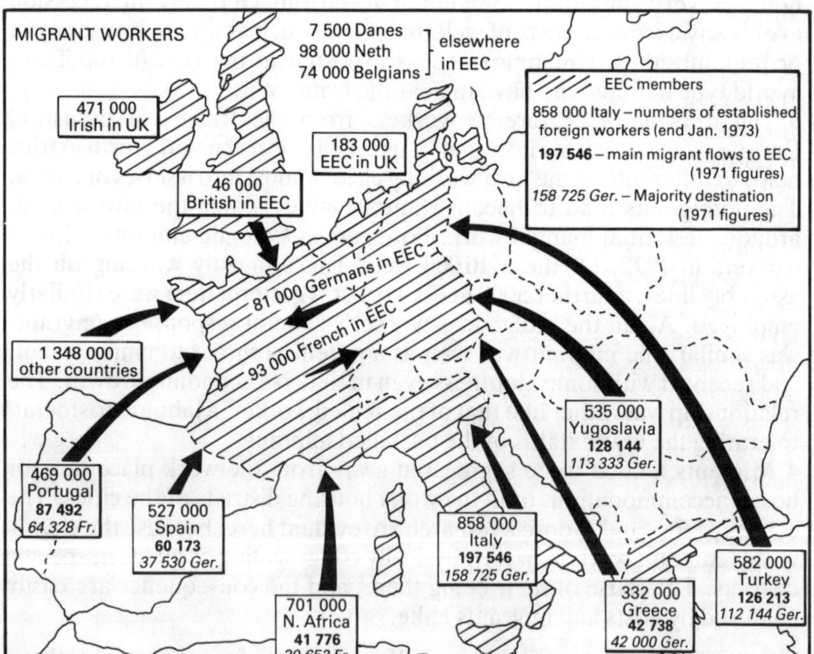

want to move and are often prepared to take low status work refused by the indigenous working classes of industrial Europe. The temptation is understandable. There are better material rewards and some migrants improve their earning capacity in comparison to the lack of opportunities in their own societies. Additionally the mass migration promotes the social mobility of the industrial workers. The interesting difference between British racial attitudes, as denoted by Castles and Kosack, and those of other European nations is inevitably one of colour. Blackness, combined with ex-colonial status more emphatically differentiates the New Commonwealth immigrant. This must not be taken too far, as they believe that in Europe although racial ractors are less evident the workers respond by visible hostility to the migrants and by criticising their physical appearance as being different and not of 'their race'. These authors insist that this reveals the true cause of racism; it is a consequence of the recruitment process of capitalist nations who exploit the labourers of the Third World, as well as their raw materials. Race is still an ascriptive ideological label used by rich industrial societies to exploit such labour and fractionalise the subordinate proletariat as a whole. The Turk in Germany receives almost the same stigmas as the Asian in Britain. Labour mobility; reserve armies of exploitable workers; the structural inequalities and capitalist ownership of wealth are the pieces of the jigsaw that make the whole picture clear. Colour and culture are presented as disguising the hidden, internal economic causes of racial antagonism.

Although many sociologists do not accept this 'economic' argument, there is much agreement that migrants to the UK tend to be lumped together as blacks and accorded similar treatment. Charles Husband recently pointed out that "In the context of the 1970s and the economic crisis of the 1980s with its attendant massive unemployment, and in the context of a general erosion of civil liberties, 'racism' is not some legacy of a colonial era which has merely failed to fade and die. It has a specific vitality and is daily regenerated in the perceptions of white Britons"(74). R Blackburn and M Mann, taking a Marxist perspective, talk of the 'bonded labourers' in Western capitalist nations, migrants who are recruited on conditions laid down by employers that place such workers at significant disadvantage when trying to improve their wages or conditions of employment(75). This is a very complex argument, but there is some evidence that indicates the existence of a quite distinct labour market for migrant workers. This dual labour market is quite literally two types of job opportunities. In Switzerland, about 40% of all factory labourers employed in the 1970s came from abroad as 'guest workers'. Although the overall picture is unclear there is evidence that a disadvantaged labour market exists. Rex and Tomlinson's study of the Handsworth district in Birmingham found that the immigrants circumstances were "characterised by a different kind of position in the labour market, a different housing situation and a different form of schooling"(76). Although not taking a Marxist perspective Rex does accept that an underclass has been created, largely of West Indian and Asian origin occupying a disadvantaged segment of an unequal society. In 1974, as Stuart Hall has noted 21% of British black youths between the ages of 15 and 19 were unemployed. He points out that the economic squeeze has a disproportionate impact upon the disadvantaged underclass. The question is whether the second and third generations of migrants children have now become permanent internal exiles in the inner-cities.

The problem that is not resolved in many sociologist's minds is whether or not migrant workers are occupants of different labour markets within white industrial societies. Following this we have to decide whether racism pushes such workers down into specific employment, or perhaps underemployment. Generalised arguments are unconvincing. A detailed report by the Policy and Economic Planning group published in 1977 written by D J Smith(77) found minority ethnic groups heavily concentrated in low status, semi or unskilled manual work.

The statistics need to be carefully interpreted. Smith found evidence that immigrant workers in Britain have been prepared to work anti-social hours, and had chosen to enter lower-status occupations than they were qualified for in order to be with their cultural group or for reasons of language retention. Discrimination against them was widespread but the dual-labour market theory was not entirely valid. Again whereas the neo-Marxists would stress that alienation and dehumanisation was the consequence of capitalist pressures there is some room for doubt. The bouts of civil disobedience, commonly referred to as the race riots in places like Brixton and Handsworth during 1981 need to be examined with care. G Gaskell and P Smith had researched the views of young people in Brixton during 1979/1980 and concluded that West Indians certainly felt that they were deprived the freedom of movement because of excessive police harassment, but these youngsters valued the aspirations of work and educational qualifications. They could see some merit in the view that obstacles to their employment were partly under their own control. In other words they were not the depressed proletariat of popular Marxism(78). This is not to say that economic deprivation and racial discrimination contribute significantly to such disturbances but such evidence does cast doubt on the view that internal colonies exist within urban industrial societies shut off from the mainstream culture and social structure.

The general emphasis of this argument is quite powerful. It is now accepted that immigrants from Asia, and the West Indies are disadvantaged within British society whether at work, school or leisure. The Scarman Report into the Brixton disorders quoted research into the registered and unregistered young unemployed blacks which suggests 55% of such males in Brixton were so placed(79). Although the precise position is unclear Martin Kettle has recently pointed out that the proportion of blacks in the prison system is rising significantly as a whole. "In April this year, according to the Home Office, 50% of the population of Ashford remand centre was black. Brixton (another remand prison) and Aylesbury prisons were between 25 and 30% black"(80). This can be interpreted as evidence of a tendency towards coercing those ethnic deviants who have been systematically 'criminalised' by their drift into petty delinquency which is treated by the courts as rather more insiduous than it is. Stuart Hall argues that if we look at the 'mugging' statistics and the way they are presented in the culture then "public opinion is carefully orchestrated" to distract analysis from the structural causes that underpin such deviance.

The arguments are complex and if there is no precise answer perhaps two points need to be remembered. European migrants have been denied the right to vote, they have often been quartered in poor housing, neglected by host trade unions and restricted to particular occupations. They tend to be disposable. Firstly, it is relevant to question whether the New Commonwealth immigrants in Britain who have rights of citizenship denied their European peers are a socio-racial category that has been superseded. The discretionary legislation on British immigration resulting in the 1981 *Nationality Act* may produce similar types of residents in Britain in the future. Migrants seeking work will require a permit; the Department of Employment fixes quotes of migrants for particular occupations; and citizen rights will be strictly controlled. This may amplify racial tensions within British society particularly if the migrants are measured against ethnic criteria. A second factor to consider is whether the theories explaining the origins of racial antipathy are better supported by theories of stratification, or cultural difference. It seems to be the case that perceived 'race' marks the status of ex-colonials, they bear the excluding stigmas of ethnicity, colour and class. Robert Moore has tentatively suggested that ". . . it could be said that blacks are simply on the receiving end of treatment that has always been meted out to the poor and the deprived. They are now the victims of rapid inner-city decay and dislocation. In other words, this is still a class issue, not a 'race' one"(81).

Some concluding remarks

This chapter has tried to provide a context for you to develop a broad view of the varied perspectives of race theory. We have marked some of the principal theories for discussion. Research into this topic has tended to confirm that the circumstances of ethnic monorities are as constrained how as they were in the early 20th century. Despite three very important Acts of Parliament (1965, 1968 and 1976) passed to outlaw discrimination on the grounds of race, ethnic or national origin, the increase of tolerance amongst diverse majority and minority groups has been difficult to establish. The Chinese rarely appear in discussions about immigration; perhaps it is because as a self-contained group they tend not to enter public services occupations or manufacturing. If the Communist Chinese withdraw our lease from Hong Kong it will be interesting to see how British society copes with another group with claims to British residence.

The overall impression from sociological research tends not to be optimistic, casting doubt on Roy Jenkins view expressed in 1966, when he was Home Secretary, that we should try to achieve "equal opportunity accompanied by cultural diversity in an atmosphere of mutual tolerance." Decayed inner-city districts like Toxteth in Liverpool 8; low pay and low status work; high youth unemployment; alongside stringent policing and added to much petty discriminatory treatment of a nagging, persistent kind offers little optimism for the future.

Nor should any depiction of the styles of living of ethnic minorities be left solely to academic commentators like sociologists. Students must take into account how such groups perceive this socially constructed discrimination 'from the inside'; we must note how the recipients of structured antipathy react to the pressures of British society. Ken Pryce's study of the West Indian population residing in Bristol, appropriately entitled *Endless Pressure* points to experiences common to many similar populations in different cities of the UK. Using the interactionist method of data collection, the technique of participant observation, Pryce researched the St Paul's West Indian scene very thoroughly getting to know the clubs, pubs, churches and homes of those living in this community. Rex and Moore's research strategy fifteen years earlier in Sparkbrook was not too dissimilar.

Pryce's conclusions were constructed around a neo-Marxist theory, linking the ex-Third World, black migrants to the social pressures of the industrial first world he argued that ". . . it cannot be said that West Indians are 'making it' either in Bristol or Britain generally because the super-problems of class and colour that face them in Britain do not differ fundamentally from the structure of constraints that drove them out of the West Indies in the first place"(82). In Pryce's view integration has failed. Those immigrants who are here are poor and embittered, either 'locked-up' in the isolation of their hot gospel, Pentecostalist religions or perhaps acting out the hustler's deviant role of street wisdom (drugs, petty theft, and prostitution) in their decaying 'shanty town' of St Pauls. Many young blacks seem to reject semi-skilled work as 'slave labour' drifting into petty-delinquency and poverty; many of their elders try to hang on to their jobs as unemployment rises, struggling to maintain their hold on work, and their respectability. All are strategies of coping, but as the recession has a disproportionate impact upon black youth, politicised teenyboppers tend to be pulled into Rastafaria. White society's rejection of blacks may ultimately accelerate this cult of celebrating 'black virtues,' a code of *negritude* (a term describing the behaviour of black youths retreating into praising negro history and culture as the only ideal worthy of following) of dissent from within the sub-culture of reggae. Those who are prone to be on the margins of poverty often seek some 'solution,' however temporary, to their problems.

Numerous other studies predating Pryce's work produced similar evidence that ethnic minorities are thrust up against much vulgar racism at all levels of their day to day life. One common experience that immigrants regularly come up against is the contradictory argument that 'they' are idle, and welfare state scroungers, and yet come over here to steal 'our jobs.' Stereotypes and ideologies do not operate on the principles of logic.

The stereotypes, of course, exist in reverse. Chevannes and Reeves cleverly indicate how this takes place in their reporting of the case of a Jamaican nurse training in England, accustomed to believing that the English are fair minded and intelligent by the schooling of her own culture. Her experience quickly tempered these youthful ideas(83). Patients avoided her black hands, nursing tutors suggested she might cope better with the lower level SEN course rather than SRN training; employment on the wards involved her in menial work; there was much avoidance of social contact by white colleagues. Inevitably her first impressions of the English, in the context of these experiences developed her own stereotypes. She believed that whites were unhygienic, after all they washed their underwear in the same sinks that dishes were rinsed when in her country this was absolutely taboo on health grounds. She saw whites as divorce prone and sexually promiscuous both outside and before marriage whereas her own culture intensely supported lasting unions between partners.

The sociology student, when looking at race relations should take note of the kind of antipathy a black person can encounter, for example "And I've had people in the middle of town trying to run me over and other people don't believe it . . . Drivers have made U-turns to come back at me, shouting 'you wog, you bastard, you nigger' and people just walk on – I just walk on . . . You can't go into a shop without being the focus of attention because people expect you to steal something. If you go into a restaurant for a meal then you are shunted off into a corner where you won't offend the other all-white clientele"(84). It may well be that the black academic community use the title *The Empire Strikes Back* to point out that enough is enough.

As students of sociology one final point worth emphasising is that the acquisition of all attitudes and values is systematic whether they be those of class or race. The socio-economic development of British society has tended to construct what sociologists call a *symbolic reality*, a view of the world that many people come to hold as a result of being reared in a particular culture. It has elements of common-sense, it reflects historical experiences passed on through successive generations and such a world-view tends to be emotional and permanent. After all, if we are informed that out opinions on politics or race are foolish we often resent the criticism; it is difficult to be self-analytical. Just as the phrase 'we are all middle class now' was the common-sense view of the early 1960s disguising much relative poverty, so the extent of racial antipathy may be much underestimated in the mid 1980s. The consciousness of those who encounter this exclusive social prejudice is a relevant starting point for any discussion of race.

Bibliography

(1) A starting point for students could well be *Police Against Black People*, *Race and Class* (1979) pamphlet No. 6 available from the *Institute of Race Relations*

(2) P Barker (ed) *The Other Britain* RKP (1982) p. 11

(3) *The Race Question in Modern Science*; UNESCO (1956) pp. 11–53

(4) C Husband, *Race in Britain* Hutchinson (1982) p. 12

(5) M Banton and J Harwood, *The Race Concept* David and Charles (1975)

(6) See R Miles, *Racism and Migrant Labour* RKP (1982) Ch. 3

(7) S Hall in *New Socialist*, July (1982) p. 5

(8) Many accessible articles from the students viewpoint are to be found in P Baxter and B Sansom, *Race and Social Difference* Penguin (1972)

(9) R Miles, op. cit. p. 14

(10) J Gabriel, *The Concepts of Race and Racism*, unpublished thesis. An analysis of Classical and Contemporary Theories of Race, Liverpool University (1976)

(11) Again a clearly written text for students is K Richardson and D Spears (eds), *Race and Culture and Intelligence* (1972). W F Bodmer's article is Chapter 5

(12) J Rex and S Tomlinson, *Colonial Immigrants in a British City* RKP (1979)

(13) T W Adorno et al., *The Authoritarian Personality* Harper Row (1950)

(14) S Hall et al., *Policing the Crisis, Mugging, the State and Law and Order*, MacMillan (1978)

(15) P Willis, *Learning to Labour* Saxon House (1978)

(16) D Milner, *Children and Race* Penguin (1975) p. 31

(17) M Weber, *Economy and Society*, Vol. I Univ. of Calif. Press p. 385

(18) J Rex and R Moore, *Race, Community and Conflict* OUP (1967) p. 273

(19) F Engels, *The Condition of the Working in England* (Panther, 1969) p. 117

(20) D Fernbach, (ed) Karl Marx. *The First International and After* Penguin (1974) p. 169

(21) Ibid. p. 169

(22) N File and C Power, *Black Settlers in Britain 1555 to 1958* (Heinemann, 1981) pp. 6–7

(23) Ibid. Section 19, fig. 192

(24) Ibid. Section 27

(25) R Miles, op. cit. (1982) p. 129

(26) T Coleman, *The Railway Navvies* Penguin (1972) see Ch. 6

(27) P F Speed, *Social Problems of the Industrial Revolution* Pergamon Press (1975) p. 133

(28) R Roberts, *A Ragged Schooling. Growing Up in the Classic Slum* Fontana/Collins (1978) p. 111

(29) T Rees, *Immigration Policies in the United Kingdom*, in, C Husband(4)

(30) G Stedman Jones, *Outcast London* OUP (1971) p. 145

(31) P Foot, *Immigration and Race in British Politics* Penguin (1965)

(32) See G Jerrom, *Scapegoats of the '30s and '80s,* in P Cohen and C Gardner (eds), *It ain't half racist, mum* Comedia (1983)

(33) B Cox, *Civil Liberties in Britain* Penguin (1975) p. 132

(34) S Moore and N Hendry, '*Sociology*' Hodder (1982) p. 164

(35) The Runnymede Trust, *Britain's Black Population* (1980) Heinemann p. 34

(36) R Moore and T Wallace, *Slamming the Door: The Administration of Immigration Control* Martin Robertson (1975)

(37) J Walvin, *Black and White* Allen Lane (1973) p. 173

(38) Action Group on Immigration and Nationality. *Briefing*, Panther (November 1978) p. 4

(39) N Deakin, *Colour Citizenship and British Society* (1970) p. 54

(40) S Rushdie, *New Society* (September 9th, 1982) pp. 417–420

(41) Quoted in *The Observer* (20th November 1983) p. 9

(42) Centre for Contemporary Cultural Studies, *The Empire Strikes Back* (1982)

(43) K Pryce, *Endless Pressure* Penguin (1979)

(44) T Parsons, *Full Citizenship for the Negro American? A Sociological Problem* in *Daedalus, Journal of the American Academy of Arts and Sciences* (1965) pp. 1009–1054

(45) Parsons, Ibid. p. 1038

(46) R Miles and A Phizaklea *Racism and Political Action in Britain* RKP (1979)

(47) R Moore, *Becoming a Sociologist in Sparkbrook*, p. 90, in C Bell and H Newby (eds) *Doing Sociological Research* Allen and Unwin (1977)

(48) D J Smith, *Racial Disadvantage in Britain* Penguin (1977) p. 93

(49) J Rex and S Tomlinson, op. cit. p. 107

(50) N Hedges and H Benyon, *Born to Work* Pluto Press (1982) p. 54

(51) *The Observer* (20th November, 1983)

(52) C Bell and H Newby op. cit. p. 105

(53) J Rex and R Moore, op. cit. p. 279

(54) J Rex and R Moore, ibid. p. 36

(55) A Giddens, *Sociology. A Brief but Critical Introduction* MacMillan (1982) p. 116

(56) R Moore, op. cit. (1977) p. 106

(57) J Rex and S Tomlinson, op. cit. p. 141

(58) D J Smith, op. cit. p. 243 (59) ibid. p. 215

(60) D Lockwood, Race, *Conflict, and Plural Society* in S Zubaida (ed) *Race and Racialism* Tavistock (1970) p. 57

(61) H Townsend and E M Brittan, *Organisation in Multi-Racial Schools*, Slough (1972) quoted in *Open University Educational Studies, Race, Children and Cities* (1978) p. 77

(62) B Coard, *How the West Indian Child is Made Educationally Subnormal in the British School System* New Beacon Books (1971)

(63) *Britain's Black Population* op. cit. p. 102

(64) H Eysenck, *Race, Intelligence and Education* Temple Smith (1971) p. 46

(65) M Kettle and L Hodges, *Uprising. The Police, The People and the Riots in Britain's Cities* Pan (1982) pp. 148–149

(66) *Britain's Black Population* op. cit. p. 99

(67) J Rex and S Tomlinson op. cit. p. 203

(68) *Oxfam Information Brief*, (November 1980 and September 1982)

(69) P Baran and P Sweezy, *Monopoly Capital* Penguin (1968)

(70) E Genovese, *Roll, Jordan, Roll: The World the Slaves Made* André Deutsch (1975)

(71) P Baran and P Sweezy, op. cit. p. 252 (72) Ibid. p. 260

(73) S Castles and G Kosack, *Immigrant Workers and Class Struggles in Western Europe* OUP (1973)

(74) C Husband, op. cit. (1982) p. 21

(75) R Blackburn and M Mann, *The Working Class in the Labour Market* MacMillan (1979)

(76) J Rex and S Tomlinson, op. cit. p. 276

(77) D J Smith, op. cit.

(78) *Race and Riots 81, A New Society Social Studies Reader* (1982) Article by G Gaskell and P Smith pp. 8–9

(79) Lord Scarman, The Scarman Report HMSO (1981)

(80) M Kettle, *The racial numbers game in our prisons. New Society* (30th September, 1982)

(81) R Moore, *Immigration and Racism*, p. 44 in R Burgess (ed) *Exploring Society* The British Sociological Association (1982)

(82) K Pryce, op. cit. p. 277

(83) Chevannes and Reeves, *Footprint in the Sand*, in R Meighan et al. *Perspectives on Society* Nelson (1979)

(84) C Husband (ed), op. cit. p. 177

(85) S Patterson Dark Strangers: *a study of West Indians in London* Penguin (1965)

3 The sociology of youth culture

Introduction

The comparatively short history of the study of youth and youth culture has seen a surprising variety of approaches. Early authors tended to see youth developing its own cultural traits, distinct norms and values, as a response to the social-structural changes brought about by industrialisation. They ranged from the functionalists who stressed the necessity of a period of transition from childhood to adulthood to conflict theorists who argued that youth represent a new proletariat with interests of its own in opposition to those of adults. This conflict perspective on youth was common in the 1960's when students were resisting American involvement in Vietnam, fighting for civil rights and the abolition of race and sex discrimination and were joining the workers behind the barricades in the streets of Paris. For some neo-Marxists like Marcuse in *One Dimensional Man*, the young represented the only real radical force in capitalism, the workers having been largely co-opted into the system by the lure of material well being. The depression of the 1970's saw a decline in the radicalism of students who seemed more concerned with establishing a career than forcing social change. It became clear to sociologists that not only had the rebellion been temporary but that in fact only a minority of youth had been involved in it. It had been a revolt of the advantaged. Sociologists recognised that young people do share some common attributes, and that these made it possible to see them as a coherent group. They also began to see that the temporary nature of these attributes plus the cross-cutting factor of social class made it a fruitless task to attempt to generalise about the social role of the young. The experience of youth came to be seen as linked to parental social background. Sociologists began to talk not of youth *culture*, with its implied distinct norms and values shared by all members, but of youth *subcultures*, which suggested that only some members of the category 'youth' joined them and that there were important links with the parent culture.

At last there was a recognition that many 13–19 year olds are really very similar to their parents in the values they adopt and in behaviour, and that girls in particular seem often to be excluded from full membership of what had been called youth culture. The focus of attention for study, then, came to be the reasons for this diversity and the links between the young and the old rather than the divisions between them.

In this chapter we will use the term culture when referring to those theories which recognise the existence of a stage passed through by all people during adolescence, a stage which involves behavioural and attitudinal characteristics which are distinct from those of adults. Youth subcultures will be the term used when discussing those theories which try to distinguish between separate groups of youth and (sometimes) separate groups of adults.

The history of youth as a separate section of society

In *Centuries of Childhood*, Philippe Aries(1), argues that the importance we attach to age groups and the actual differences between them are recent developments. Neither childhood nor adolescence were separately recognised in life in the Middle Ages; beyond infancy all individuals of the same class were treated alike. The modern concept of the child as a dependent individual with special characteristics and requiring special treatment only developed in the 17th century. The concept of adolescence developed in the late 18th century. In the 17th century the upper classes began to dress their children differently than adults, this practice was slowly copied by the lower social classes in a process which has been termed *stratified diffusion* (2). The pastimes of all age groups were also the same, apart from the babies. Games and amusements played a much more important part in life than they do today. Once again, the upper classes first abandoned what we would consider the 'childish' playing of games.

The distinction between adolescence and childhood on the one side, and adulthood on the other, began largely because of large-scale conscription at the end of the 18th century. However, awareness of youth as a *general* phenomenon only really began at the end of the First World War. Aries writes:

> "The awareness of youth began by being a feeling common to ex-servicemen, and this feeling was to be found in all the belligerent countries."(3)

The age of adolescence gradually expanded after the First World War. It encompassed both older and younger people as time went on. The very distinctive youth styles that we know today appeared after the Second World War. One of the earliest were the 'beatniks' of the mid-1950's who wore jeans, sloppy jumpers and duffle coats, and whose values were similar to those of the hippies, who are seen by some as a development from them. 'Teddy boys' (or 'teds') wore quiffed hair and Brylcreem, drainpipe trousers, thick crepe-soled shoes, and Edwardian jackets. They were aggressive and often attacked beatniks and black immigrants. Their preferred music was the rock-and-roll of the time.

The 1960's saw the appearance of 'mods' with their short hair, smart mohair suits, Lambretta or Vespa scooters and parkas. They preferred American 'soul' records or West Indian ska, an early and less commercialised form of reggae. Later English white groups, such as The Who, were their idols, their album *Quadrophenia* was concerned with mod culture. 'Skinheads' were a development of mod culture, but their hair was much shorter, they were less smart in appearance and were more oriented to violent behaviour and patriotism. They wore dyed Levi jeans and Doc Marten boots. 'Rockers' or 'greasers' had a culture which centred on the motor-cycle. They wore black leather jackets with studs and chains, long unkempt hair and dirty jeans.

The late 1960s saw the development of the 'hippie' culture with its 'back to nature' ethic. Peasant clothes were worn with beads and flowers, long hair was the norm. Their preferred music was played by bands like Grateful Dead and The Doors. The 1970s and 1980s have seen a resurgence of skinheads with a more political flavour. 'Glamrock' culture was quite distinct from this, it was bisexual in style and mirrored Hollywood concerns with image and clothes. The favoured pop artist and indeed the model used by these young people was David Bowie.

Punks' favoured a rejection of consumerism and claimed to be a do-it-yourself culture. Ripped clothes, zips, safety pins and brightly coloured hair with spikes were their trademarks. Their music, like their fashion, was home-made and it was deliberately discordant. Meanwhile, black West Indians started becoming Rastafarians in large numbers. This contains religious elements as well as stylistic ones. It involves wearing 'dreadlocks' and a 'tam' (a woollen hat); listening to reggae music and smoking marijuana (ganja). White society (Babylon) is rejected as exploitative and they dream of a new life in Africa.

These are some of the important developments in youth culture in Britain since the Second World War. The future will see the development of many more – some similar, and others totally original. In this chapter we will examine some of the explanations of and perspectives on these developments. We will begin by examining and criticising an account of youth culture which stresses the biological characteristics of adolescents. Then we will examine the work of writers who have stressed social and economic change as the causative factor in the rise of youth culture. From this perspective we will move to theories of youth *subcultures*, which stress their class-based nature. These theories, unlike the earlier ones, recognise the class-divided nature of society as a whole and seek the explanation of youth subcultures within this analysis. Finally, we will review the interactionist account offered by Stan Cohen in his *Folk Devils and Moral Panics* and look in detail at two studies which, while accepting the interactionist account, also adapt and add to it. These are *Policing the Crisis* by Stuart Hall and others and *The Rules of Disorder* by Marsh, Rosser and Harré.

Theories of youth culture

The biological approach

The earliest theories about youth culture concentrated on the physical differences between youth and adults. One theory was put forward by G Stanley Hall in his book *Adolescence* which was published in 1904 (4). For Hall the 'problems' which youth present are unbridled sexuality, rejection of parents and teachers, difficulty in concentrating on and completing one job, extremes of emotion and violence, and general unpredictability. They are the result of the bodily changes undergone in becoming a sexually and physically mature adult. He links this to the theory of evolution in an account which has striking similarities to the Lombrosian theory of deviance. He writes:

> "Adolescence is a new birth, for the higher and more completely human traits are now born . . . the adolescent is neo-atavistic (ie a throwback in evolution) and in him the later acquisitions of the race slowly become prepotent (ie more powerful than those of pre-human characteristics which the child displays). Development is gradual and more saltatory . . . Important functions previously non-existent arise . . . Every step of the upward way is strewn with wreckage of body, mind and morals . . . Sex asserts its mastery in field after field, and works its havoc in the form of secret vice, debauch, disease and enfeebled heredity . . . There are new repulsions felt towards home and school, and truancy and runaways abound. The social instincts undergo sudden enfoldment and the new life of love awakens. It is the age of sentiment . . . of rapid fluctuation of mood, and the world seems strange and new . . . Character and personality are taking form, but everything is plastic. Self feeling and ambition are increased, and every trait and faculty is liable to exaggeration and excess. It is all a marvellous new birth."(5)

Hall also argues that the increased pressure caused by the sedentary life, the closed spaces and bad air of advanced industrial society have made the problem of the time of physical transformation of the individual even worse than ever. The adolescent can no longer work out the stresses and conflicts of biological change in a physical way, being confined to the school, office or shop and by the claustrophobic city streets:

> "Now, instead of head-hunting, winning a new name, wrestling alone with spirits or other of the drastic initiations of savages, the

> civilised and more sedentary youth must vent his intensification of the personal feeling in dreams of greatness."(6)

Hence the problem, while having always been present, is a growing one in so called civilised countries.

Hall's theory has many pitfalls. Theoretically, his thesis is flawed because it is a biologically incorrect description of babies' and adolescents' development. Babies and adolescents are as human and as far along the evolutionary chain as adults. The idea that the development of the baby within the womb follows the course of evolution that the race as a whole followed over million of years has been found to be incorrect. Though there are traces of pre-human physical characteristics at some stages of the growth of the foetus (for example, groups of muscles found in fish), these are only echoes of the past, being weak and partly formed. Certainly, any idea of atavism within, and especially outside, the womb is out of the question. Methodologically, Hall records the physical details of many thousands of adolescents but then averages out the details of weight and height, for example, in each age group. This technique allows him to describe adolescence as a period of life which involves regularities of bodily size and shape or awkwardness. As a result, he misses differences between individuals and treats these averages as true of *all* members of the group. Similarly, differences in the behaviour patterns of a number of individuals are ignored(7).

Modern research in physiology and psychology suggests that the storm and stress we associate with adolescence is not determined by the physiological changes which occur during this time of life, but is *socially* conditioned. Even during the 1920s more careful investigators than Hall found that particular social conditions can cause reactions amongst youth *not* found elsewhere in the same age group. For example, F Thrasher(8) who was a member of the Chicago school studied Chicago youth gangs and isolated the causes for their development in the social disorganisation of downtown areas, the breakdown of the family, bad schooling and the lack of leisure facilities. Youth in Chicago responded to these social conditions by creating a new and different world for themselves which allowed them escape from the humdrum existence of the normal citizen. Thus the idea of distinct and separable periods of life passed through at the same stage by all individuals with social environment having only a slight influence, has been shown to be incorrect.

Although it has been the subject of some severe criticism recently, Margaret Mead's study of female adolescents in the Pacific Island of Samoa(9) provides further evidence of the importance of social environment in the production of youth culture and an example of the way that cross-cultural comparison can lead to the advancement of knowledge in sociology. This is one of the few detailed studies of the social position of youth which devotes itself to *girls*, most others barely mention them.

Mead made a study of fifty girls in three small neighbouring villages on the island over a period of nine months. She showed that while there *is* social ranking by age in Samoan culture, there is no period of conflict or rebelliousness there – no youth problem. Girls tended to stick together in age groupings or gangs until just before puberty, at which point these groups broke up due to the individual nature of the tasks which they were then allotted and to the secrecy of their (quite liberated) sex lives. For boys, the age-based groups tended to last through life due to the more co-operative nature of the tasks they had to do. Despite this, there were no delinquent or delinquescent gangs, no distinctive youth culture at all in Samoa:

> "The community ignores both boys and girls from birth until they are 15 or 16 years of age. Children under this age have no social standing, no recognised group activities, no part in the social life . . . But at a year or two beyond puberty . . . both boys and girls are grouped into a rough approximation of the adult groupings, given a name for their organisation, and are invested with definite obligations and privileges in the community life."(10)

In their various groupings (based on social rank), the adolescent boys and girls learn their adult roles, such as how to make speeches, to serve and drink Kava or to learn the names of chiefs of other villages. By the time they are 16 or 17, Samoan boys and girls have also learned the job of controlling the young ones. They constantly interrupt their own conversations to tell the young children to "keep still", "sit still", "keep your mouth shut", just as adults do in our society. Each child is disciplined and socialised in this way both by the older children and by having responsibilities for younger ones given to them. This delegation of the parental role (as we see it) begins at 6 to 7 years of age. The housekeeping is done by children below the age of 14.

Mead concludes that the concept of the biologically induced awkward age is a nonsense, as there is no such age in Samoa whose inhabitants are genetically almost identical to every other member of the human race. She writes:

> "Can we think of adolescence as a time in the life history of every girl child which carries with it symptoms of conflict and stress as surely as it implies a change in the girl's body? Following the Samoan girls through every aspect of their lives, we have tried to answer this question, and we found throughout that we had to answer it in the negative."(11)

The reason for its absence is a social one.

American society is a stressful and, in many ways, inhuman one. This means that imminent entry into the rat race is a frightening and stressful experience for an adolescent. Faced with a bewildering variety of occupational choices, with fierce competitiveness, with numerous standards of morality and sets of norms to choose from, it is not surprising, she argues, that the youth of America appear unsettled and troublesome. In Samoa, there are no choices and growing up is a casual affair in a society with very liberal codes of conduct.

Recently, Mead's findings have come under critical fire. In a book published in early 1983(12), Professor D Freeman suggests that Mead went to Samoa with preconceived ideas about the cultural relativity of adolescent behaviour and wished to use empirical evidence gathered on the island to prove a point. This led her to be easily taken in by the adolescent informants who made something of a game out of telling her lies. Mead only studied fifty girls, lived with ex-patriots, did not speak the girls' language and only stayed for nine months (two of which were spent orientating herself). These facts also meant that little importance could be attached to her findings, according to Freeman. The work was simply not up to the standards of more recent ethnography.

Current research suggests that adolescent behaviour is neither totally culturally nor totally biologically determined but is the product of both the cultural environment and biological changes during puberty. While it is an open question as to the relative strengths of the two factors, it is clear that the cultural environment is important, whatever the criticisms of Mead's research. In Germany under the Nazis, both boys and girls entered semi-military clubs and organisations at an early age. They had to conform to the customs of these groups. This inculcated loyalty to Hitler and the Nazi state and stressed physical development and endurance. These adolescents were turned into servicemen and women even before they were fully mature, a feat strikingly similar to Mead's account of adoption of adult responsibilities by the young. It is also the case that children in the USA, from its pioneering years to today, have had to take an active and independent role because their parents were less familiar with the new customs and language than they were. Like children of Asian immigrants in Britain today, the children were nationals of the new country. They attended its schools, spoke its language, were familiar with its norms and technology and thus were in many ways dominant and independent. This situation led to a much greater opportunity in America for youth to develop in a different direction from their parents, a development which was troublesome from their parents' point of view.

Despite all the problems associated with it, the theory of the biological determination of behaviour has influenced educational 'common sense' and academic thinking throughout this century. For example, the division between primary and secondary education at the age of 11 years recommended by the Butler Education Act was based on notions of important biological and psychological changes at that time of life(13). Parents are still often heard referring to the 'difficult age' around 13 to 16, with its implied biological causes. One example of quite a recent academic work which continues to support the biological theory is the Marshall

Cavendish Learning System(14). This argues that with the onset of puberty, girls become concerned about their appearance and are particularly anxious not to appear foolish. Boys seek approval and thus join gangs and follow them into smoking, drinking and drug-taking. Restlessness, boredom and disinclination to work are common features of the adolescent, as is some degree of awkwardness and clumsiness and the 'burning urge to reform the world.' They are sensitive to comments about clothes, appearance, hairstyles and friends; moody, sulky, quarrelsome and obstinate behaviour are common. Sexual licence, illegitimate pregnancy and venereal disease are serious problems but:

> "... perhaps the most difficult problem of adolescence is the possibility of serious domestic friction within the family."(15)

In fact, every one of this 'Learning System's' statements is equally true of adults and one could argue that the biological theory has justified the labelling of adolescents as a deviant and troublesome group. Such spurious ideas *appear* to be supported by criminal statistics: today the age group from 14 to 16 years has the highest rate of serious crime it has had for more than 20 years(16). Again this is only true of advanced industrial societies and we should bear in mind the criticisms of criminal statistics that come from the interactionist school of sociology. These point out that the existence of a negative label will bring about actual effects; the so-called 'self-fulfilling prophecy'. The biological theory is not only misleading, then, but can be positively harmful.

Modern industrial society and youth culture: social and economic change

Early *sociological* theories about youth culture concentrated on recent changes in society to account for the development of youth as a quite distinct, often troublesome and oppositional group. These changes included:

1 The affluence of teenagers and the presence of a commercial system to supply the goods demanded by them;
2 the influence of the Second World War on socialisation patterns;
3 the effects of the extension of education, and
4 the effects of the mass media on styles and leisure time activity.

This section will examine some of these theories in detail.

The most important early statement of the theory that new affluence amongst young people and their parents (who may subsidise spending) led to a change in the pattern of life of the young came from Mark Abrams in his book *The Teenage Consumer*(17). Abrams writes of teenagers in 1959 that:

"... as compared with 1938, their *real* earnings (ie after allowing for the fall in the value of money) have increased by 50% (which is double the rate of expansion for adults) and their real 'discretionary' spending has probably risen by 100%."(18)

This led to:

"distinctive teenage spending for distinctive teenage ends in a distinctive teenage world."(19)

The ability to spend money on records, clothes, magazines, entertainment and transport gave teenagers the ability to buy themselves a new 'world' of their own and break free of the adult one until the time came for them to take on adult responsibilities. Teenagers, with all their spare cash, bought the kind of items just mentioned while their parents bought consumer durables such as carpets, fridges, suits as well as the day-to-day necessities of family life.

It would not be true to say that Abrams completely ignores the factor of class differences in all this. He does state that it is the working class teenager who participates most in this new world of consumption:

"... the teenage market is almost entirely working class. Its middle class members are either still at school and college or else just beginning their careers: in either case they dispose of much smaller incomes than their working class contemporaries."(20)

The overall message of the book suggests that class differences are not that important any more and that the process of embourgeoisement is rapidly breaking down any differences that do remain. In a later work of Abrams, we read ...

"In the post-war world class barriers have tended to lose their clarity ... Some working class families have incomes as high as some white collar families and there is little to choose between their styles of living."(21)

And again ...

"Under conditions of general prosperity the social study of society in class terms is less and less illuminating. And its place is taken by differences related to age."(22)

The theme of the affluent teenager was taken up by the press and TV and became part of accepted knowledge. The attitude of the media was ambivalent. It sometimes regarded youth as a problem, sometimes it condoned their frivolousness in an amused and patronising way. Even today the media presentation of early youth culture presses home the affluence theme. A Channel 4 programme called *The Sixties* shown in December 1982 stated that the income of the average 16 year-old doubled between

1956 and 1966 and that 60 million singles were sold in 1963. It showed scenes of Carnaby Street boutiques selling goods faster, almost, than they could get them in the back door. As we shall see in the chapter on the media, the affluence thesis fits nicely into the consensus view of British society which is characteristic of the attitude of most media personnel.

The fact that youth culture became a noticeable problem ten or so years after the Second World War led some writers to see it as an important causative factor. One such example comes from the work of T R Fyvel in *The Insecure Offenders*. The theory was that absence of fathers from the home resulted in incomplete socialisation for the war children. This, combined with greater levels of insecurity about the future felt by this generation (made worse by the invention of the atom bomb), resulted in disturbed youths forming teddy boy gangs in the 1950s. Abrams, too, argues that the 16 million post-war children had a more than normal sense of alienation due to the disruptive effects of the war on the British population(24). The obvious question, though, is why later generations of youths joined youth culture. For Fyvel, the answer is that the disruption of the traditional culture has never been put right because of the commercialisation of post-war Britain, linked to the new-found affluence.

Fyvel's view appears to be tinged with a rosy romanticism about some past golden age where everyone was properly socialised and there was no deviance among the young. Many modern conservatives would share his critique of the mass culture generated by the consumer society, as we shall see later (page 134).

Another factor which is often seen as crucial in the creation of youth culture is formal education. P Aries sees developments in education in the 15th and 16th centuries as crucial in separating young people from their elders in terms of behaviour and attitudes. In medieval times, even those children who went to school were treated in the same way as adults and no age-related distinctions were made between pupils. However, the development of colleges, which began between the 13th and 14th centuries, saw a change in this. Order was imposed on the internal workings of the institution and young people in it (who were between the ages of eight and fifteen years) were "submitted to different laws from those governing adults". The development of the school class in the 16th century saw the beginnings of separations within the general category 'Young People'. At first the division was on the basis of position in the school and increasingly subtle distinctions were made by the authorities in the treatment given to each age grade. This is seen by Aries as a result of the general tendency in history towards classification and separation. In this case, it made adolescents see themselves as a distinct and different group.

The extension of compulsory schooling during the 20th century has increasingly provided a youthful environment between family on the one hand, and work on the other. Gangs and cliques were the natural product and trends of fashion and speech were quickly disseminated among large groups of adolescents. Thus one commentator writes that the high school pupil is cut off:

> ". . . from the rest of society, forced inwards towards his own age group. With his fellows, he comes to constitute a small society, one that has its most important interactions *within* itself, and maintains only a few threads of connections with the outside adult society."(25)

The increasing separation of the young in society has, in the view of many writers, been assisted by the parallel development of the mass media. Widespread possession of TV and radio, expanded readership of fiction and the spread of the cinema have led to the rapid diffusion of youth 'style'. Thinkers on the left and the right of the political spectrum see the mass media as substituting a plastic and worthless *mass culture* for the old cultural values. The styles we associated with youth culture are seen as mere media products rather than stemming from the genuine interests and desires of young people. As we have just seen, Fyvel takes this view, as does Paul Johnson, writing about the '*menace of Beatle-ism*' in 1964:

> "Both TV CHANNELS now run weekly programmes in which popular records are played to teenagers and judged. While the music is performed, the cameras linger savagely over the faces of the audience. What a bottomless chasm of vacuity they reveal. Huge faces bloated with cheap confectionery and smeared with chain-store make-up, the open, sagging mouths and glazed eyes, the hands mindlessly drumming in time to the music, the broken stiletto heels, the shoddy, stereotyped 'with-it' clothes: here, apparently, is a collective portrait of a generation enslaved by a commercial machine."(26)

Marxist theorists of the Frankfurt School (Marcuse, Horkheimer and Adorno) see capitalist society as a mass society. It is full of people who are virtually indistinguishable from each other in their tastes and behaviour due largely to the pervasive influence of the media.

> "The gradual dissolution of the family, the transformation of personal life into leisure and of leisure into routines supervised to the last detail, into the pleasures of . . . the movie, the best-seller and the radio, has brought about the disappearance of the inner life."(27)

Both left and right, then, see this subversion of 'real' culture by the mass media as a *bad thing*. Their analysis of the reasons, possible cures and the nature of 'real' culture are different. Even a Vice-President of the USA has joined in this critique:

> "In too many of the lyrics, the message of the drug culture is purveyed . . . at its worst it is blatant drug culture propaganda . . . and all the while that this brainwashing has been going on, most of us have regarded it as good, clean, noisy fun."(28)

Songs such as *Lucy in the Sky with Diamonds* (LSD) fuelled this drug theme criticism. So too, did the untimely deaths of Janis Joplin, Jimi Hendrix and Brian Jones.

To conclude, then, the theories of economic and social change pointed to the factors we have analysed above, and to the associated decline in the importance of the family as a socialising agent and an agent of more overt discipline. This has combined to bring about the development of youth culture. This culture was largely seen as a classless phenomenon involving most, if not all, teenagers to a greater or lesser degree. Berger and Berger feel able to write:

> "To a considerable degree, the youth culture cuts across class lines . . . it has created symbols and patterns of behaviour that are capable of bestowing status upon the individuals from quite different class backgrounds . . . Thus the young people of all classes can participate in the collective ecstasies of a rock festival."(29)

There are many flaws in the theories of youth culture which link its development with recent social and economic changes, not least of which is the attack on the embourgeoisement thesis made in recent years. One of the main critical appraisals of this thesis was that of Goldthorpe and Lockwood (30). This study concludes that:

> ". . . there remain important areas of common social experience which are still fairly distinctively working class; that specifically middle class social norms are not widely followed nor middle class lifestyles consciously emulated; and that assimilation into middle class society is neither in process nor, in the main, a desired objective."(31)

So even amongst affluent workers there are important class differences remaining in British society. Goldthorpe and Lockwood's study only shows, though, that affluence amongst some members of the working class does not give rise to 'middle classness.' Other studies have shown that general affluence as a characteristic of British society is a myth, and was a myth in the 1950s and 1970s too. For example, B Abel-Smith and P Townsend's book *The Poor and The Poorest*(32), P Townsend's most recent book *Poverty in the United Kingdom*(33) and the Coates and Silburn study *Poverty: The Forgotten Englishmen*(34) all show this to be the case. The publication of Abel-Smith and Townsend's book marked the re-discovery of poverty in Britain, finding that the numbers of poor *increased* from 4 million in 1953/54 to 7.5 million in 1960. Coates and Silburn write:

> "During the 50's the myth that widespread material poverty has finally and triumphantly been overcome was so widely accepted by politicians, social commentators and the general public alike, that for a decade and more, public controversy and political discussion were engrossed by the new problem of what people were still pleased to call the 'affluent society'".

These problems, of course, included that of youth culture. It took the publication of careful work done by the social commentators we have mentioned to remove this myth. Peter Townsend found that 6.1% of his sample were *in* poverty in 1968–69, and 21.8% were on the margins of poverty, even taking his harshest definition of poverty of an income of less than the Supplementary Benefit level plus housing costs. This leads Townsend to estimate a total of 3.32 million people living below the Supplementary Benefit level, with another 11.86 million people on its margins (ie within the range of up to 40% above the Supplementary Benefit level.)

Townsend considers the existence of such poverty is due to the hierarchical nature of our society and to the highly unequal distribution of resources. People also try to live up to a style of life which they are led to believe is the only acceptable one (with a car and the possessions that advertising and other sources lead us to believe in as normal) but the attempt only produces more poverty as they take on commitments they cannot afford.

As for the influence of war on youth culture, it is clearly inadequate as an explanation of contemporary developments. Young people appear to be deviating further and further from the norms and values of their parents, yet the war is little more than a distant memory, even to the parents themselves.

On the face of it the argument about the extension of the period of schooling seems to have more substance to it. The problem, though, is that young people respond to the experience of secondary education in different ways. Only some of those at school join anti-school subcultures. Others have no contact with it all and spend their school careers in the way that their teachers would like all pupils to do: working hard and not deviating at all from the adult model of appropriate behaviour(35).

The mass culture argument is also an interesting one but open to criticism. Left and right wings of the political spectrum are agreed that mass culture cretinizes us, ruins our tastes, blunts our senses and paves the way to totalitarianism. They also agree that the mass media are the principal 'carriers' of the disease. For both, the 'real' culture (traditional working class norms and values for one, high culture of opera and classical music, etc for the other) is threatened by the waves of 'teen' magazines and advertisements and programmes like *Crossroads* and *Top of the Pops*. The counter argument, though, suggests that, firstly . . .

> ". . . with the development of mechanical reproduction on a mass scale, culture has become more democratised: TV and radio have made drama, music and opera more accessible (one Shakespeare play or Mozart opera is seen by more people in a single evening's television viewing than the total contemporary audience for all Shakespeare's plays and Mozart's operas); through the mass production and sales of records and cassettes, the symphony, chamber

music, song and opera have been fully democratised; the so-called 'paperback revolution' brings the cheap book within the range of the whole population: from 6000 titles in print in 1960, the number has reached almost 40 000 in the 1970's."(36)

Secondly, and perhaps more importantly, is the question of what makes opera 'better' than the Sex Pistols, or what is 'good' about traditional working class culture. Indeed, did the latter exist or is it just an invention of many leftist writers, at least in the form they depict it? Criticism of mass culture and of mass youth culture stems from what is no more than a subjective assessment of the relative merits of one form of culture or another.

Functionalist theory: modern industrial society and the role of youth

In 1942, Talcott Parsons coined the term youth culture(37) and began the functionalist attempt to account for its rise in advanced industrial societies. This attempt has been continued by many writers, including Eisenstadt(38), Sugarman(39) and P and B Berger(40). The main themes of the functionalist approach to this question will be brought out here.

At the centre of the theory stands its analysis of the contrast between the social life of the family unit and that of the wider industrial society of which it forms a part. The family is argued to be a warm, close grouping based upon the traditional choices of action outlined in Table 1. Within the family, relationships are warm and emotional, each of its members works for the group as a whole, family members treat each other as individuals and judge them in terms of their characters and positions within the family rather than on more general criteria. On the other side of the coin, though, the modern industrial society is an emotionally cold place. People are self-interested, they judge each other not as individuals but as role performers and the possibility of displaying all sides of one's character is limited by the restrictive nature of the roles the individuals play. Table 1 illustrates the distinctive features of the family on the one hand and society on the other. They are presented by Parsons in the form of five sets of 'pattern variables'. These represent choices individuals can make in their dealings with others. In practice, the individual does not really have a choice because the culture of the society determines which pattern of action is considered normal in a given context. Thus in a simple society the traditional choice would be characteristic both of behaviour in the family and in wider society. In modern industrial society, it is only found in the family.

Any attempt to move directly from one pattern of action in the family to wider society would lead to feelings of unhappiness, isolation and loneliness. If there were no way of easing the process, society would suffer

Table 1 Talcott Parsons' 'pattern variables'

Name of variable found in traditional societies and the family	*Characteristics of the traditional choice of action*	*Name of variable found in advanced industrial societies*	*Characteristics of the modern choice of action*
Affectivity	Social interaction is an end in itself and serves no other purpose. Eg relationships within the family are emotionally (affectively) rewarding and are enjoyed for themselves	*Affective neutrality*	Social interaction is undertaken for a secondary purpose. The interaction (eg between a salesman and client) is not enjoyed in and for itself
Collectivity orientation	Action by the individual is in the interests of the group. Eg the wage-earner works for the whole family and not only him/her self	*Self orientation*	Action is self-interested. Eg the salesman's actions are motivated by the desire for personal gain
Particularism	The individual is dealt with as a unique person, not as someone performing a generalised role. Assessment is based on *who* the person is, not how well they perform the role	*Universalism*	The individual is dealt with as part of a general classification and assessed as such. Eg a doctor is judged by reference to a notion of how doctors should behave
Diffuseness	Individuals have a number of roles to play, often simultaneously. Eg the roles of father, husband, grandfather, teacher, brother, employer, etc	*Specificity*	Individuals may be clearly identified as performing one role at any one time. Eg the teacher performs only that role in the classroom, no other enters into the relationship
Ascription (quality)	Individuals are dealt with according to ascribed criteria. Eg they will be treated differently if they are girls rather than boys, children rather than adults	*Achievement (performance)*	The individual is dealt with according to how well he/she performs. Eg as a driver rather than a *lady* driver, as a tennis player rather than a *black* tennis player

because unhappy individuals do not operate efficiently. It is the function of youth culture to provide a period of acclimatisation. It allows the individual to become used to independence from the family and to expect a certain amount of responsibility. It also helps to relieve the personal anxiety experienced by teenagers about their imminent move into the adult world.

This distinctive period of change is a purely modern phenomenon. In traditional societies there was no such divide between the patterns of action found in the home and those of the wider group. In societies like Britain the gap between family and wider society is experienced more sharply by boys according to functionalist writers. They argue that most boys have to face the outside world in their present instrumental role as wage earners whereas girls stay at home providing emotional comfort for the other members of the family (the so-called *affective* role). This helps to explain why girls do not participate as much as boys do in youth culture(41). The following extracts illustrate some of these points:

> "... the definition of youth in modern society has been greatly different from that existing in any other society that we know of. Not only is youth inserted between childhood and adulthood as a distinctive biological phase, but that phase has been expanding in both directions and has increasingly created a sub-cultural world of its own."(42)

> "Having first separated the family from the institutional areas of the economy and the state, the industrial revolution has created an ... interstitial area (an interval between the family and the economy) in which 'private life' could flourish in a variety of forms. Youth is one of many 'luxuries' of this situation. It is similar to childhood in one fundamental characteristic, namely, its segregation from the 'serious' activities of economic and political institutions."(43)

On the other hand, its relative independence from the family also gives it some similarities to the adult world:

> "Both the uncertainty of the future and possibility of present rivalry (at school) favour the development of groups centred on teenage culture interests to provide both pleasant distractions from anxiety about the future and a non-competitive framework of social interaction."(44)

Furthermore, youth culture helps to complete the process of socialisation which family and school can no longer properly complete in a complex and highly diversified society. These two institutions are themselves too slow to adapt to change and cannot keep up with the most recent developments which the new entrant needs to be aware of. Therefore, youth culture at least partly exists to finish the job of socialisation.

> "While socialisation in most pre-modern societies has been highly integrated and consistent, providing the individual with strong pat-

terns to grow into, socialisation in modern society has been characterised by high degrees of discontinuity and inconsistency . . . Primary socialisation as well as the early stages of secondary socialisation do not, as it were, complete the job. They leave the personality 'open ended'. If that is so, it would follow that a period set aside for the individual to complete the process would be highly functional."(45)

All this does not assume that the functionalist approach to youth culture accepts it wholeheartedly as a good thing. While it is argued that its existence fulfils vital functions for modern industrial society, the functionalist often expresses a feeling that youth also presents a problem. Sugarman writes:

"In most folk societies children learn their adult roles by working alongside their parents . . . (they) get married and step into adult status at an early age. Then there is no youth problem".(46)

Being positivist in nature, the functionalist approach allows predictions to be made. Firstly, we can expect to find similar youth culture in all advanced industrial societies. This is because youth culture is a product of the nature of advanced industrial society, and because all advanced industrial societies require broadly similar structures and action patterns. The functionalist theory of youth culture thus incorporates a convergence theory since it is seen as the product of "Industrial Society and its institutional dynamics"(47). Secondly, we can expect that the duration of the interstitial period will expand as youth are absorbed into the labour market at an increasingly later age. This point was made by the Bergers in the early 1970s for the USA and seems particularly apt in the Britain of the early 1980s.

The main fault with the functionalist approach is the almost complete absence of *class* in both its descriptions and explanations. The word youth appears to mean *all* members of a particular age group, as does the word adult. Reading this literature leaves us with an image of advanced industrial society that looks like this:

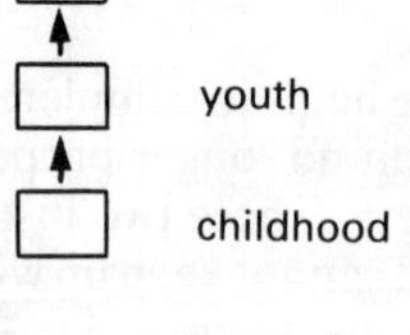

This is the structure of the age-set form of stratification found in simple societies where social status is usually a function of age and sex. It ignores the important differences between groups of people (both young and old) based upon ownership of wealth and upon occupation which exist in more complex societies. Berger and Berger's description of youth culture, for example, seems, in reality, to be discussing only middle class youth. Black and poor white American youth are forgotten. They say, for example, that youth are subsidised by their parents so that they can afford to buy the material necessities of youth culture. But as well as this:

> "... there is a large and constantly expanding network of subsidisations through the educational system, most of it financed by the state."(48)

This clearly is not true of most lower working class and black individuals either in Britain or in the USA. In Britain, 'subsidisations' (ie subsidies) are currently given to these groups by the Manpower Services Commission to Youth Training Scheme Trainees in an apparent attempt to *eliminate* the interstitial period before the 'entry into the economy'. Discretionary educational grants are more and more difficult to come by as LEA's cope with spending limits imposed by central government. This means that practically the only beneficiaries are degree students, over 70% of whom come from middle class backgrounds.

A second criticism is the description of the different worlds of family and society. Parsons' pattern variables are inadequate as a description of industrial society. Ascriptive criteria, such as sex and colour, are still important (the chapter on race deals with the latter in great detail). Family background also plays a major part in determining one's life chances, as the quote from Heath on page 41 in the development chapter illustrates. Peter Laurie writes:

> "... in the short space of time between acquiring the beginnings of an adult viewpoint and the final settling into a role in life, he must experiment with a good many of the available avenues: almost every day marks another choice made, if only by neglect. And the more specialised our society becomes, the more difficult is the choice."(49)

Both Willis and Corrigan (50 and 51) state that the findings of their studies indicate that there is no real choice for working class kids. Another point is that in everyday life we are not really emotionless automatons conditioned by society in the process of socialisation. Emotions affect our behaviour all the time, and notions of belonging to and acting for the group are important for all of us (witness the Falklands spirit of the 'war' months of 1982 and beyond). Furthermore, the rather rosy picture which Parsons paints of the family is also open to criticism. Many children simply cannot leave it soon enough, as Laing's studies (dealt with on pages 214–216. show.

Thirdly, not only is class forgotten, but so are girls (except with reference to their place in the home). It may be true that girls do not play as active a part in youth culture as boys, but this fact needs explanation. When these writers *do* address themselves to this subject, the explanation is in terms of the different social role of girls. However, as women, especially young women, enter the economy (as they have done increasingly in Britain during the period of the rise of youth culture as a mass phenomenon) this type of reasoning ceases to hold much water.

Our discussion of convergence theory leads us to question the functionalists' claim that similar youth cultures will develop in all modern industrial societies. As we shall see later, similarities may be present but this is probably due to non-determined factors such as the international sale of youth culture products (for example records and clothes) and the mass media's role in spreading trends across cultures. In France and Italy, for example, youth subcultures are not found on anything like the scale of Great Britain's. This suggests that the theory of institutional dynamics can be criticised.

Theories of working class subcultures

Recent field research has questioned the idea that youth culture is a classless and inclusive phenomenon, and has suggested that it is intimately connected to class structure in society. One of the earliest challenges in Britain to the 'classless teenage consumer' model came in Peter Willmott's *Adolescent Boys of East London*(52). Based on research started in 1959 and carried out over more than 5 years, it studies adolescent boys in Bethnal Green. Boys were interviewed both unsystematically and, later, in a more systematic way after a random sample of 246 had been chosen and traced. These boys were asked to keep a diary for a week and to come to Willmott's Institute of Community Studies so that the researchers could get to know them on a personal level. Local boys were also 'observed' wherever and whenever possible. Most of the systematic interviewing was done in 1964. This was a time at which the pop culture was at its height and, therefore, one could most expect these boys to be participating in the classless and independent youth culture described by Abrams, Sugarman, Laurie and the Bergers. What Willmott's research showed, was that although the Bethnal Green boys had easy access to discotheques, beat clubs and boutiques, only a minority used them. The rest were more likely to do their dancing to local beat groups and to buy their clothes from the local menswear shops. The life, the culture of the boys, was closely linked to the working class culture of the East End. As Murdock and McCron put it:

> "Rather than replacing class-based cultures, the new teenage leisure culture was being laid over the top, setting up an increasingly complicated interaction between the two."(53)

While many of the boys *were* teenage consumers, that consumption was mainly locally based and limited in its nature. The boys tended to spend a lot of their time with their peer group. They tended to go to the local cinema, dance hall or boys club or simply 'hang about'. This was, in fact, the main activity of the 14 to 15 year age group. Among the 18 to 19 year-olds, the local pub (the City of Paris and The Crown) was a central interest. Willmott also argues that there are three different types of adolescent. They are distinguishable by their basic attitudes, despite the fact that each may come from a similar background:

1 *The working class boy* goes to secondary modern or possibly comprehensive school and leaves at 15. He does not dislike school. He is most likely to have a skilled or semi-skilled manual job, often as an apprentice. He expects to marry before he is 25. He is more likely to spend money than save it and says one should 'enjoy oneself' rather than work hard. He is quite likely to be a teenage consumer because he lives at home, giving his mother some money for his keep and, therefore, has some spare cash to spend on whatever he wants.
2 *The middle class boy* goes to grammar school or comprehensive school and leaves only when he is 16 or perhaps older. He likes his time at school. He has a lower middle class job and his father is often a shop-keeper or a clerk. He believes in saving money and studying and working hard to 'get on'. He is unlikely to participate in any form of youth culture, he is usually very 'adult' in appearance and attitude.
3 *The rebel* goes to the secondary modern and left at 15. He did not like it very much. His job is manual and probably unskilled. He does not enjoy his job and often changes jobs. He does not think he will marry and rejects completely the idea of abstaining from sex. He is likely to be a consumer of records, drugs and the 'in' books of the time (Jack Kerouac books are mentioned by Willmott). One example of the rebel type said:

> "Well, I might decide to take the day off and to go up the park and sit and meditate. Or go round my friends' pad for an all-night session. A group of us drink whisky and smoke tea (marijuana) and talk about what's happiness and things like that".(54)

Willmott concludes that:

> "Most boys in Bethnal Green remain members of their families and of the wider kin-group. Their lives are set in a locality in which they know many other people, including shopkeepers stallholders and publicans. Though some are antagonistic to school and others un-enthusiastic, there is little sign of widespread hostility to the schools or teachers . . . There is little sign of what has been called 'the war of the generations'."(55)

Willmott's study demonstrates firstly that we should not class all people of the same age together under the blanket term *youth*. There are important differences between them. Secondly, he shows that these important links between the world of adults and the world of young people do exist. Thirdly, he explicitly brings the question of class into the analysis in studying Bethnal Green as the archetypal working class area. These themes are followed up by the theories of youth subcultures which we will now examine.

Much American work on deviance during the late 1950s recognised that social class was an important determinant in whether or not a particular youth participated in delinquent subcultures, and that some youth *never* joined such subcultures. The work of Albert Cohen and Cloward and Ohlin(56) attempted to explain this. Much of this work started from the assumption that initially the youth wanted the goals of American society. As they lacked the means to achieve them they became alienated and began to deviate. Deviant youth subcultures were seen as a means of dealing with this failure. These theories are based on a *consensual* view of society because of the assumption of an initial agreement on the goals and the means of achieving them, even among the poorer sections of society.

During the 1960's, sociologists questioned this consensual model and suggested that some groups in society *never* share the dominant norms. Walter B Miller(57) argues that there is a distinctive 'lower class' cultural system with its own 'focal concerns', ie major areas of interest and involvement. Youth particularly, tend to live out these focal concerns because of their association in gangs where conformity to group norms is essential. Lower class youth subculture is simply a product of the class subculture from which they come. This concept of separate *parent* subcultures which give rise to particular *youth* subcultures and which have strong links with them is central to much later theorising particularly by British writers.

Mike Brake(58) argues that working class youth are faced with a future doing society's boring, alienating and frustrating jobs after a school career in which their chances of success are much lower than those of middle class youth. Working class youth subcultures are an attempt to inject some excitement and colour into this bleak world during the short period between school and 'settling down.'

Like Miller's work, this approach adds the notion of class-determined failure which does not exist in Cohen's work or that of Cloward and Ohlin. But it misses Miller's point that not only does class position determine possible life chances, but also gives distinctive meanings, values and focal concerns which *shape* the subculture as well as creating it. A distinctive stage in the class-based analysis of youth subcultures in Britain came with the publication of *Resistance Through Rituals* by Stuart Hall and Tony Jefferson (eds)(59).

The Centre for Contemporary Cultural Studies (CCCS) at the University of Birmingham had been devoting itself to the study of youth subcultures and was particularly concerned that youth subcultures should be interpreted *structurally*. It considered that concrete social factors in society as a whole should be recognised as playing a crucial part in their generation and form. This work had a strong materialist influence and derived from the work of Marx. It was argued that features of culture are merely *epiphenomena* (dependent spin-offs) of infra-structural causes. Because this approach sees such close links between concrete factors and cultural forms, its supporters believe it is possible to 'read' the signs in youth culture and trace its elements back to their causes:

> "Youth cultures can be 'read' . . . in terms of their relation first, to 'parent' cultures, and through that, to the dominant culture, or better to the struggle between dominant and subordinate cultures."(60)

This stress on the possibility of 'reading' subcultural elements, ie seeing them as symbols or signs of some structural message, leads the work of the CCCS to be dubbed *semiotics* or, as here, *semiology*. The inventor of this approach to culture says this:

> "A science that studies the life of signs within society is conceivable; it would be a part of social psychology and consequently of general psychology; I shall call it *semiology* (from the Greek semeion 'sign'). Semiology would show what constitutes signs, what laws govern them. Since the science does not yet exist, no one can say what it would be; but it has a right to existence, a place staked out in advance."(61)

The foundations of the CCCS approach can be seen in an article by Phil Cohen which attempts to explain working class youth cultures in terms of structural changes in the economic base and social life of London's East End.

P Cohen's article(62) analyses the traditional working class culture of the East End of London and argues that it is founded on three factors:

1 The extended kinship network, which provides a system of mutual aid and support;
2 the working class neighbourhood with its close social relations also providing support and security;
3 a self-sufficient local economy which meant that travel outside the East End was unnecessary for that area's inhabitants.

During the 1950s, however, this social structure began to change. Redevelopment of the area meant the destruction of meeting places that were focal points of the social life of the community. The extended family began to break up into isolated units as couples moved into new housing estates on the periphery of London. The tight social network began to break down too. The economy of the area also underwent drastic change during this period. The small craft industries were destroyed, the family business and corner shop were replaced by large concerns, often outside the area. New jobs were created outside the East End community which were highly skilled and specialised and consequently well paid. Securing one of these jobs elevated the East End working class boy or girl to membership of a new suburban working class elite. For those without the educational qualifications for access to these jobs, there were only dead end, low paid and unskilled jobs, usually in the labour-intensive service industries doing jobs such as van boy, office boy, packer or warehouseman. The traditional character of the East End community was further eroded by the influx of immigrant labour to take up the large number of low paid jobs which had been created by the post-war expansion of industry. The close community of the old East End was destroyed and in its place was a much more impersonal, less self-contained and fundamentally divided social system. The young experienced these changes in a much more direct way than the old. For the lucky few they meant travel out of the area to the new jobs, for the rest there were dull routine and low paid jobs (as many had been before) but without the support of family and neighbourhood.

Phil Cohen's central thesis is that the variety of youth subcultures which have emanated from London's East End since that time have been an attempt to deal with this new situation; to retrieve some of the cohesive elements lost at that time and, in the process, adding some aspects of the new situation.

Thus the argot (slang) and ritual forms of the mods stressed many working class values but their dress and music reflected the *image*, but not the reality, of the affluent consumer. The mods' subculture was an exploration of the upward direction that some East End youths had been able to take into the new well-paid jobs. It was an imitation of their lifestyle as those left behind perceived it. The skinhead subculture, on the other hand, explored the downward direction. It was an imitation and a re-creation in an exaggerated form of the traditional working class lifestyle and community as these young people believed it to have been. In neither case was there a generation gap as such. These youths shared the cultural heritage of the older generation but, being at the sharp end of social change within capitalism, they developed and modified certain aspects of it. This is best illustrated by the skinheads whose 'no-nonsense' looks and values were a distorted reflection of the hard life of manual labour and recovery from it of the traditional working class. The braces, the Doctor Martin industrial-looking boots, the short (prison style) haircut, the jeans, all suggested manual work, the hard life and a rejection of the effeminate long-haired cushy life of office work and academia. The violence, the aggressive territoriality, the defence of that space which the skins pretended to rule (OK?) attempted to recapture the communality, the closeness and other-exclusion of the old East End. The blacks were, and are, seen by skinheads as destructive of traditional English life. Thus coloured immigrants, particularly Asians (most of all, Pakistanis), were the object of the skinheads' most violent behaviour.

Mods, though coming from the same unskilled and socially isolated group as the 'skins', attempted to cover the gap between themselves and those who enjoyed the affluent life associated with the newly available, well-paid, highly skilled work. The 'flash' clothes, the sparkling scooter, the rejection of the crudely aggressive masculine image of the skins and the rockers all spoke of the affluent young trendy. Perhaps most importantly, this thesis is confirmed by the image of the glorious nightlife which the mod indulged in, at least in the mythology of the mod subculture. The mod's ideal week involved a merry-go-round of dancing and pill-popping – The Scene Club, the Hammersmith Palais and the Mecca were the favoured haunts and London mods liked themselves to be thought of as constantly frequenting such venues. In fact, few could afford such a life-style. The reality was an old scooter, greasy fish and chips and an old parka, talking on a street corner and dreaming about the life of luxurious nightclubs, gangsterism and beautiful women.

Phil Cohen's analysis adds a strong class element to earlier theories in two senses:

1 He points out that members of youth subcultures come from the lowest strata of the working class; those with the dead-end jobs and low pay. Youths who become socially mobile do not join such subcultures.
2 The youth subcultures are a response to an attempt to deal with the class situation imposed on the proletariat by government and developers. These represent the outside forces of capitalism which destroyed the traditional supportive framework of working class culture.

Cohen's study has been subject to a number of criticisms, not least from sociologists whose political position has been not very far removed from his own. Like Fyvel's, it is a dated analysis. The situation of youth in and out of London has changed dramatically since the 1950's and 1960's. Subcultural styles have changed but remain long after the social and economic changes he describes. The problem youth have to deal with now is unemployment and increasingly there is no upward option for them to explore as the highly skilled and well paid jobs are not available any longer for the vast majority of young people. As Hall and Jefferson point out, there is no explanation of *why* some people explore the upward option and become mods while others explore the downward and become skins or Teds. In an account which seeks to 'read' style by relating it to social structure, the reasons for choosing one option rather than another also require explanation. Finally, both these authors and D Hebdige(63) point out that Cohen has not adequately demonstrated the relationship between the changes in the structural base of society and the ideological superstructure. He does not prove the links he suggests exist in any way. How does he *know*, for example, that braces and boots reflect an attempt to recreate some elements of traditional working class culture? Hebdige believes that Cohen is stretching a point in linking substructure and superstructure in such a close way. In many ways the skinheads and mods displayed characteristics unconnected to and separate from the working class base. They affirmed their own distinct generational identity.

> "For example, the skinheads undoubtedly reasserted these values associated with the traditional working class community, but they did so *in the face of* the widespread renunciation of those values in the parent culture – *at a time when* such an affirmation of the classic concerns of working class life was considered inappropriate."(64)

The mods, too, went to the West End (at least some of them did) and to the East Coast resorts and not the traditional working class focal points.

This criticism does not mean that theories of youth subcultures must return to the old generation gap or teenage consumer type of approach; with the addition that just lower working class youths join such groups and only some of these can afford to genuinely participate in their cultural life. The later work of the CCCS elaborates on and modifies this early theory of Cohen's. They add to it a version of Marxist theory based on Antonio Gramsci's discussion of *Hegemony*, a concept which requires explanation before the CCCS work can be fully appreciated.

Gramsci was an Italian Marxist who was most active in the early part of this century. He adapted Marx's theory to the Italian situation and added many important elements. His revision of Marxism became the model for the work of the Italian Communist Party and for the Eurocommunist movement as a whole. Perhaps the most important changes made by Gramsci involved the suggestion that the hold of the ruling class, the bourgeoisie, over society is not certain or stable. It is a hold which depends upon the maintenance of ruling class ideology in the minds of the oppressed sectors of society. This ideology keeps people in their places and leads them to accept, or at least, not to recognise, their exploited positions. It is maintained by the educational system, the mass media and religion. One commentator writes:

> "The concept of hegemony is really a very simple one. It means political leadership based on the consent of the led, a consent which is secured by the diffusion and popularisation of the world view of the ruling class."(65)

Ruling class ideas become generally accepted as 'right and proper' while others are seen as 'subversive', 'odd' and 'ridiculous'. In contemporary Britain support for the party system, the House of Commons, the monarchy and the juridiciary are normal. Our support for some of these institutions might be qualified in some cases, but overall the status quo is considered legitimate. There are those who argue that the House of Commons is dominated by males (there were only 23 female MP's at the time of the 1983 election) and by whites (there were no black MP's at that time); and that the House has very little power anyway, being eclipsed by outside economic forces over which there is no democratic control. Such challenges to the hegemonic dominance of the bourgeoisie have no hope of gaining acceptance themselves unless they too are supported by social institutions which can propagate this questioning and critical stance. However, the point that Gramsci makes, and the CCCS takes up, is that such a challenge *is* possible and that a constant struggle does go on between bourgeois ideas and those of the working class. Holes can be torn in the fabric of bourgeois ideology, and the tear can be of a permanent nature if there is a strong alliance of social forces to sustain opposition to the ruling class.

Today, the Italian Communist Party sees itself in this role – trying to create an alliance of social groups which can challenge the ideas of the ruling class. The CCCS maintains that less organised 'fabric-ripping' also takes place in the form of spontaneous youth sub-cultures. These are an attempt to 'win space' from bourgeois hegemony; both cultural space in the sense of authentic working class neighbourhood norms, values and institutions, and actual space on the street corner. They are a form of resistance, not political or terroristic in form but *ritualistic* and, as a result, not really changing or solving anything except at a symbolic level.

In this interpretation youth subcultures are a V sign at the bourgeois establishment, a symbol of defiance and a source of unity for groups of youths who feel exploited but are not sure by whom or why.

Tony Jefferson uses the specific example of the teds to illustrate the case(66). He argues that the ted style can be 'read' as an attempt to symbolically defend, a constantly threatened space and a declining status. The group-mindedness of the ted is an attempt to recapture traditional working class communities destroyed by war as well as the extended family destroyed by redevelopment of the inner cities. Both the physical space and the cultural space of proletarian communities were taken over by the bourgeoisie. The ted's subculture was symbolic resistance to this. The extreme touchiness about real or imagined insults, is an attempt to maintain and defend their status which has been deprived by the capitalist environment. Blacks, too, were seen as threatening and therefore, were the object of violence from the teds.

An important element of all youth subcultures is the style of dress. Jefferson says that this element came from some Savile Row tailors in 1950 who wanted a new style for aristocratic men about town. They adapted the Edwardian suit for them so that it consisted of a long, narrow-lapelled waisted jacket, narrow trousers, ordinary shoes and a tie with a 'Windsor' knot. Working class youths took up this fashion some time in 1953 and changed it slightly, adding thick crepe-soled shoes, skintight drainpipe trousers, bootlace ties (which came from the slick city gambler figure in Western films, Jefferson thinks), and moleskin or satin-collars. The distinctive hairstyle was also added; long on top, short at the sides with a quiff and lots of grease. Jefferson writes:

> "I see this choice of uniform as, initially, an attempt to butt status (since the clothes chosen were originally worn by the upper class dandies) which, being quickly aborted by a harsh social reaction, was followed by an attempt to create their own style via the modifications just outlined."(67)

According to this argument the unskilled working class youths attempted to cover the gap between themselves and their upper class contemporaries. Being rejected and ridiculed, they then parodied the dandy style and, by their violence and the fear it created, became a significant group in their own right. Their style, then, was a resistance to bourgeois ideology which cast them in the role of status-less and insignificant groups at the bottom end of society.

This approach has also been applied to the sociology of education by Paul Corrigan(68) who argues that working class kids play truant from school because they are *made* to go to school. School is compulsory because the bourgeoisie use it to:

1 Provide a bourgeois moral and religious code;
2 create a disciplined and punctual workforce; and
3 create a hierarchy of civilisation based upon education.

The working class always find themselves at the bottom because education is a game in which the bourgeoisie make the rules so that they always win.

It is not suprising that kids muck about in class or play truant. They are, in effect, waging guerilla warfare on the teachers who are imposing an alien and unwanted culture upon them. Corrigan sees the classroom as the battleground of this war. One side is trying to get the other to accept its view of the world and behave in the way that it wants them to behave, the other rejects the legitimacy of that attempt in whatever way is to hand. Because teachers have the power their position gives them, the children must use guile (leading the teacher on, mucking about but not getting caught). The world of 'footy' and pop helps the boys that Corrigan studied in two working class Sunderland schools to find a clear identity and to stand up against the teachers and the culture they represent. Both football and the music scene reinforce the distinct world of the working class youth. This separateness assumes political and tactical importance on Monday morning; without the experience of the pop concert and the Roker Park ground the boys would be much 'easier' for their teachers in the guerilla war between them. Subcultural activities outside the school gates and the deliberate disruption behind them are both aspects of the boys' *resistance*, the first ritualistic, the second more purposive.

Three questions immediately spring to mind after reflection on the CCCS approach to youth subcultures.

1 Why did not earlier generations of the working class resist bourgeois hegemony in the way today's young do?
2 If youth subcultures are resistant to bourgeois hegemony, why are there also subcultures among the youth from middle class (or bourgeois) backgrounds?
3 If youth subcultures are 'resistance through rituals' by the working class, why do the female members of that class rarely take a full part in this project?

In answer to the first question, Hall and Jefferson argue that:

> "... Youth encounters the problems of its class culture in different sets of institutions and experiences from those of its parents; and when youth encounters the same structures, it encounters them at crucially different points in its biological careers."(69)

Thus the young, unlike the old, have education imposed on them for long periods, they are hit by unemployment more, they have not been absorbed into the routine of work and they are exposed to more sources of conflicting socialisation, such as the media and travel. Today's young may suffer the oppressions of bourgeois society more than the last generation and they are more flexible in the patterns of their resistance to it.

In reply to the second question, Hall and Jefferson point out that middle class subcultures, such as hippies, drop-outs or drug culture tend to be more individual than group-centred and more retreatist in style. They do not oppose the system, they merely drop out of it or try to set up small scale alternatives in the hope of 'changing the world by example'. Such middle class subcultures are the result of the fragmentation of that class by the increasing complexity of capitalism. Fractions of the larger middle class culture come to attack some of its own central elements. The themes of anti-weapons, anti-sexism, anti-education, anti-consumption and anti-heterosexuality are seen as a reaction to the new materialistic and privatised culture of the modern middle class by its own youth. At the same time, however, elements of the new order (for example permissiveness and anti-authoritarianism) are contained in these youth subcultures. Middle class youth subcultures are possibly an attempt to bridge a structural gap just as working class ones, and they can be 'read' in the same way. Both types of subcultures are intimately connected to their parent culture and ritualistically resist problems which result from their social position.

In answer to the third question, two female sociologists, A McRobbie and J Garber(70) argue that girls retreat into passive, giggling cliques (rather than a full blown subculture) or aggressive sexuality (eg in front of the young male teacher to embarrass him) as a *female* response to *male* ideological hegemony. In this case the bourgeois and the working class male collude in the domination of girls, and the girls need to 'make space'. They achieve this by listening to records, joining fan clubs, etc. The idea that girls' groups are home-centred can be seen as a reflection of the supposed central position of the home in the life of females. According to this argument, hanging around doing nothing outside, as the boys do, would be more difficult for girls for whom such activity evokes echoes of prostitution. In many ways, the behaviour of the girls is simply a reflection of media images of 'what girls do'. Despite this the authors maintain that the 'bedroom culture' *is* a type of ritualistic resistance. Generally it is less oppositional and more retreatist than the boys' subcultures, but it can be put to oppositional use. For example, when the girls' obsessions with particular stars are used as a means of alienating the teachers and creating a defensive solidarity. Like the other youth subcultures studied by the CCCS, the girls' 'bedroom culture' contains elements of both the parent culture (the dependence relationship with popstars, the home-centredness) and new oppositional elements.

A further point made by McRobbie and Garber is that girls are not entirely absent from all male subcultures. There are female mods (a fairly feminine youth subculture in style anyway), though few female hell's angels or teds. Despite this admittedly minority role they are almost *entirely* absent from the literature dealing with these groups. As in many other areas of sociology (such as the family and education) women have until recently, been ignored by this male dominated profession. Where girl members *are* mentioned in the early literature, they are dealt with in an amazingly contemptuous way. Peter Laurie writes of the teddy girl, for example:

> "... she emphasised her bosom and bottom, her heels were preposterous, and she was blonde if it could be humanly arranged."(71)

While Fyvel comments:

> "In my glimpses of them they seemed crudely painted up, pathetically young, appallingly uneducated, some of them probably in danger of drifting into prostitution – in any case, as I looked at their expressionless faces, I felt sorry for their future families."(72)

In the light of this sort of approach it is quite understandable that the present generation of feminist sociologists have decided quite consciously to abandon the old sociological ethic of 'value freedom' (always something of a myth anyway). They take a committed feminist stand in their work in order to counteract the decades of chauvinist attitudes embodied in sociological work.

One of the most recent works on youth subculture, by Dick Hebdige, broadly follows the CCCS approach but adds two significant ingredients.

Firstly, he shows that when we 'read' subcultural styles we must take account of the fact that the mass media structures the way society is perceived by youth. Their subcultures are not based on the reality of their social situation but on a meditated perception of it. A diagrammatic representation of this point looks like this:

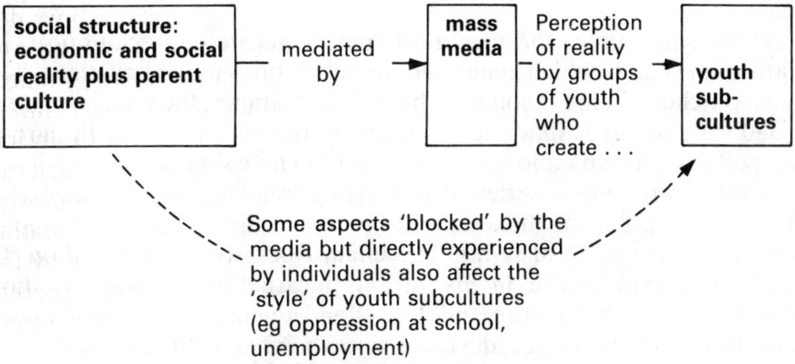

Early youth subcultures such as the teds were not affected in this way because of the relatively low exposure to the mass media by the working class. Today it is an important factor in determining the shape of the subculture. Youth cultures have to deal both with the actual reality of the structural situation *and* the mythologies.

The second point Hebdige makes in qualifying the CCCS position is that the youth subcultures are not allowed independence by the capitalist world in which they exist. They represent a threat, a form of resistance to bourgeois hegemony and they are not accepted passively by the bourgeoisie. There is a counter attack. This takes the form of an attempt to incorporate or co-opt the new styles into the capitalist world, thus neutralising them. This incorporation takes two forms: the commodity form, achieved by commercial institutions, and the ideological form, achieved by the mass media.

The commodity form of incorporation is the method whereby cultural signs (dress or music) are converted into mass-produced objects that are sold to young people, at first by small entrepreneurs and later by big business. The capitalist market takes the artefacts of the culture away from young people, alienating them from their own sub-culture. Furthermore, it 'normalises' the symbols of resistance by turning them into fashion, and neutralises them by turning them into a 'leisure-time only' style. Hebdige quotes the headline of an article in *Cosmopolitan* in the Summer of 1977 which illustrates the point nicely: "To Shock is Chic." This argument is different from that of Sugarman and other functionalists and some Marxists who argue that commercial interests *generate* subcultural styles (the mass culture argument). Hebdige is saying that these interests contain and incorporate autonomous rebellious movements.

The ideological form of incorporation works in two ways. The media can propagate the idea that the subcultures consist of semi-humans, they then proceed to provoke a righteous moral panic against these folk devils. Alternatively, they try to show that these are 'normal kids underneath', the sons and daughters of Mr and Mrs Average, just going through a phase.

At the same time, the media attempt to negate appreciation of the features of society which generated the subcultures in the first place. The 'rags to riches' theme is common here – for example, the unemployment UB40 sang about is made less serious by the very fact that the group escaped from it into fame and wealth and can now sing about it.

Hebdige provides a series of interesting 'readings' of subcultures to illustrate the points he makes about the role of the media and the incorporation of the cultural styles. The Glam Rock style was based on the figure of David Bowie in his various incarnations (Ziggy Stardust, Aladdin Sane, Mr Newton and The Blond Fuehrer). It consisted of a sexually ambiguous image, devotees wore their hair in bright colours, had platform shoes or 1950s plastic sandals and held their cigarettes just so. Disguise and dandyism were the main themes, sexuality and gender typing were the main objects of opposition. Hebdige reads this subculture as a challenge to the traditional Puritanism of the working class, particularly the way the media took up this Puritan theme and magnified it. The young people took and adapted images, styles and ideologies available elsewhere in the media and used them in the fight against these things. For example, the high fashion made available by Cosmopolitan, for *girls*, was taken and used by *both sexes*. The nostalgia cult propagated by the media was reflected in the 1950's fashion and the Hitler theme which were part of this style.

> "They were, in short, challenging at a symbolic level, the 'inevitability', the 'naturalness' of class and gender stereotypes."(73)

A second subcultural style Hebdige analysed is that of the Punks. He describes their sartorial style as 'confrontation dressing'. The use of pegs, razor blades, TV components, tampons, safety pins and bin liners was a deliberate attempt to shock. They turned conventional ideals and ideas inside out by wearing fragments of school uniform defiled by graffiti, fake blood and swastikas, and by wearing make-up to be seen. They challenged traditional sexual roles and exaggerated stereotypes by their blatant use of bondage gear, fishnet stockings, chains and dirty raincoats. Their dances were the obverse of the courting dance; the pogo and the robot could be described as 'anti-dancing.' Their music was challenging in every respect – the names of the groups (Sex Pistols, The Rejects, The Clash, The Slits, The Dead Kennedies), the quality of the music ("we're into chaos, not music" – Johnny Rotten), the lyrics ("I wanna be sick on you",

"Belsen was a gas") and the performances (which usually included spitting on the audience and sometimes vomiting.) The fanzines, such as *Sniffin Glue*, turned destruction of the English language into an art form and the whole system of signs added up to an image of worthlessness – as the words Punk and Rotten themselves suggest. Punk norms and values, then, were a form of 'semiotic guerilla warfare'. Hebdige says this of them:

> "Whereas the skinheads theorised and fetishized their class position in order to effect a 'magical' return to an imagined past, the punks dislocated themselves from the parent culture and were positioned instead on the outside: beyond the comprehension of the average (wo)man in the street in a science fiction future. They played up their otherness, 'happening' on the world as aliens, inscrutables."(74)

They escaped their origins and created a chaos, an anarchic and alienated world in which coherent form was destroyed. This was the challenge to the ruling ideology, an attempt to destroy, or at least rock the established order. It was not long, though, before the shops began to sell trousers with zips in large numbers carefully sewn into them. Safety pins became all the rage and were sold in the form of key rings and pendants. Meanwhile the record companies were signing up the Punk groups, having recognised their market potential, and the music and lyrics were toned down (or perhaps *up*) to appeal to a larger audience. The capitalist world was moving against the challenge.

Hebdige takes and modifies the CCCS approach then, while at the same time adding some new elements to it. In doing so he answers some of the criticisms of the earlier approach made by Stan Cohen in the third edition of his book *Folk Devils and Moral Panics*(75). Cohen contends that there is much in common between the functionalist and the Marxist accounts of youth culture. Both maintain that the structure of society imposes certain conditions upon youth (such as deprivation and failure in education). Both see the particular cultural forms adopted by youth as a response to this structural context; and both see the biography of the individual youth as living out this culture. Cohen considers the CCCS have taken insufficient account of the power of commercialism in their approach. Youth subcultures and changes in them are often *not* a response to structural developments but are *manufactured*, dictated by and in the interests of consumer society. American cultural imperialism is another important factor which is given short shrift in this work, according to Cohen. Often the kids are just adopting styles which have been imported from America and have little or nothing to do with events in this country or the class situation of some of its younger inhabitants. Moreover the CCCS approach, while convincingly demonstrating that most skinheads are working class youths, does not tell us why not all working class youths are skinheads. Murdock and McCron make the same point when they write:

> "Subcultural studies start by taking groups who are already card-carrying members of a particular subculture such as skinheads, bike boys or hippies, and working backwards to uncover their class location. The approach therefore excludes adolescents who share the same basic class location but who are not members of the subculture."(76)

Cohen also asks, why is it that the violence displayed by members of some youth subcultures is so often directed at other *youths* if, as the CCCS argues, the subculture is symbolic resistance to the bourgeois world?

Finally, and crucially, what, if the kids themselves do not see their behaviour as a form of reaction to structural demands or conditions (and they do not), gives these authors the ability to see an explanation which the participants themselves are blind to? This is a specific instance of the general criticism which phenomenologists make of those who seek to use positivist approaches to the study of society. They argue that we cannot establish laws concerning the causation of social behaviour: we cannot explain the determinants of behaviour because behaviour is *not determined by anything*. People act in a certain way only because of the conscious motives they have for acting in that way, and they could easily change the patterns of their actions if they wanted to do so. In fact many young people *do* swap subcultures almost overnight. The corollary of this is that it is not for the sociologist to discover reasons for behaviour, or to theorise on its causes but only to describe the motivations and perceptions of the people involved. Nothing more than this exists. In fact Cohen does not go all the way down the road of this argument because, as we shall see in a moment, he explains the styles of youth subculture by reference to the mass media, an influence which the participants themselves may not recognise.

Other critics of the CCCS work(77) have pointed out that the authors concentrate very heavily on Britain South of Watford Gap. If skinhead subculture is a response to London's lost traditional community we are left wondering why there are skinhead gangs in Northern industrial towns where such a community remains alive. We are not really told why a single parent culture gives rise to many different manifestations of youth subcultures, nor what influences an individual to join one rather than another. Methodologically too their work leaves much to be desired. Ethnography makes fascinating reading and can give useful insights, but it is an insubstantial basis for a *general* sociological theory.

Interactionist and related approaches to the study of youth

The subtitle of Stan Cohen's book *Folk Devils and Moral Panics: The*

Creation of Mods and Rockers, suggests its principal theme, that youth subculture must be seen as a media creation rather than as a reaction by the working class section of youth to their economic and social environment. The mods and rockers subcultures were only made up of groups of youth with different clothing styles before the exaggerated claims of the press began the process of their formation into the subcultures we know about today. This process began after a few scuffles broke out on Easter Sunday 1964.

Press editorials and comment exaggerated and distorted events, using words like 'riot', 'battle' and 'siege' to describe what were, in reality, minor events. There were no gangs as such; the mods and rockers polarisation did not exist. Only a minority had motorbikes or scooters and they were not affluent, as the press claimed. Newspapers predicted that similar 'riots' would happen again and, of course, this led to the classic 'self-fulfilling prophecy'. Youths went down to the east and south coast resorts of Clacton, Brighton, Margate or Hastings to join in the fun. The press increasingly criticised their clothes, their hairstyles, their scooters and motorbikes until the ensemble was associated with these 'folk devils' – the object of unanimous vilification by the public.

Cohen states there are two reasons for the exaggeration of events by the press: firstly, the 'institutionalised need to create news; and secondly, the existence of the inferential structures of the newsmaking process. Newspapers with little news in them are boring and do not sell, therefore when there is little or no news it is necessary to *create* it. The mods and rockers did not become news because they were new; they were presented as new to justify their creation as news. The inferential structures of the news-making process refers to the fact that journalists naturally take the side of the police, the magistrates and the local residents because they share the same world view. This consensual definition of the situation is reported, rather than either objective events (if such exist) or the definitions of events held by mods and rockers themselves. By exaggerating the concerns and fears of the agencies of social control, the media create a 'moral panic'. Mods and rockers, like all the youth subcultures, act as scapegoats for society to blame its troubles on. They also strengthen the boundaries of the acceptable by bringing them into focus.

Cohen summarises his theory in this way(78):

> "... the societal reaction in general and the mass media in particular, could plausibly be thought to have had the following sorts of effects on the nature, extent and development of deviance:

1 Reinforcing and magnifying a predisposition to expect trouble: 'something's going to happen.'

2 Providing the content for rumours – thereby structuring the 'something' into potential and actual deviance: such rumours and images facili-

tated by deviance solidifying the crowd and validating its moods and actions.
3 Creating a set of culturally identifiable symbols which further structured the situation and legitimised action.
4 Spreading hostile beliefs and mobilising the participants for action.
5 Providing the content for deviant role playing by transmitting the sterotypical expectations of how persons in particular deviant roles should act.
6 Magnifying the Mods-Rockers dichotomy and giving the groups a tighter structure and common ethos then they originally possessed.
7 Polarising the deviants further and further against the community and – through the actions of the police and courts – setting up a spiral of deviancy amplification."

The mass media act as the socialising agents for the subcultures adopted by youth rather than their peers or any previous generation of subculture members. Cohen, therefore, rejects the substructure-superstructure account of Marxist-influenced writers and attributes independence to the norms and values which, for a Marxist, would be superstructural products of substructural forces.

In *Policing the Crisis* Stuart Hall, Chas Critcher, Tony Jefferson, John Clarke and Brian Roberts try to unify interactionist and neo-Marxist perspectives by accepting Cohen's analysis but adding a conflict view of society(79). Looking primarily at the 'new' crime of 'mugging' (a label for a variety of pre-existing crimes) and the associated themes of troublesome youth and the race problem; they analyse the moral panic about mugging which arose in 1972 and lasted for over a year. They argue, like Cohen, that the label preceded the crime and acted to bring it about:

> "If a label precedes a crime, and the judicial arm of the state is increasingly locked in a struggle with a section of the community which then produces its criminals, and the society shows a clear predisposition to panic about this aspect of 'rising crime' before it discovers a particular instance of the crime to panic about, then it is necessary to turn, first, not to the crime but what seems most problematic: the reaction to crime. Thus we pose the problem now in its most paradoxical form: could it be possible – historically plausible – that a societal reaction to crime could precede the appearance of a pattern of crimes?"(80)

Their focus of attention is not why the 'crime wave' started or the study of how a label can amplify deviance(81); it is the reason for the predisposition to panic.

While agreeing that Cohen's account has considerable value, they argue that we need to take historical and structural factors into account when theorising about the nature and causes of moral panics. Their argument is that there are moments of panic followed by a tightening of the grip of the control culture (the police, the judiciary and the media acting with increased vigour against deviants) whenever there is a crisis in society. Such panics have:

> "signalled, time and time again in the past, periods of profound social upheaval, of economic crisis and historical rupture"(82)

These periods are the result of the internal contradictions of capitalism which result in falling rates of profit, economic slumps, currency crises, inflation and stagnation and breakdowns in wage bargaining. All of these weaken support for the social and economic system. Given the threat to bourgeois hegemony and the very structure of the class system it becomes necessary to label and 'criminalise' (ie to simply make illegal what is in reality the expression of a social and economic conflict) those who pose a threat or who might be easily depicted as posing a threat. These are the young, the black, the political dissidents and those from poor environments. By this means consensus can be artificially reconstructed and the nature of class domination once again 'hidden' behind the consensual veneer. If this is not done:

> "The masks of liberal consent and popular consensus slip to reveal the reserves of coercion and force on which the cohesion of the state and its legal authority finally depends"(83)

At this point, in Althusser's terms, the ideological state apparatus has failed and the repressive state apparatus is revealed for what it is. The creation of a moral panic, though, is:

> "one of the principal forms of ideological consciousness by means of which a 'silent majority' is won over to the support of increasingly coercive measures on the part of the state, and lends its legitimacy to a 'more than usual' exercise of control"(84).

Mugging is only one subject of an increasingly rapid succession of moral panics. There have been panics about drugs, hippies, the underground, pornography, long-haired students, layabouts, vandalism and football hooliganism. In each case the area of concern was identified and 'firm steps' were called for. One interesting aspect is the tendency for the activities of a small number of 'troublesome' individuals to be seen as representative of the group as a whole. Thus while *some* young people may become, for example, punks or long-haired students (possibly as a result of the label), these images are quickly expanded to encompass a whole generation and they become a social problem, about which 'something should be done'. Such Folk Devils are increasingly necessary because of the ever-worsening crises in capitalism, but while the repressive nature of the state may be masked and its class conflicts once again disguised by a created consensus, the working through of social anxieties do not succeed for long:

> "The 'trouble' about youth is not appeased by the teddy boys, and 'mods' and 'rockers' sent down in court; it surfaces again, now about hooliganism, vandalism, long hair, drugs, promiscuous sex. The fears about race are not expiated by a succession of panics about blacks . . . or calmed by tougher and tougher measures of control on the entry of immigrants"(85).

No wonder that we find moral panics about Folk Devils throughout the history of capitalism; there was, for example, a garroting panic in the mid 19th Century.

The authors of *Policing the Crisis* are not proposing a conspiracy theory of the creation of panics, however. The media do much of the ideological work of reconstructing bourgeois hegemony in a non-deliberate way. The media tend to reproduce the definitions of the situation held by the powerful because of the hierarchy of access to newspapers and TV programmes. The press and broadcasting media automatically adopt the position held by *primary definers* such as politicians, the police and business leaders. The press accepts their view of what constitutes "important news", their statistics uncritically and sanctions their view of the malaise in society caused by mugging and youth. For example, once race relations in Britain have been defined (by Powell) as a problem of numbers, even liberal spokesman are forced to discuss the issue in these terms and not in terms of the multiple disadvantages suffered by black people discussed in this book. Indeed, the authors argue that when such perspectives *are* successfully introduced the media manage to sever causal links in a quite remarkable manner. The complex structural links between young blacks, poor living environments, educational and employment opportunities and crime are reduced to an implied link between dirt and crime:

> "The litter in the street becomes the sign of . . . criminality . . . a derelict house or street infects the inhabitants with a kind of moral pollution."(86)

Hall and the other authors of *Policing the Crisis* very much agree with Golding and Elliot (see pages 267–268.) They see the media as unconsciously performing an ideological task, transmitting and re-inforcing dominant ideas, bourgeois hegemony:

> "Hierarchical structures of command and review, informal socialisation into institutional roles, the sedimenting of dominant ideas into the 'professional ideal' – all help to ensure, within the media, their continued reproduction of the dominant form."(87)

Such factors are far more important than overt censorship or formal control over the content of newspapers or TV news.

According to these authors, the crisis that needs to be policed by the control culture of police, judiciary and the media is the crisis of capitalism; an economic system unable to contain the contradictions inherent in it. The *apparent* crises merely function to strengthen the weakening consensus and to legitimate 'tough measures' against those who dissent or who can be easily shown to be the 'cause' of this country's problems. Through this argument, Hall et al achieve a synthesis of interactionism and neo-Marxism, moving beyond Cohen's focus on the media and adding the extra dimension of the dominant class. For Hall the media literally *mediate* between the dominant and the subordinate class, while for Cohen they appear to be acting as independent agents, motivated mainly by news values and the search for a good story.

Marsh, Rosser and Harré in *The Rules of Disorder*(88) wish, like Hall et al, to achieve the synthesis of a variety of sociological perspectives in the study of one aspect of youth culture; football hooliganism. They adopt elements of a structural, interactionist and phenomenological approach. They categorise the first two approaches as the 'outside' approach, they call the last the 'inside' approach and concentrate on it in the book. They write:

> "... it is clear that an understanding of any 'deviant' phenomena will require two avenues of investigation. The first involves sociological theory of societal creation of deviance and the processes by which this is achieved. The second requires a social psychology of the symbolic universe in which acts are endowed with meaning and the commonsense accounts which are offered within such a universe to render the imposed concept of deviance intelligible".(89)

They approvingly quote the structuralist theory of football hooliganism given by Ian Taylor(90). This author argues that hooliganism can be understood as a form of resistance (more than merely ritualistic this time) to the increasingly professionalised and commercialised nature of football clubs which were once 'of the people'. Players were at one time ordinary people whom the fans knew personally, now they are highly paid stars in the service of the entrepreneurs of the football business. Marsh, Rosser and Harré concur:

> "Contemporary 'problems' on the terraces can thus be seen, in this historical context, as a coherent resistance of change and as an attempt by fans to reclaim their soccer heritage."(91)

The similarities to the CCCS accounts of the rise of skinheads and mods are worth noting.

The authors of *The Rules of Disorder* are also in full accord with the deviancy amplification theory of interactionist work such as Stan Cohen's and Jock Young's(92). They stress that:

> "The deviancy amplification model would seem to require only a small number of incidents (which might even arise by chance) in order to develop the familiar pattern of escalation".(93)

The bulk of the book however, is concerned with the nature of the fans' reality, particularly Oxford United fans. The book presents an inside account of social order and meanings on the terrace in the ethnographic style of anthropology and phenomenology so that we may understand the fans' world. They find that a fan can progress through a 'career', marked by successful risk taking (or 'hazarding'). One can progress from Novice (inexperienced boy) to Rowdy (noisy fans – hooligans in the press terminology) to Town Boy (extremely loyal and 'hard' fan.) Within the Rowdy category there are social roles such as Chant Leader, 'Aggro' Leader, Nutter, Hooligan and Organiser. One achieves social mobility in this world by getting into situations where one could lose face. For example trying to start a chant by shouting out 'Give us an O' (in preparation to spell Oxford) and getting no response would be extremely embarrassing, while success on a number of occasions would eventually lead to the social role of Chant Leader. The authors show that despite the media's image of uncontrolled mindless violence and despite remarkably similar rhetoric amongst the fans themselves (the result of a conspiracy by the fans to hide the truth from each other), there are in fact very strong Rules of Disorder which contain aggression. This means that most potentially violent situations never escalates because all the participants are familiar with the rules. For example, if you keep your jacket on you demonstrate to the other side that you do not intend real violence. Marsh et al describe the sequence of events on match days and the rules which are embedded in this sequence, repeated every Saturday. Throughout they insist that "Action is neither chaotic nor senseless but rather is structured and reasoned". The fans also know the rules for action held by non-fan participants like policemen and ambulancemen who, in their turn, know something of the fans' rules.' *Real* disorder only occurs where one or more of the participants does not know the rules or deliberately chooses to ignore them. The overall conclusion is that aggro is a form of ritualised aggression, part of the social mechanism whereby aggression in society is controlled and managed:

> ". . . we suggest that aggro is one contemporary social means available to man for coping with aggression. . . . Whilst animals may rely on instinctive patterns of motor co-ordination to direct their ritual displays of threat and submission, man develops social systems which rely on culture for transmission. But the end product is the same – order."(94)

It is interesting to note that the authors insist that this explanation of the fans' behaviour is recognisable to the fans themselves. They agree with the phenomenologists point that any explanation *must* fit the commonsense reality of the inside social world of the participants. If this is not the case the sociologist is merely imposing a set of meanings on the participants, when in fact the absence of any objective reality means that both sets of meanings are of equal value. They are just two of many possible ways of constructing the social universe:

> "If one was to listen carefully to the fans and on the basis of this build up an account of the inside reality but then found that this reality was unrecognisable when offered back to fans, one would have to admit one had got it wrong."(95)

From ethnographic studies such as these and others(96) it seems that the CCCS "got it wrong" for this very reason, as Stan Cohen suggests.

The two studies we have just examined have attempted to combine a variety of sociological perspectives into an over-arching theoretical framework. Clearly, each has a preferred angle; structuralism in the first, phenomenological in the second. It is doubtful whether a *genuine* synthesis is possible in view of the basically contradictory tenets of the perspectives: consensus versus dissensus, exploitation versus cooperation, social reality shaping man versus man shaping social reality, subcultures embodying a group's constructed reality versus subcultures as shaped by outside forces, the possibility of a sociologically revealed truth versus its impossibility. At the very least these sit uneasily alongside each other, at the worst they are completely incompatible.

Chapter review

We have examined a number of the competing perspectives on youth culture and youth subcultures. We first examined biological theories and concluded that while biological factors have *some* role to play in engendering the differences between young and old, social factors are of far greater importance. We then examined theories which tried to isolate specific post-war social and economic developments as the causative factors in the presumed birth of youth culture in that period. We looked particularly at the putative general post-war affluence, the effect of the war itself, the extension of state education and the expansion of the mass media as possible important catalysts. In each case we identified important flaws in the argument. The functionalist perspective on youth culture, although more theoretically sophisticated than those just mentioned, was nevertheless found to lack analysis of a number of important splits in modern industrial society and to contain an implicit determinism. In examining some of the structuralist theories of youth subculture which incorporate semiotic analysis of these social phenomena we found that problems were nonetheless connected with this approach too. These problems primarily concerned the imposition of the social perspective and political viewpoint of the sociologists onto the subjects of their study as well as the lack of any real evidence of their applicability. In the final section we reviewed the work of Stan Cohen who took an interactionist stance, seeing youth subcultures as largely a media creation; and that of Stuart Hall et al. who sought to add a structural element to the interactionist account. We also gave an account of *The Rules of Disorder* which sought to synthesise interactionism, structuralism and the ethnographic approach of phenomenology.

It is quite clear from this short review of some of the literature that the sociology of youth culture is as, if not more, divided as other areas of sociology by the variety of perspectives that exist within the discipline as a whole. In the study of youth culture, this lack of a paradigm, an agreement on the basic concepts and foundations for research is compounded by the lack of detailed empirical studies of specific youth subcultures which approach them *without* having decided the findings of the research before actually doing it. These two factors make the area of youth culture studies one of the more fragmented sub-disciplines within sociology.

Bibliography

(1) P Aries *Centuries of Childhood* Jonathan Cape, 1973 (first published in the U.K. 1962)

(2) B M Young & P Willmott in *The Symmetrical Family* Penguin, Harmondsworth 1975

(3) P Aries op. cit. p. 28

(4) G Stanley Hall *Adolescence: Its Psychology and Its Relation to Physiology, Anthropology, Sociology, Sex, Crime, Religion and Education* D Appleton & Co., NY. 1904

(5) Quoted in C M Fleming *Adolescence* Routledge & Kegan Paul, 1967 pp. 37–38

(6) Ibid. p. 38

(7) A study conducted in 1922 tested 3500 children in three cities entering the first grade of school and tested them annually thereafter until they left. The study found great individual differences and also found that physical development was gradual rather than saltatory in character. This was reported in W F Dearbon and J W Rothney et al. *Predicting the Child's Development* Sci-Art Publishers, Cambridge, Massachusetts 1941.

(8) F Thrasher *The Gang* University of Chicago Press 1927

(9) M Head *Coming of Age in Samoa* Penguin, Harmondsworth 1928

(10) Ibid. p. 64

(11) Ibid. p. 158

(12) D Freeman *Margaret Mead and Samoa: The Making and Unmaking of an Anthropological Myth* 1983

(13) See O A Wheeler *The Adventure of Youth* London University Press 1945 for an account of the relevance of such theories to the formulation of the Act

(14) Marshall Cavendish Learning System: Man and Machine *Who is the Adolescent* Marshall Cavendish Books Ltd

(15) Quoted in J L Thompson *Examining Sociology* Hutchinson 1980 pp. 110–112

(16) In 1981 the figures for the number of persons found guilty of indictable offences in England and Wales per 1000 in that age group were as follows (source: Social Trends 1983 HMSO)

Years of Age	*Number*
10–13	30
14–16	75
17–20	73
21+	13

(17) M Abrams *The Teenage Consumer* London Press Exchange 1959

(18) Ibid. p. 9

(19) Ibid. p. 10

(20) Ibid. p. 13

(21) M Abrams *The Newspaper Reading Public of Tomorrow* Odhams, London 1964

(22) Ibid. pp. 57–8

(23) T R Fyvel *The Insecure Offenders: Rebellious Youth in the Welfare State* Penguin, Harmondsworth 1966

(24) In Abrams 1974 op. cit.

(25) A Coleman *The Adolescent Society* Glencoe Free Press 1961

(26) P Johnson 1964 *The Menace of Beatleism* New Statesman 28 February 1964

(27) M Horkheimer *Art and Mass Culture* in *Critical Theory* Herder & Herder 1972 pp. 277–8

(28) Speech by Vice President Spiro Agnew Sept. 1970 in Las Vegas. Quoted in S Denisoff *Sociology: Theories in Conflict* Wadsworth Publishing Co. Inc. 1972 p. 23 Belmont, Calif.

(29) P Berger and B Berger Sociology: *A Biographical Approach* Penguin, Harmondsworth 1976

(30) J Goldthorpe & D Lockwood et al. *The Affluent Worker in the Class Structure* Cambridge University Press 1969

(31) Ibid. p. 157

(32) B Abel-Smith & P Townsend *The Poor & The Poorest* G Bell & Sons 1965

(33) P Townsend *Poverty in the United Kingdom* Penguin 1979

(34) Coates & Silburn *Poverty: The Forgotten Englishmen* Penguin 1970

(35) D Hargreaves *Social Relations in a Secondary School* Routledge & Kegan Paul 1967 and Colin Lacey's *Hightown Grammar* Manchester University Press 1970. Both found this to be the case

(36) Alan Swingewood *The Myth of Mass Culture* Macmillan 1977 p. 108

(37) T Parsons *Age and Sex in the Social Strucutre of the United States* in *Essays in Sociological Theory* (revised edition) Free Press New York 1964 pp. 88–103

(38) Eisenstadt *From Generation to Generation* Glencoe Free Press 1956

(39) B Sugarman *Sociology* Heinemann 1968

(40) P Berger & B Berger op. cit.

(41) See, for example, Sugarman op. cit. p. 70

(42) Berger & Berger op. cit. p. 240

(43) Ibid. p. 241

(44) Ibid. pp. 244–5

(45) Ibid. p. 240

(46) Sugarman op. cit. p. 71

(47) Berger & Berger pp. 250–251

(48) Ibid. p. 250–251

(49) P Laurie *The Teenage Revolution* Anthony Blond Ltd., London 1965 p. 11

(50) P Willis *Learning to Labour* Saxon House, London 1977

(51) P Corrigan *Schooling the Smash Street Kids* Macmillan 1979

(52) P Willmott *Adolescent Boys of East London* Penguin, Harmondsworth 1969

(53) G Murdoch & R McCron *Youth and Class: The Career of a Confusion* in G. Mungham & G. Pearson *Working Class Youth Culture* Routledge & Kegan Paul 1976 pp. 10–27

(54) P Willmott op. cit. p. 175

(55) Ibid. p. 179

(56) Albert Cohen *Delinquent Boys* Glencoe Free Press 1955 and Cloward and Ohlin *Delinquency and Opportunity* Glencoe Free Press 1961

(57) W B Miller *Lower Class Culture as a Generating Milieu of Gang Delinquency* 1962

(58) M Brake *Cultural Revolution in Alternative Delinquency* in R Bailey & J Young (eds.) *Contemporary Social Problems in Britain 1973*. D Hargreaves & C Lacey (op. cit.) follow a similar argument

(59) S Hall & T Jefferson *Resistance Through Rituals* Hutchinson 1976

(60) Ibid. p. 16

(61) Ferdinand de Saussure *Course in General Linguistics* p. 16 quoted in T. Hawkes *Structuralism & Semiotics* Methuen & Co. Ltd. 1977 p. 123

(62) P Cohen *Subcultural Conflict and Working Class Community* Working papers in cultural studies no. 2. Centre for Contemporary Cultural Studies, University of Birmingham 1972

(63) D Hebdige *Subculture: The Meaning of Style* Methuen 1979

(64) Ibid. p. 79

(65) A Bates *Gramsci and the Theory of Hegemony* Journal of the History of Ideas 1975 pp. 351–67, p. 352

(66) T Jefferson *Cultural Responses of the Teds* in S Hall & T Jefferson op. cit. pp. 81–86

(67) Ibid. pp. 85–6

(68) P Corrigan op. cit.

(69) S Hall & T Jefferson op. cit. p. 49

(70) A McRobbie & J Garber *Girls & Subcultures* in Ibid. pp. 209–229

(71) P Laurie op. cit. p. 25

(72) Fyvel op. cit. pp. 96–7

(73) D Hebdige op. cit. p. 89

(74) Ibid. pp. 120–21

(75) S Cohen *Folk Devils & Moral Panics* 3rd edition 1979, first published 1971

(76) G Murdoch & R McCron op. cit. p. 25

(77) For example Bernard Davies *Youth Cultures, Myths and Political Realities* in *Youth and Society* No. 16 1976 pp. 13–16. Quoted in O'Donnell *A New Introductory Reader in Sociology* Harrap 1983

(78) S Cohen *Sensitisation: The Case of Mods & Rockers* in S Cohen & J Young *The Manufacture of News: Deviance, Social Publicity and the Mass Media* Constable 1981, first published 1973 pp. 957–8

(79) Stuart Hall, Chas Critcher, Tony Jefferson, John Clarke and Brian Roberts *Policing the Crisis: Mugging, the State and Law and Order* Macmillan 1978

(80) Ibid. p. 182

(81) They do explain this in terms of the increased police attention on this particular crime, leading to more arrests of people who would have not been caught before. Also, some youths who see themselves as locked in a struggle against the forces of law and order take to mugging because this becomes the defined site of a continuing battle with "the law" and the social system it protects. In addition the "catch-all" nature of the term "mugging" means

that there is an increased tendency by the police and courts to define a variety of crimes as mugging which leads to an apparent increase in its incidence

(82) Ibid. p. 186

(83) Ibid. p. 217

(84) Ibid. p. 221

(85) Ibid. p. 323

(86) Ibid. p. 115

(87) Ibid. p. 60

(88) P Marsh, E Rosser and R Harré *The Rules of Disorder* Routledge and Kegan Paul 1978, paperback edition 1980

(89) Ibid. p. 11

(90) Ibid. p. 14

(92) Stan Cohen *Folk Devils and Moral Panics* op. cit. J Young *The Role of the Police as Amplifiers of Deviance* in S Cohen *Images of Deviance* Penguin 1971

(93) Marsh, Rosser and Harré, p. 117

(94) Ibid. p. 128

(95) Ibid. p. 118

(96) See for example I Walker *Three Young Men of Southall* and *The Voices of Toxteth* in New Society 24 September 1981 and 26 November 1981

4 The sociology of health

Introduction

The sociology of health has only recently become a subject of increased importance. The general view was that health and illness were purely physical and mental questions and, therefore, did not concern sociological enquiry. If sociologists did look at the subject at all it tended to be in a very limited way. This involved studying the roles of the doctor and the patient and their patterns of interaction or studying conceptions of illness, particularly mental illness.

More recent work has recognised the social nature of various aspects of the topic of health which this early, predominantly American work, did not deal with at all. The fact that both physical and mental health are *social constructs* was recognised, as was the political and social importance of this. It became clear, too, that health was distributed across the class structure in a very unequal way. The necessity of discovering the links between the health patterns of the community and the class structure became a priority for sociologists. The system of health care, like other social welfare measures, was recognised for what it was – the outcome of political negotiation conducted within the framework of the financial constraints of a particular type of economy. Sociologists recognised the need to study the public and private organisation of health care; the way in which resources were allocated and who benefitted from this allocation.

This chapter explores some of these themes. We will begin with an examination of the definitions of health and illness, looking at the medical, Marxist and functionalist views. We will then examine the history, current organisation and resource allocation of the National Health Service (NHS) in Britain. This is followed by a more theoretical discussion of Social Democrats', Market Liberals' and Marxists' views on health policy in this country. The following section will look at the data on the social distribution of health changes, reviewing the information on morbidity and mortality across the social classes and then look at some of the propositions which have been made to explain these data. The fifth section will look specifically at the topic of mental health and examine the work of two of the major authors in this field – R D Laing and Thomas Szasz. The sixth section will review Parsons and Illich, two very different approaches to the role of formal health care in advanced industrial societies. The final section briefly summarises the ground covered in the chapter.

Definitions of health and illness

The medical definition

Although superficially health seems an easy thing to define, on closer examination it is a particularly elusive concept. It is often defined in a negative way as the absence of sickness, but this is not very useful. Attempts at a positive definition tend to become so broad as to be equally useless. The World Health Organization, for example, defines health as:

> "Not the mere absence of disease but total physical, mental and social well-being."

This begs the question as to what constitutes physical well-being – let alone mental and social well-being which could mean virtually anything you want it to mean. The medical profession and the public in general often consider health to be the normal state of affairs which is sometimes disrupted by apparently random attacks from outside which result in sickness:

> "Disease is understood as a failure in and of the individual, an isolatable 'thing' that attacks the physical machine more or less arbitrarily from 'outside' preventing it from fulfilling its essential 'responsibilities'."(1)

Even mental illness has come to be seen in this light in some quarters. Physical intervention, such as frontal lobotomy and leucotomy (removal of part of the brain and severing of nerve fibres respectively) as well as electro convulsive therapy (ECT) are used in its treatment.

Medical science treats the body like a machine which most of the time runs smoothly but occasionally suffers damage from outside. Spare part surgery in both name and function illustrates this analogy well. Doctors are trained into the belief that a sound knowledge of the physical nature of the body, its biological, physical and chemical processes, will enable them to cure disease once they have correctly diagnosed it through the scientific analysis of symptoms.

Modern Western medicine has assumed the status of a science; it examines only observable phenomena, it attempts to establish correlations between them in order to identify causes. Facts and laws thus established are built up into a body of knowledge about disease which can then be put into practice.

This approach to medicine appears to be of fairly recent origin. Lesley Doyal notes that before the industrialisation of Britain:

"Most healing and care of the sick was undertaken . . . on an informal or semi-formal basis, often by women. Their knowledge of healing was based largely on tradition, and involved the use of empirically based 'natural' remedies (such as herbs) as well as religious or supernatural methods – amulets, spells or prayer for example."(2)

In one way the early and later stages of medicine have something in common; both view sickness as a form of possession, in the first instance by spirits, in the second by germs. N Jewson(3) has suggested that we can see scientific medicine as going through the following stages:

1 Bedside medicine (Middle Ages to the late 18th century) in which medicine was only for the wealthy and was based on patronage. The account given by the *patient* of the symptoms was the most important aspect of diagnosis, and psychological factors rather than objective physical ones were paramount. Disease was thought to be due to a disruption of the balance between mind and body. The therapeutic value of medical treatment was virtually nil, but confidence in the doctor probably helped the patient to feel better.
2 Hospital medicine (1800 to 1900) which was the result of the development of unhealthy cities and large numbers of sick poor people needing treatment. Doctors became more organised as a profession and the patients became treated as 'cases' rather than people because they were no longer paying the doctor and had lower status. The doctor took control and the patients' subjective view of their diseases became unimportant. The mechanistic view of ill-health (ie treating the sick body in the same way as a malfunctioning machine) took over from the psychological view. Developments such as the thermometer, stethoscope and laryngoscope were made at this time so that the doctor could more effectively seek out and examine the defective part. Despite these developments, medicine remained fairly ineffective.
3 Laboratory medicine (1900 to the present day) was the third and final stage and marks the final victory of the mechanistic approach in medicine. The experimental method is now utilised to the full and medicine is viewed as one of the natural sciences. The sick person is now viewed not even as a set of organs but as millions of cells, and so is treated even less like a person than in the second stage. Now people are merely objects to be manipulated by medical technology.

The modern scientific/mechanistic view of health as the normal state of the body seems to be mistaken. The 1978 General Household Survey reports that:

"Overall 56% of men and 70% of women reported that they had a health problem at the time (of the survey) or that one kept recurring. Yet only 9% of men and 12% of women questioned had seen their doctors in the preceding 14 days."(4)

It appears that at least subjectively, illness appears to be the norm. In this sense it is not the equivalent of the machine gone wrong – we are hardly ever 'right'.

In another sense, too, the mechanistic view can be criticised. It takes ill-health to be an objectively identifiable thing, something which you have either got or you have not. Clearly, someone who has lost a leg or who cannot eat because of lockjaw is not healthy, but definitions of ill-health beyond this elementary level are difficult to arrive at. If we compare two people who have nothing 'wrong' with them in an identifiable sense, one may be able to run further while the other becomes quickly winded. One may frequently feel tired and suffer headaches and backaches while the other does not. Can we really say that they are both healthy?

The Marxist model

Marxists reject the simple mechanistic view of health and illness and argue that these are categories which are selectively applied to individuals in the interests of the owning class. Peter Sedgwick, the Marxist author of Psycho Politics(5) writes:

> "The blight that strikes at corn or potatoes is a *human invention*, for if we wished to cultivate parasites (rather than potatoes or corn) there would be no blight, but simply the necessary foddering of the parasite crop . . . the invasion of a human organism by cholera germs carries with it no more . . . the stamp of 'illness' than does the souring of milk by other forms of bacteria . . . All sickness is deviancy. That is to say, no attribution of sickness to any being can be made without the expectation of some alternative state of affairs which is considered more desirable."

In capitalism, the alternative state of affairs which is considered more desirable is a worker who is efficient, so illness becomes defined as the inability to work. The role of the doctor is crucial here. He/she has been given the power to declare the presence or absence of ill-health in a person. The individual's subjective perception of his/her own state of health is not considered trustworthy or important and it is for the doctor to decide who is ill and who is malingering.

The modern capitalist needs a skilled, well-educated and healthy workforce and it is the task of the doctor and the health service to ensure that he gets it. In the 18th and 19th centuries the major requirement of the workforce was physical strength to heave, pull and push. The rapidly increasing population of the time, combined with the indiscriminate use of women and children as well as men in the mines and factories meant that as soon as one worker fell ill he/she was easily replaced by another.

The ill were simply sent back to their families to recover or die. In advanced capitalism, with its high technology machines and complex organisation, workers are not so easily replaceable. Frequent absence from work or a low level of work efficiency will mean a reduced level of surplus value extraction for the capitalist.

Medical care became central to the interests of advanced capitalism (hence the introduction of health legislation in the 19th century) and it was no longer enough to simply throw the suffering worker back on his or her own resources. Hence the need for the state to take responsibility for the health of the workers. This development led to the danger that workers would take advantage of the provision of health care by taking days off work and draining the resources of the state for no benefit to the capitalist. In this view, the doctor takes the role of gate-keeper, validating or otherwise the claims of workers to access to time off work (often paid), medicines and the attentions of qualified medical staff.

This Marxist approach criticises as performing an ideological role the mechanistic model of illness held by medical men and women. By treating ill-health as an external thing which strikes the individual more or less at random it diverts attention from the social conditions which destroy health. It focuses attention on the individual and not on the macroscopic structures of society in which he/she lives. About 10% of all GP's prescriptions and 20% of annual NHS expenditure on drugs goes to tranquillisers, anti-depressants or hypnotic drugs, mainly for women. The Marxist view suggests that oppressive conditions, a depressing and unstimulating environment, routine housework, the stresses of child care, the lack of paid employment or, where it exists, its physically and emotionally draining nature are the real causes here, *not* something internal to the individual alone. Even where the environment and living conditions *are* identified as contributing to illness by the medical world, it is often still the individual who is the focus of attention. The person is blamed for his own ill-health because he smokes too much, eats the wrong food or does not get enough exercise. Lesley Doyal, author of *The Political Economy of Health*, which states the Marxist view of health issues strongly, writes:

> "Contemporary epidemiology (the study of the causes of disease) has . . . incorporated environmental factors into its understanding of ill-health, but it interprets them narrowly and selectively, usually emphasising those aspects which can be seen as the individual's own responsibility."(6)

The functionalist definition

Parsons was one of the earliest writers on the sociology of health and his account of the *sick role* is given here. Like the Marxists, Parsons considers illness to be the result of a deliberate decision, but a decision on the part of the patient:

> "To take the simplest kind of case, differential exposure to injuries or to infection is certainly motivated, and the role of unconscious wishes to be injured or to fall ill in such cases has been clearly demonstrated. Then there is the whole range of 'psychosomatic' illness about which knowledge has been rapidly accumulating in recent years. Finally, there is the field of 'mental disease', the symptoms of which occur mainly on a behavioural level."(7)

Thus illness is *motivated behaviour* and may be legitimately regarded as a form of deviance. The motivation to become ill stems from a desire to avoid 'normal' role obligations because they are too demanding or stressful. The sick role is an escape mechanism for the individual, its primary feature being *dependency* – other people take over one's responsibilities and become themselves responsible for one's well-being. Allowing the individual to 'opt out' into the sick role is dangerous because the functioning of society may be upset by the withdrawal of too many people. It does, however, confer positive benefits. Before examining the functions of the existence of a sick role let us outline its characteristics. Parsons defines it as "a set of institutionalised expectations and the corresponding sentiments and sanctions" which have the following features:

1 "the exemption from normal social role responsibilities which, of course, is relative to the nature and severity of the illness. This exemption requires legitimation by and to the various alters (others) involved and the physician often serves as a court of appeal as well as a direct legitimating agent."(8)
2 "the sick person cannot be expected by 'pulling himself together' to get well by an act of decision or will."(9)

He must, therefore, be taken care of.

3 "the definition of the state of being ill as itself undesirable with its obligation to want to 'get well' ensures that the sick role is only a temporary one."(10)
4 there is an:
"obligation – in relation to the severity of the condition of course – to seek *technically competent* help, namely, in the most usual case, that of a physician and to *co-operate* with him in the process of trying to get well. It is here, of course, that the role of the sick person as patient becomes articulated with that of the physician in a complementary role structure."(11)

The function of the sick role is primarily to prevent the formation of a subculture of the sick which could be disruptive to the social system. The sick are, for Parsons, deviants and it would be dangerous to let them get together and solidify a set of deviant norms and values (eg where incapacity, dependency, fatalism, apathy and retreat become acceptable). In the sick role, the ill person is tied up not with other sick people but with a group of non-sick: doctors and friends and relations(12). The second function of the sick role is to deny legitimacy to being sick. As we saw, one of the features of the sick role was that being sick should be seen as undesirable so that it simply does not make sense to assert a claim that the way to deal with the frustrating aspects of the social system is for everybody to get sick. If one could assert such a claim, the effects on the social system would be devastating.

To summarise, the function of the sick role is to isolate, neutralise and reintegrate groups of people who have defined themselves as being ill so that they can escape the burdens and pressures of normal roles. Medicine is fulfilling the function of an agency of social control in the interests of society as a whole, not any sectional group within it. This aspect of medicine's work occurs regardless of any therapeutic value of the treatment itself. Needless to say, Parsons accepts the claims of medicine to scientific status and curative efficiency.

We will now move on to examine the history of health care provision in this country and its current organisation. We will concentrate on the question of how competing demands on the allocation of resources have been resolved so that in the following sections we can analyse different approaches towards the reasons for this course of development and for the contemporary structure of health care provision.

The National Health Service

History and current organisation

1847 saw the first appointment of a medical officer in the country by a local government body. The appointment was made in Liverpool. Health care, like most other areas of concern, was in the hands of local bodies whose powers were discretionary. About 190 *Improvement Acts* had been passed by 1847 to set up elected bodies with powers to levy rates for the paving and draining of particular areas. Many places did not have such sanitary authorities. In 1848 the *Public Health Act* was passed. Its main provision was to set up a temporary National General Board of Health with powers to form local boards of health where the death rate was higher than the national average (at that time 23/1000 per year). In 1858 two significant acts were passed. The *Medical Act* set up a Medical Register overseen by a Medical Council to lay down standards for qualified doctors and cut out the 'quacks' and charlatans. The *Public Health Act* passed the medical responsibilities of the General Board of Health to a committee of the Privy Council.

In 1867, Poor Law infirmaries, asylums and hospitals were set up to deal with the workhouse sick. Gradually they were opened to all in need.

In 1872 central government took control of the chaotic local situation and passed the *Public Health Act* which obliged all local authorities to appoint medical officers of health and sanitary inspectors. 1902 saw the *Certification of Midwives Act* which set the standards for midwives as the earlier acts had done for doctors. In 1906 and 1907, the newly elected Liberal government passed the *Education (Provision of Meals) Act* and the *Education (Administrative Provisions) Act*, the latter providing for medical inspections of children.

The 1911 *National Insurance Act* required weekly contributions from employees, employers and the government and covered people earning less than £160 per annum. It gave benefits of 50p per week and free doctors' services in the event of illness. It was, however, administered by private insurance companies, not by a department of the state. This took the pressure off Poor Law authorities in terms of health provision for those who could not afford to pay, but it did not cover everybody, did not include all risks (eg there were no death benefits) and the benefits given tended to be inadequate, inconsistent and short-lived. Administratively, it was untidy and wasteful and made no attempt to link health, employment and insurance services. About 12 million people (25% of whom were women) were covered for health insurance.

In 1918 the *Maternity and Child Welfare Act* was passed. In 1919 the Ministry of Health was established to supervise the health care of the nation. It was also given control over housing and permitted (but did not compel) councils to build houses for rent. In 1928 the *National Health Insurance Act* was passed, extending the provision of state-controlled insurance against ill-health. The 1929 *Local Government Act* permitted local authorities to build and develop their own hospitals and made them responsible for health in their own areas. The 1944 *Education Act* made the provision of school meals and milk compulsory (though the former has since been removed by the 1980 *Education Act*). 1942 saw the publication of the Beveridge Report and 1946 the passing of the *National Health Service Act*. The Appointed Day (the official start of the Health Service in Britain) was the 5th July, 1948.

The public hospital provision, prior to the 5th July, 1948 was divided into two – voluntary hospitals and municipal hospitals (ie ones built and run by local authorities). On the Appointed Day 1143 voluntary hospitals (90 000 beds) and 1545 municipal hospitals (390 000 beds) were taken over by the NHS in England and Wales(13). Voluntary hospitals had varied in both size and function. Funding was based on voluntary subscriptions, donations or endowments and payments by patients, whereas municipal hospitals included ones set up under the Poor Law and under the 1929 *Local Government Act*. This Act allowed local authorities to charge the patients for what they could reasonably afford. Some people took out private insurance to meet this eventuality (about 7 million people). Where GP's consultations were not covered by insurance (either private or under the *National Insurance Act*) then fees had to be paid unless waived by the GP in the name of humanitarianism.

The NHS from the Appointed Day

The Beveridge Report on Social Insurance and Allied Services of 1942 was critical of the existing provision of health services. Even by 1939 more than half of the population were not covered by National Health insurance, including employees earning over £8 per week, the self-employed and the families of contributors. The extent of provision varied tremendously, death benefits and dental services were often not covered and there were large regional inequalities in provision. Because the different provisions were not centrally organised the administrative costs were high. In 1942 the Minister of Health published a draft plan for a unified Health Service. In 1944 a revised plan was published (after strong opposition to the first from doctors) and in 1946, the new Labour Minister of Health, Aneurin Bevan, published his NHS Bill. Once again there was strong opposition from doctors who feared loss of earnings and status. Consequently the Act, when it was passed, was full of compromises. These concerned the continued existence of private medicine, especially in the form of pay beds within NHS hospitals, and the freedom of doctors to devote part of their time to private work; as well as the continued independence of the teaching hospitals and the retention of some health functions by local authorities.

The main provisions of the 1946 Act were:

1 That hospitals (excluding the teaching hospitals) were taken over and run by Regional Hospital Boards and Hospital Management Committees.
2 Family practitioner services were provided by individual GP's or groups of them working together in Local Authority Health Centres. Payment was to be on a capitation basis: the number of people on the doctor's list determined the fee he/she received.
3 Local Authorities were to be responsible for Health Centres and ambulances as well as their other duties in terms of public protection from unhealthy conditions, immunisation, school health and maternity services.
4 All health services were to be free to the patient.

The diagram on p. 178 depicts the three-fold administrative structure of the NHS as it was from the Appointed Day until 1974.

The aims of the NHS at its inception were stated to be:

1 The provision of optimum standards of services "to secure improvement in the physical and mental health of the people and the prevention,

		Ministry of Health	
Sector	**Hospital services**	**Family practitioner services**	**Local authority services**
Administrative body	Regional hospital boards and hospital management committees	Local executive councils	County and borough councils and London boroughs
Responsible for	Teaching hospitals and special hospitals – Broadmoor, Rampton and Moss Side were outside this system (having their own governing bodies)	Doctors Dentists Ophthalmic opticians Drugs Frames and lenses Medical appliances	Health centres Maternity services Health visitors Home nurses Vaccination Ambulances

diagnosis and treatment of illness" thereby meeting health needs "wherever and whenever they arise".

2 The service was to be comprehensive in scope and universal in coverage so that *all* health needs could be met *anywhere*.

3 Services were to be free of charge so that *anyone* could make use of them.

4 Funding for the NHS was to come mainly from taxation, supplemented by insurance contributions.

5 Freedom was to be built into the system because patients had the freedom to change doctors or opt for private medicine and doctors could refuse patients and devote some or all of their time to private medicine. In this way excessive state control was to be avoided.

We shall see that there are different views as to how far these aims have been achieved and whether there were other latent aims underlying these manifest ones.

Changes in the Health Service since 1946

Prescription charges were soon introduced due to the high cost of drugs to the Health Service and the feeling that they were being over-prescribed by doctors. Just as it was a Labour government which introduced the principle of free services, so it was a Labour government which first introduced charges, a fact which led to the resignation of both Aneurin Bevan and Harold Wilson in 1951.

The structure of the NHS quickly came under criticism. It was felt by the government that there was wasteful duplication of administrative structures under the three-fold division and that there was inadequate coordination between the three branches which led to inefficiency and demoralisation. Patient care was felt to be the victim of this inefficiency and lack of integration – for example, patients would have to remain in hospital longer than was necessary because community services, such as Home Nurses, were not available to accept them. Clearly from the government's point of view, integration of the tripartite structure was necessary and this was achieved by the 1974 reorganisation of the NHS which paralleled the reorganisation of local government in the same year. The administrative structure after 1974 was divided into three sections once again, but this time the division was hierarchical rather than functional.

DHSS	*Number in England*	*Function*
Regional health authority	14	Determining regional priorities, planning and overseeing major building projects, etc. Co-ordinating and controlling AHA's
Area health authority	90	Planning and organising health provision in the area (which is broadly based on council boundaries)
District management teams	270	Taking responsibility for the day-to-day running of the health service in the districts

In addition there are the Family Practitioner Committees (committees of the AHA's) which mainly administer GP's contracts and dentists' and opticians' fees and allowances. The public's interests are represented by the Community Health Councils (one for every DMT) whose function is to monitor health service provision by visiting hospitals, hearing evidence from complainants and other people involved and, where necessary, publishing reports. They must be consulted by the AHA when plans for closure are envisaged. Evidence suggests that CHC's are neither representative of the public at large nor particularly efficient in their function. 33% of their members are nominated by local voluntary organisations, 16% by the RHA concerned and the remainder by the Local Authority. None are elected by the public and consequently very few of their members are manual workers.

Since 1974 it has become increasingly clear that the new structure is wasteful and inefficient in some ways. Because the RHA's do the macro-planning on the long-term and the DMT's do the day-to-day running of the middle tier of the system, the AHA's were redundant. Newly created District Health Authorities are now replacing them with the role of District Officer being central to the work of this new body.

The allocation of resources within the NHS

In this section we will look at three different aspects of resource allocation in the NHS – the distribution of resources among the different sectors of the NHS's work, the way resources are distributed around the country and, finally, the differential availability of the services of the NHS across the social classes. This discussion concentrates on how resources are *divided up* and does not consider *alternative* ways in which the funds available to the NHS could be spent. In the year 1978–79 a total of £8980 million was spent by the NHS, amounting to 13.3% of total public expenditure (compared with £498 million and 10.2% in 1951).

Sectoral allocation

Most of the money spent by the NHS goes to its hospital service; in 1948, 55% of the total went to hospitals; today it is around 65%. In 1971 the balance of NHS expenditure was as follows:

Hospitals	65.5% of total expenditure
Pharmaceutical	9.8%
GP services	8.1%
Dental services	4.8%
Ophthalmic services	1.3%
Local Authority Health Services	6.9%
Other	3.6%

Even within the hospital sector there is great inequality. London teaching hospitals and acute hospitals spend much more money on the care of patients per head than mental hospitals or those for the handicapped. In 1973–74 the patient in the teaching hospital had £142.86 spent on him/her per week, in an acute hospital £104.78, in a mental hospital £36.60 and in one for the handicapped, just £33.68(14). In 1979 there was a total of 2046 non-psychiatric hospitals with 296815 beds and 497 psychiatric hospitals with 158960 beds in Great Britain(15). It is clear that hospitals dealing with acute illness as opposed to long-term problems or mental illness, get the lion's share of the money. Yet every year 5 million of us present ourselves to our GP's with a mental health problem, 24 million working days are lost each year through mental illness. One in six women and one in nine men will spend some time in a psychiatric ward, and even though 53% of all hospital beds are occupied by the mentally ill and handicapped, only 25% of the total hospital budget is spent on their care. L Garner, a critic of the NHS, writes:

> "Everything indicates that a mental health problem brings with it a lowering of the quality of life on every front, and that those generally observed aspects of life in mental health institutions – the poor surroundings, the lack of highly qualified medical staff, the high proportion of immigrant staff – are common to most countries of the world."(16)

Geriatric services suffer the same kind of problem, a disturbing fact in view of the increasing number of old people in our society. 50% of all hospital beds, excluding maternity and psychiatry, are occupied by the over 65's, while they use 47% of beds in the psychiatric hospitals. Despite their great need for the resources of the NHS, Garner comments that:

> "It is very difficult for those responsible for squeezing capital funds out of the health service to get money for old people. Mostly it is a question of make do and mend, of adapting existing buildings and squeezing into corners that no one else wants."(17)

The reasons for the relative generosity of funding for acute medicine and the paucity of that for psychiatric, handicapped and geriatric care can really be summarised under the two headings: 'no hope' and 'no power'. The official version is 'no hope', ie this sector of medicine cannot hope to provide a cure in any sense and, therefore, the bulk of resources should go to areas where constructive work *can* be done. To quote from a research paper of the Royal Commission on the NHS:

> "There are questions . . . where the pressure on resources (whether money, staff or machines) compels clinicians to make decisions about the acceptance of treatment of patients which cross the delicate boundary between clinical discretion and social policy. These include . . . the use of substantial resources for cases where recovery can only be very limited, instead of for other purposes; . . . what resources should be given to prolonging the lives of the very old . . . instead of using scarce nursing and medical resources for other purposes?"(18)

and:

> "Slow progress is expected in the improvement of services for the mentally ill and the mentally handicapped which the DHSS has identified as national priorities because resource allocation . . . are going to Regions which are also short of acute care, for which there is greater pressure."(19)

There seems little chance of fundamental changes in the near future at least, despite the fact that one of the aims of the 1974 reorganisation was to shift resources towards the chronically sick and disabled and the consultative document entitled *The Way Forward* issued by the DHSS recommended giving priority to the mentally ill.

The 'no power' explanation for the continuing inequalities in this aspect of resource allocation suggests that the old and the mentally ill and handicapped cannot 'fight their corner' in the same way that the acutely sick or their representatives can. This view sees resource allocation as the outcome of a very unfair competition as far as the disadvantaged groups we have been discussing are concerned. From the point of view of higher medical staff there is no status in caring for the incurable and so they pressurise for more facilities in the acute sector where they can be seen to be doing something. As a result status within the profession as individuals and within society as a group will rise through association with efficient technological acute medicine.

The geographical allocation of NHS resources

The geographical allocation of NHS resources is closely linked to questions of social class (to be examined in the next section). In those areas with a large working class population there tends to be a correspondingly small provision of health care resources such as GP's, dentists and hospitals. This is despite the fact that manual workers tend to be more unhealthy than non-manual workers. This leads Julian Tudor Hart to refer to the *Inverse Care Law* in an article in the medical journal *The Lancet*(20). This law states that the availability of good medical care tends to vary inversely with the need of the population served.

Geographical inequalities within the NHS are found both at a national and at a local level. The Regional Health Authorities spend widely varying amounts as do the Districts, even ones quite near to each other. Districts which are mainly rural tend to have far fewer facilities per head of the population served than urban ones. To quote Lesley Garner:

> "At the last count, the region where most money was spent on health per head of the population was the London based region of North East Thames at £90 per person per year. In Trent, the health region which covers an area of England from Yorkshire down to Leicestershire, each individual accounts for only £63 per year. But if you take the comparison down to district level, the discrepancies vary even more widely. Within North East Thames the citizen of the London Borough of Camden accounts for £136 per annum while the citizen of Essex only receives £50 worth of health care, even less than the supposedly disadvantaged citizen of Trent".(21)

Doctors point out that it is easy to get more provision if you have got something already because money is spent on improving provisions which already exist. For this reason, if for no other, the NHS still suffers the inadequacies of the legacy of health provision handed down to it on the Appointed Day. The National Federation of Women's Institutes conducted a national survey of medical facilities in rural areas and found that:

> "Over half the settlements they surveyed had no doctor's surgery, 89% had no optician, 84% had no dentist who would accept National Health patients, 75% were without a chemist . . ."(22)

Figures for both per capita expenditure on General Hospitals and for the distribution of GP's country-wide show that the NE of the country, the NW and the Midlands suffer in respect of both types of facility(23) while the South and SE (areas of middle and upper social class preponderance) are much better provided with health facilities. In 1971, twice as much was being spent on major buildings south of the River Trent than north of it(24). It is probably true that hospitals and consultants tend to be *more* accessible to the working class than doctors because they are concentrated in metropolitan areas. Geographical accessibility is not necessarily translated into *actual* accessibility. One of the main reasons for the inadequate provision of GP's in working class areas is their reluctance to work there and their preference for more affluent and pleasant surroundings. Because they are independent contractors rather than employees, paid a fee rather than a salary, they can go wherever they like (although they can be prevented from setting up practice in areas where the DHSS considers there to be over-provision of doctors). Incentives are provided in the form of a designated area allowance, but the inequalities remain. In the light of this, the Resources Allocation Working Party (RAWP) was set up after the 1974 reorganisation to look into the question of geographical allocation of resources, though its major task was to impose cuts overall rather than to give more to under-resourced areas. It published a consultative document in 1976 which proposed cuts in the high spending regions and relative increases in under-resourced areas. But, to quote David Widgery, a socialist doctor and author of *Health in Danger*:

> "RAWP is a classic social-democratic cock-up . . . As so many (such) schemes in times of crisis, it turned out to be a case of robbing an impoverished Peter to pay a broke Paul. The regions who receive money through RAWP are not getting more money, just less cuts."(25)

Widgery also points out that RAWP imposed cuts on areas which appeared to be overspending, but in fact were not doing so when the social class of their inhabitants (and consequently, the greater need for health care) was taken into account: Liverpool and Inner London, for example, suffered in this way.

Differential access to NHS resources by social class

The question here is: who uses the services of the NHS more, the middle class or the working class? The answer overall seems to be that the working class make more use of things like GP's services and hospital beds and out-patient services. When one takes into account the relatively poorer health of this section of the population compared with the middle class, it appears that the working class under-utilise and the middle class over-utilise the available resources. Moreover, it seems that the types of services generally received by the manual and non-manual sectors are different too:

> "Middle class patients make more use of services such as mass miniature radiography, cervical cytology, conservative dentistry, antenatal and postnatal care and family planning."(26)

In an article in *New Society*, Ann Howlett and John Ashley(27) show that working class patients tend to get post hoc treatment for an existing medical problem whereas middle class patients are more likely to use medical services for preventative treatment. Accessibility to the teaching hospitals, which spend more money per patient and have a lower mortality rate, represent another aspect of social class inequality. The following figures on this are given in the same article(28):

Hospital Type	*Social Class of Patients*		
	I/II (%)	III (%)	IV/V (%)
Teaching	70	50	40
Regional Board	30	50	60
Number of cases studied	20	102	90

Quality of care is another point: in working class areas there tend to be fewer doctors and this results in larger lists for each doctor. Surgeries tend to be less well-equipped and doctors tend to be less well qualified, often being immigrants who find it difficult to get a practice in the more attractive areas of the country. A study by Ann Cartwright entitled *Human Relations and Hospital Care*(29) showed that doctors in hospitals are more likely to explain the nature of their condition to the patient if he/she is middle class than if he/she is working class. In general practice the study found that elderly middle class patients got longer consultations with the doctor than elderly working class ones. Westergaard and Resler(30) explain the more abrupt and inferior treatment received by members of the working class in terms of the cultural divide that exists between them and the middle class doctor:

> "... the benefits which most ordinary people receive (from the health service) include no participation in control. Nor do the services work in a way to give such people the kind of everyday familiarity and ease of contact which are needed for power of individuals and families to make the best use of what is going; to press the demands to the limits of provision, and then beyond; to manipulate the resources of the services in the ways that the upper and middle class people can ... in their use of state provision for health and education and in dealings with the tax authorities."(31)

Let us now consider some of the contrasting approaches taken towards health care provision by writers in the field of sociology and social policy.

The welfare state and the social order: three views on the role of the National Health Service

The Marxist view

On the face of it the provision of health care for the working people by the state presents an anomaly for Marxists. Why should the State provide apparently free services and cheap medicine to the working class when according to Marxist theory, the state merely represents the interest of the owners of the means of production whose main concern is the efficient exploitation of the working class? Marxists have responded in three ways to this question.

1 The NHS, like other aspects of the Welfare State, is a concession fought for and won by the genuine representatives of the working class, the unions and the Labour Party.
2 The NHS is a form of ransom paid by capitalists to avoid political and economic disturbance from an increasingly impoverished working class.
3 The provision of health services is in the interests of capitalists and therefore no contradiction exists in the fact of state medicine within a capitalist society.

We will examine in detail the third of these arguments. The first two arguments are close to other viewpoints we will be examining and a summary of them can be found in Graham Room's *The Sociology of Welfare*, pages 42–48. Westergaard and Resler point out that the setting up of the NHS, like many other 'socialist' measures introduced under the 1945–51 Labour Government was:

> "... not an autonomous creation of the (Labour) movement, forced through in the teeth of Conservative opposition or designed to cut sharply into the privileges of the upper and middle classes. In large part – with the exceptions that included the more radical features of the NHS Act – it was the product of bipartisan agreement originating in the period of wartime coalition."(32)

This fact seems to suggest that the Conservatives recognised the necessity of a national health service under modern conditions. Marxists argue that such a health service is considered desirable by the capitalist class due to their need for a healthy and strong workforce. As the workers cannot individually maintain their own health, owing to the low level of income given to them, it falls upon the state to provide this service. Lesley Doyal, the Marxist commentator writes:

> "... physical fitness can affect the amount of surplus value extracted in a working day. Frequent sickness absence from work may also make it difficult to control the labour process efficiently. It is, therefore, a matter of some concern both to the individual capitalist and to capital as a whole, that the physical health of the labour force should be maintained at a 'satisfactory' level."(33)

By funding health care through the state from taxation, both direct and indirect (ie taxation on incomes and purchases respectively), the capitalists ensure that the financial burden imposed by the NHS falls squarely on the shoulders of working men and women. Westergaard and Resler make the point that while:

> "Benefits from the national health services were estimated in terms of their cash value, to be much the same across the range of incomes."

payments for these benefits:

> "fall relatively hardest on the weakest shoulders."(34)

This is because the service is financed through both direct taxation which is progressive (more is taken from the richest people) *and* indirect taxation, which is regressive (more is taken from the poorest people because they spend more of their income in percentage terms on items which are subject to indirect taxation). 89.5% of the funding of the NHS comes from tax revenue and Westergaard and Resler state that the progressive forms of taxation made up little more than 40% of total tax revenue between 1950 and the early 1970's. Regressive taxation of various kinds made up the bulk of the rest. Their conclusion is that the *very* poorest, particularly pensioners, received a net gain from state benefits. Above that there was very little distinction between the small wage earners and the executive and professional range in terms of tax paid as a percentage of total income and benefits received, despite the fact that the poorer you are the more benefits you usually need. These findings are supported by J C Kincaid, the author of *Poverty and Equality in Britain*(35) and Frank Field, Molly Meacher and Chris Pond, joint authors of *To Him Who Hath*(36).

A second strand of the Marxist argument is that the provision of a national health service is of benefit to the capitalist class in that it provides an extensive and lucrative market for drug companies and for industries producing high-technology medical equipment. The Public Accounts Committee, Parliament's financial watchdog, published a report in May 1983(37) showing that the profitability of drug companies rose from 21% in 1978 to 23.3% in 1980, with some large companies earning as much as 35%. This was in an environment of general decline in the profitability of industries. Many of these companies are huge multinationals such as Hoffman La Roche, Glaxo, Wellcome, Beecham, ICI and Ciba-Geigy. Many of them sell the drugs to their UK affiliates which raises the possibility of transfer pricing (see page 28). In 1970, Roche products (UK) were purchasing the raw materials for Librium and Valium at £370 and £922 per kilo respectively from the Swiss parent company, when the prices in Italy were £9 and £20(38). Increasingly, they are taking a monopolistic form – a feature which Marx predicted would become common in all industries in late capitalism. In Britain, five companies control about 30% of the drugs market: in the USA, 10 firms control over 40%, while the three largest Swiss firms together account for 15% of World sales(39). This monopolisation is enhanced by the high costs of research and development: small firms find it impossible to invest in sufficient amounts. Products resulting from the research efforts of large companies are protected by patents which help them to maintain their pre-eminent position:

> "Once monopoly privileges leave the world of the individual inventor (a romantic memory of the past which, however, still influences government policy) and enter the real world of multiple patent ownership by large corporations, the main function of patents is not to encourage inventive activity but to aid profit maximisation through the minimisation of competitive forces."(40)

La Roche's products Librium and Valium account for about 70% of the value of NHS prescriptions of tranquilisers and hold over 33% of the world tranquiliser market. Librium was sold by La Roche to the NHS at £10 per 1000 when the cost of production was 20p(41). Other companies cannot make these products and compete by selling them at lower prices thanks to the patent laws, so price levels remain artificially high.

Companies like La Roche justify high price and profitability levels by arguing that they represent return on high research and development costs, both historic and future. However, the patent laws themselves help to generate these costs by encouraging companies to research and develop equivalents of successful drugs which are chemically just different enough to dodge the patent law but similar enough to be as effective as the original. The NHS cannot directly take advantage of these cheaper equivalents because chemists must issue *exactly* what the doctor has written on the prescription. Generic prescribing (giving an equivalent drug in place of the branded one prescribed by the doctor) is not permitted and so the doctor controls the make of drug which is most in demand. Small wonder that about £800 per year per doctor is spent by the drug companies on advertising. The total sales and promotional effort amounted to £71 million in this country in 1977.

Millions of pounds are spent every year by the NHS on such things as whole body scanners as well as sophisticated equipment needed for modern surgery such as lasers and the latest obstetric equipment. Acute medicine is increasingly dependent on such equipment and doctors pressure the NHS for the most modern technology on the grounds that the best possible care must be provided. Such equipment is expensive – a computerised tomography (CT) scanner costs £1.5 million pounds to buy and £100 000 per annum to run. The firms that produce this equipment are oligopolistic multinationals, not humanitarian research organisations; they include EMI, Phillips, Siemens, General Electric and Hoffman La Roche.

The central point Marxists make on the question of having a national health service within a profit-oriented economic system is that the stated aim of the first (health) suffers as a result of the aim of the second (profit). Doctors are encouraged to prescribe more and more drugs(42) and these cause harmful 'side' effects as well as distracting attention from the social causes of disease. Funds are diverted into non-productive and even harmful areas which, for the Marxist, also includes the high-technology equipment. Let us examine these arguments in more detail.

The fact that drugs sometimes have harmful side effects is well known from cases like the Thalidomide and more recent Opren scandals. These are often seen as exceptions but in fact, are only more extreme examples of the norm according to the Marxist. The word 'side' effect suggests that it is secondary and of minor importance but, as Ian Kennedy in *The Unmasking of Medicine*(43) points out, the undesired consequences are as much an effect of the drugs used as the desired ones. Adverse reactions to drugs account for 5% of the admissions to hospital medical wards, while something between 10% and 15% of patients in hospitals suffer adverse reactions to drugs. Ivan Illich (not a Marxist but concurring very strongly with this point) in *Limits to Medicine*(44) calls this clinical *iatrogenesis* (doctor-caused illness) and says that doctors do more harm than good through the use of drugs. This may be overstating the case as far as the developed world is concerned, but in the underdeveloped one, the stringent controls and tests we have are absent. Doyal gives an example:

> "The drug *Dipyrone* . . . is licensed in the US only for patients with terminal malignant disease whose fever cannot be reduced by safer measures. In Brazil, on the other hand, it is recommended for numerous complaints from rheumatism to toothache. Yet this drug has a mortality rate as high as one in two hundred."(45)

Anabolic steroids are widely used in the Third World. The injectable contraceptive Depo Provera, whose effects include upsetting the menstrual cycle, reduction of the milk supply and even pérmanent sterility and cancer(46) is also used. This lack of restriction is attractive to drug companies as is the possibility of larger profits, thanks to the possibility of transfer pricing(47).

Marxists argue that the use of drugs distracts attention from the real causes of disease: diet, housing, industrial injuries, traffic, pollution and oppressive environments. Chemicals will not solve the problems, they can only be a first aid which treats the symptoms and only after the illness has begun. By relying on them, we are blinded to the more fundamental problems (and solutions). For these reasons the National Health Service should really be called a National Sickness Service, according to the Marxist. Its function is to repair the damage done by society rather than to promote health in a positive way. Widgery, a doctor himself, illustrates this point by quoting from drug company advertising:

> "'Valium for the prisoners of a society of stress,' said the advertisements which skilfully picked out the pressures on commuters, locked into wordless boredom and vacant faces, and housewives, imprisoned in towering blocks of flats . . . demanding children and an

> unsympathetic spouse: 'Valium helps your patient enjoy his work. Formerly nervous and tense, he takes a greater interest in his job and is better able to meet and solve his daily problems.' If Marriage is loveless, the streets without beauty and nights without peace, take a pill."(48)

Kennedy points out that 650 people are killed at work, 6500 in the home or at play and 7500 on the roads every year. 10% of all working days lost are due to bronchitis (which is exacerbated by environmental factors), 48 million days are lost through injuries and smoking continues to increase among women. All of these could be cut down without the use of drugs.

It is interesting that the mass media seize on 'wonder drugs' and new medical techniques and technology. In doing so they reflect the views and interests of the top members of the medical profession who gain prestige from these areas of acute medicine, as well as the interests of the drug and high technology companies. The Marxist argues that the media generate public support for increased resourcing of these areas of medicine, which must be detrimental for other areas. The old, the mentally ill and handicapped as well as preventive medicine and education are the Cinderellas of the health service. Meanwhile, millions of pounds are spent on heart operations and new scanners for the benefit of a few (heavily publicised) patients. The reasons for the distribution of resources within the NHS are grounded in economic and political interests, for the Marxist, Doyal, writes:

> "... capitalist production is a cause of ill-health in a variety of ways. As a consequence, any preventive medicine which was to be substantially effective would need to interfere with the organisation of the production process itself. Insofar as curative medicine appears to deny or at least to minimise the need for such preventive medicine, it serves to protect existing economic interests."(49)

Old people and the mentally ill or handicapped have nothing to offer society; they are not productive. Therefore, any resources spent on them are wasted from a financial point of view.

No radical analysis of the provision of health care within capitalism can ignore the existence of the private sector and its influence. There are three basic ways of providing private medicine: fee for service; insurance cover (so that the insurance company pays medical fees); or premiums to private medical organisations who provide their own doctors, hospitals and equipment or 'rent' them from the NHS. British United Provident Association (BUPA), Private Patients Plan and Western Provident Association are three of the largest in Britain, accounting for 98% of all subscriptions. As with drugs and high-technology equipment, the existence of private medicine is actually *detrimental* to the health of the majority of the population, according to the Marxist. Firstly, only the comfortably off can afford it; in America, 10 million people have no health cover and many others only inadequate cover(50). A dual system is, therefore, necessary if general levels of health are to be maintained. Secondly, only some types of health problems are profitable: namely, acute medicine which requires short-term care (hysterectomies, tonsilectomies, operations on varicose veins, etc.). Other, longer-term health problems which require care rather than cure (the terminally ill, mentally ill, geriatrics) represent an open-ended commitment where costs exceed income. It is therefore necessary and in the interests of capital to have a public sector to deal with these areas. Thirdly, the private sector relies on the expensive equipment and training of doctors and nurses paid for by the NHS. While fees are paid for the use of beds (a total of £195 million in 1981 for 32 000 pay beds), overheads such as buildings and equipment, the use of auxiliary staff's time, the training the doctors and nurses receive, are not paid for. Widgery quotes the evidence of a junior doctor to a House of Commons Select Committee examining private practice in the NHS:

> "The consultant operated on the private patients in the Ophthalmic Department operating theatre after the afternoon's NHS list had been finished. The regular nursing staff were in attendance at the private operations for which extra duty they received an occasional box of confectionery."(51)

The existence of paying patients alongside NHS ones means less time and fewer resources for the NHS patient. The doctor, who is receiving a fee, will be tempted to spend more time with the private patient and therefore less with the NHS one. During that portion of time spent at the private hospital (often across the road from the NHS one), the doctor is not available to treat NHS patients. Furthermore, by allowing queue-jumping by paying patients over NHS ones, it lengthens waiting times for beds and appointments. The general level of care for the majority therefore declines.

Another criticism of private medicine is that it leads to concentration of resources in rich (and profitable) areas of the country, thus depriving those in the poorer areas of comparable treatment or necessitating long-distance travel. Also, its administrative costs are far higher than the NHS's – (about double, due mainly to complicated fee and payment structures and advertising) so fewer resources are actually available for health care. It can lead to medical inflation by giving an incentive to doctors to provide unnecessary medical services(52) and by creating the feeling among patients that they should get their money's worth. Thus, while a few people get more medical treatment than they need (or is good for them), the poor go untreated.

All this is not to say Marxists wholly support the NHS and wish simply to see private medicine abolished. Apart from questions of inadequate financing, the allocation of resources to the wrong sectors and geographical areas already dealt with, there are also the problems of sexism and racism in the NHS. Consultants are predominantly male, nurses predominantly female, most black NHS workers are nurses and porters and black doctors tend to get undesirable practices in poor areas. Moreover, in its present form, the NHS is not really amenable to public control: it is nationalised rather than socialised. The Community Health Councils which, in theory, represent the public, in fact have limited powers and mainly consist of middle class appointees. From the Marxist perspective, these inadequacies are the result of self-interested conservative groups' actions:

> "(In 1945–6) . . . there was very little discussion about the basic philosophy underlying the new scheme, and the final structure of the NHS was determined by the outcome of negotiations between the state and various establishment groups . . . most importantly, the leaders of the medical profession."(53)

To truly socialise the provision of health care would require a more fundamental reorganisation of the economy. This would include some form of socialisation of drug companies and equipment supplies, the reorganisation of education to make access to top medical posts open to all and the dismantling of capitalism as a whole in order to avoid the economic contradictions within it which lead to recurrent crises (and the consequent cuts in public health expenditure) and the circumstances which cause much of the illness we suffer which stretches resources to the limit. For the Marxist, the mode of production shapes the health service just as it shapes the education system. Only changes in the economic base can fundamentally improve the service, or even remove the need for it.

Market Liberals and the state provision of health care

For Market Liberals society must be based on the liberty of the individual to set up enterprises or to sell labour. The complexity of advanced industrial society and its high division of labour means that collaboration is required between individuals and companies. This collaboration, formalised into contractual agreements, should be regulated by market forces, not government. For the Market Liberal, the fact of private ownership within capitalism does not imply conflict of interest between those who are owners and those who sell their labour (as the Marxist argues). *All* benefit from the general prosperity produced by the production and exchange of goods. Intervention by the state only upsets the delicate balance of market forces (which match supply and demand, set prices and correct wage levels). Such intervention can only be detrimental to the economic well-being of society as well as putting limits on the freedom of the individual. Theorists in the Market Liberal's laissez-faire perspective on the economy and society include Adam Smith (*The*

Wealth of Nations), J S Mill (*Principles of Political Economy*) and Milton Friedman (*Capitalism and Freedom*). They all reject Marx's bleak prognosis for capitalism, which foresees only immiseration, pauperisation and unemployment. If given a free hand capitalism will produce wealth, happiness and freedom for everyone, with market forces ensuring that unemployment does not exist while the great productivity of modern factory organisation will eradicate any pockets of poverty which remain.

For the Market Liberal the intervention of the state in health care, like the income tax which mainly pays for it, is a dangerous and destructive thing. High levels of taxation discourage work effort among the population and lead to a fall in levels of productivity and, therefore, affluence. Provision of health care and other social policies remove the responsibility from the individual for himself/herself and family, thus leading to a dependent and non market-motivated state of mind. Furthermore, the NHS in its present form is too monolithic, giving no *real* choice of service to the patient in terms of doctors, hospitals or any other service. The NHS is felt by Market Liberals to be unnecessarily expensive because patients are not made aware of the real costs of drugs and other services so they do not exercise care or selectivity in demanding them. In other words, market forces no longer regulate demand. Some financial responsibility must be put onto the patient to limit demand, otherwise cuts imposed by central government are the only answer; an unsatisfactory one from all points of view. For Market Liberals ill health is a subjective state and health is not something which can be legislated for.

Market Liberals in general are in favour of a large and expanding private medical service. It was from a position very close to this that the Conservative Minister of Health in 1980 said that it would be desirable for at least 25% of health treatment to be borne by the private sector. The perceived advantages are that consumers have more choice and more control over their medical treatment as they directly pay for the service and because of competition between rival companies and doctors for business. The long waiting lists experienced by NHS patients for non-urgent operations would disappear. In a free market such things are quickly eliminated by consumer choice. As health care becomes a profit-making industry it contributes to the general prosperity of society rather than being a burden on public funds. Large amounts of capital are generated and can be reinvested in other industries and used to further improve health facilities and research. Where private and state medicine are found side by side, the former is beneficial to the latter because it pays for its use of beds. It supplements the finances of the state sector, and relieves the long waiting lists and excessive demands for medical care by dealing with the acute cases and allowing the state sector to concentrate its resources where they are most needed, in geriatric and psychiatric care. By the end of 1981 over 4 million people in Britain were covered by private medical insurance (7% of the population), compared with only 1.5 million in 1966. The total subscription income for 1981 was £200 million, an average of £108 per subscriber. Much of this money went to the NHS and the private companies took the responsibility for many of the medical problems of these people, despite the fact that they had also contributed to the NHS through taxation.

The Market Liberal considers the NHS to be unnecessary. It disrupts market forces and is largely used for the advancement of the interests of the various groups within it:

> "The British health industry exists . . . in the interests of the producer groups who make it up. The welfare of the patients is a random by-product, depending on how conflicts between the groups and between them and government happen to strike down at any particular time."(54)

There is, therefore, no *moral* driving force behind health service policy; it is the accidental outcome of competing forces and interests in this view. Whether this is an over-cynical view of the history of the NHS policy is a matter for debate.

The Social Democratic view of the state provision of health care

R M Titmuss (in *Problems of Social Policy*, *Essays on The Welfare State* and *Commitment to Welfare*) and T H Marshall (in *Class, Citizenship and Social Development* and *Social Policy*) are two of the founding fathers of this school of socio-political perspective. More recent members of it include Brian Abel-Smith (co-author of *The Poor and the Poorest*) and Professor David Donnison, ex-Chairman of the Supplementary Benefits Commission. Where Market Liberals stress the *civil* rights necessary to set up and follow through new enterprises, create jobs and wealth, these authors stress *social* rights. These include the right to receive basic levels of income, housing, education and health. Social Democrats are critical of the Market Liberals' overemphasis (as they see it) on civil rights, arguing that the freedom enjoyed by some involves costs to others. These costs include unemployment during downturns in the economy, poverty for those without the necessary skills or intelligence to compete in the struggle for survival and ill-health for those who cannot afford private medicine.

It is the duty of central government to protect and extend these social rights because no other institution can or will do it. Welfare services such as the NHS, pensions, state education, supplementary and unemployment benefit and social services are the manifestations of a political will to protect the poor and the weak from the adverse consequences of what is an otherwise workable system. The Social Democrats believe that provision of such services by well informed government policy will go a long way towards removing ill health. In addition, these services represent a deliberate attempt to secure popular co-operation and support for government. On this point, Titmuss writes that modern society in general and war in particular:

> "... imposes a great increase in social discipline: moreover, this discipline is only tolerable if – and only if – social inequalities are not intolerable ... It follows that the acceptance of social disciplines – of obligations as well as rights – made necessary by war, by preparations for war and by the long run consequences of war, must influence the aims and content of social policies not only during the war itself but in peace-time as well ... The aims and content of social policy, both in peace and in war, are thus determined – at least to a substantial extent – by how far the co-operation of the masses is essential to the successful prosecution of war."(56)

The problem is that the provision of a national health service does not only lead to social quiescence but throws up new demands and exposes new areas of opposition which can lead to social unrest. This is recognised by most Social Democrats as an unfortunate but unavoidable consequence of a social policy which is both the only morally defensible one and a necessity.

The attitude of the Social Democrats towards private medicine is very similar to that of the Marxists. They see it as catering only for the relatively affluent few who pursue their own interests and ignore those of the general community. Indeed, like Marxists, they see the existence of private medicine as positively detrimental to the NHS because of the parasitical relationship of the former to the latter. Unlike the Marxists, however, they are relatively happy with the present structure of the NHS, as they see increased funding as the solution to most of its problems.

The table opposite summarises the positions taken by the three schools on a number of social policy issues.

After assessing the relative merits of the three perspectives examined here, Graham Room finds that the Social Democrats' case is the most persuasive, particularly in the light of the development of the NHS since 1946:

> "Our account of the process of reorganisation (of the NHS in 1974) tends ... to vindicate social democratic arguments that social policy development had something of a sui generis (unique) character, in which the deficiencies of past measures are consciously evaluated and political choices made among alternative societal futures."(57)

He does recognise that powerful interests – particularly those of the medical profession – have tended to divert the course of health policy from a completely rational and consistent course. Furthermore, the continued existence of health and provision inequalities amongst the social

Table 1

ISSUE	*MARXIST*	*MARKET LIBERAL*	*SOCIAL DEMOCRAT*
Nature of society	Divided by classes with opposing interests	United by common interests	United by common interests and values
Social order maintenance	Coercion and ideology operate to suppress conflict	Self-interest and the common good are the same, therefore, social order is maintained by pursuit of self-interest	Humanitarian social policies prevent any conflict which may be engendered by the ill-effects of capitalism
Attitude to NHS	*Anti:* it represents the interests of the ruling class and embodies the class, colour and sex inequalities in society	*Anti:* it impedes the free play of market forces when over-expanded	*Pro:* it alleviates the ill-effects of capitalism, produces political legitimacy and prevents civil unrest
Desired changes to present system of health care	Must be changed in the context of wider social changes including socialisation of NHS and abolition of capitalist drug companies	Severe reduction of NHS or its abolition is necessary. It should be replaced by private health care	Extension of NHS provision is necessary, especially in such areas as psychiatric and geriatric care
Attitude to private medicine	*Anti:* it is available for the few and is parasitical on state resources. As with other profit-making enterprises, it is detrimental to the general good	*Pro:* it is a source of wealth, leads to better health care, improves consumer choice and is beneficial for the NHS	*Anti:* it represents the expression of private interests rather than the general public's interests

classes indicates that political will has somehow been frustrated. For the Marxist, this fact is an inevitable consequence of an economic structure which is harmful to the health of those at its 'sharp end'. Policy decisions about *health* have little effect because they do not tackle the structural causes of ill-health.

In criticising the Marxist view of the state provision of health care(58), Room writes:

> "It is by no means clear precisely how the interests of the capitalist class come to mould the state's social policies . . . it remains unclear by what means the state becomes aware of this interest (and) . . . what prevents the agencies of the state apparatus developing and pursuing their own interests and goals . . ."(59)

While Marx himself did not attempt to clarify these questions in detail, later Marxists such as Ralph Miliband in *The State in Capitalist Society*(60) have shown that the social origin of people in the top sector of state institutions is the same as the capitalist class and that there are strong personal and social ties between capitalists, top politicians and civil servants. Nicos Poulantzas in *The Problem of the Capitalist State*(61) argues that Miliband makes a series of errors and omissions. Poulantzas, also a Marxist, makes the point that:

> ". . . the *direct* participation of members of the capitalist class in the state apparatus and in the government, even where it exists, is not the important side of the matter. The relationship between the bourgeois class and the state is an objective relationship. This means that if the *function* of the state in a determinate social formation and the *interests* of the dominant class in this formation coincide, it is by reason of the system itself . . ."(62)

Harold Wilson's history of the 1964–1970 Labour Government(63) contains an account of a meeting with the Governor of the Bank of England at the beginning of the administration's term which illustrates Poulantzas' point. The meeting was called to discuss the severe fall in the value of the pound brought about by heavy selling of sterling by international speculators who were disturbed by socialist policies about to be implemented by the first Labour government for thirteen years. Wilson writes that the Governor:

> "was now demanding all-round cuts in expenditure, regardless of social or even economic priorities, and fundamental changes in some of the Chancellor's economic announcements. Not for the first time, I said that we had now reached the situation where a newly-elected Government with a mandate from the people was being told, not so much by the Governor of the Bank of England but by international speculators, that the policies in which we had fought an election could not be implemented; that the Government was to be forced into the adoption of Tory policies to which it was fundamentally

> opposed. The Governor confirmed that that was, in fact, the case. I asked him if this meant that it was impossible for any Government, whatever its party label, whatever its manifesto or the policies on which it fought an election, to continue, unless it immediately reverted to full-scale Tory policies. He had to admit that this was what his argument meant, because of the sheer compulsion of the economic dictation of those who exercised decisive economic power."(64)

In the light of this kind of analysis, it becomes clear that there are limits to social policy, including health policy, imposed by the general organisation of the economy. The implementation of policies which were not perceived by capitalists and financiers as in their interests would see a collapse of support for, and investment in, the British economy. From the Market Liberals' perspective this does not matter as state intervention is damaging anyway. For the Social Democrat it is a serious limiting factor on the achievement of general health, while for the Marxist it is a further factor which prevents the achievement of general health in capitalism even where a national health service does exist.

The social distribution of health chances

In this section, we will examine the facts of, and the suggested explanations for, the *differential morbidity* (sickness) and *mortality* (death) across the social class scales.

Statistics on morbidity are usually gathered from the various agencies of the NHS (hospitals, dentists or GP's) and therefore rely on people presenting themselves to these agencies for diagnosis and treatment. Whether or not they do this clearly depends on such factors as their threshold of pain, their ability to recognise symptoms and distinguish the important from the trivial, their attitude towards hospitals and doctors and the extent to which they treat themselves or turn to non-NHS medication (acupuncture, homeopathy, private practice). Other factors include whether their work and home commitments allow them the freedom to visit their GP's without cost in terms of children left unattended or docked wages, and whether, and after what period, they require a doctor's sick note. Knowledge of the existence and whereabouts of NHS facilities and access to transport are also important. Logic suggests that many of these will vary in a fairly consistent pattern between the classes.

Another set of problems concerns the decisions made by the doctor and the nature of disease itself. When the doctor writes "cause of death" on a death certificate in the case of an old person, it is:

> "a toss-up which (one of several existing conditions) the doctor will choose to write on the death certificate. In a person dying at the age

> of 70 there are quite likely to be 12 or 13 separate and possible causes of death . . . Because of this coincidence of ailments, they are also likely to be taking several different courses of drugs which can confuse diagnosis – and the patient – still further by their muddle of side-effects."(65)

As regards diagnosis of disease in living patients, the same one in two different cases does not mean that those cases are identical. Bronchitis, for example, can differ greatly in its severity and incapacitating effects between patients.

Some authors(66) also suggest that length of stay in hospitals and other NHS institutions by members of different social classes are not directly comparable because decisions on admission and discharge by doctors and others are affected by non-medical factors such as whether the patient has a comfortable and safe home with the amenities he/she will require. Once again, the class of the patient will have an important bearing on these matters. Length of absence from work due to ill-health will also be affected by whether, and for how long, full pay and then proportions of it are given. Those who suffer rapid and severe financial hardship and even threat of dismissal due to ill-health (primarily those in manual occupations) will have an additional incentive to spend as little time away from work as possible. The figures would simply make it appear that these groups recover more quickly than others.

Class difference in mortality

Table **2** shows very clearly that the number of stillbirths, the infant mortality rate and deaths over the whole range vary very closely with social class. To put into words some of the startling facts about mortality and social class:

1 men and women in social class V had a two and a half times greater chance of dying before retirement age than those in social class I(67);
2 at birth and for the first month of life, the chances of dying are almost double for a child with a social class V than a social class I family(68);
3 the infant mortality rate in 1970–72 was almost three times as high in social class V as in social class I, but it is now 'only' double (see Table **5**);
4 for men of economically active age there was greater inequality in mortality between occupational classes I and V both in 1970–2 and 1959–63 than in 1947–53(69);
5 for economically active men the mortality rates of classes III and combined classes IV and V for age groups over 35 either deteriorated or showed little or no improvement between 1959–63 and 1970–72. Relative to the mortality rates of occupational classes I and II they worsened;
6 for women aged 15–64 the standardised mortality ratios of combined

Table 2 Mortality by social class and age

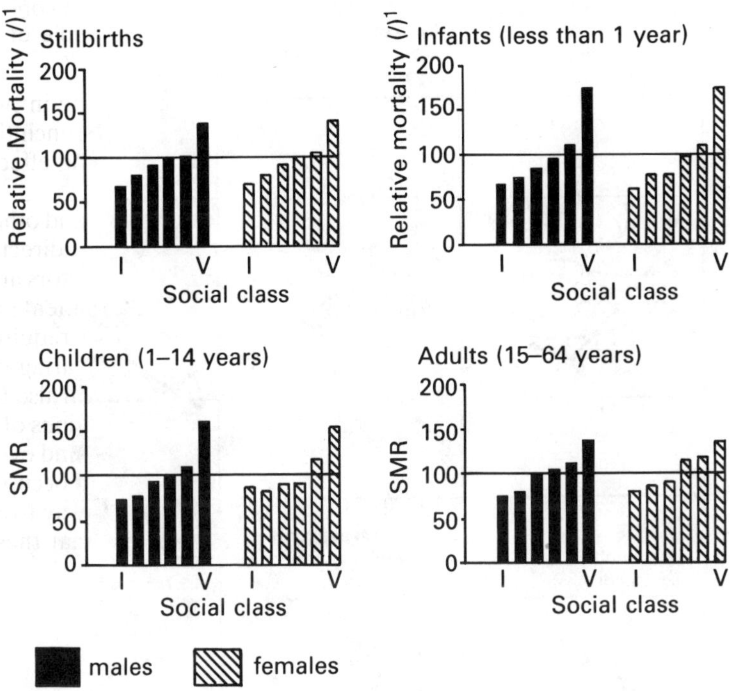

(source: *Occupational Mortality 1970–72, London, HMSO 1977*)

classes IV and V deteriorated. For married and single women of all ages in class IV they deteriorated between 1959–63 and 1970–72;
7 maternal mortality fell by more than a third during the decade 1960–1970. Although that of class I fell less sharply than other classes, inequality between the more numerous class II on the one hand and classes IV and V on the other remained at the same level.

Class difference in morbidity

The General Household Survey on ill-health showed that there is much more ill-health than is reported because formal treatment is not sought. Cause of death information tells us something about morbidity in the population but is unhelpful in respect of short-term and non-fatal illness. Table **3** shows the incidence of selected causes of death by social class and

Table 3 Mortality ratios by occupational class, age and cause of death (men 15–64, England and Wales)

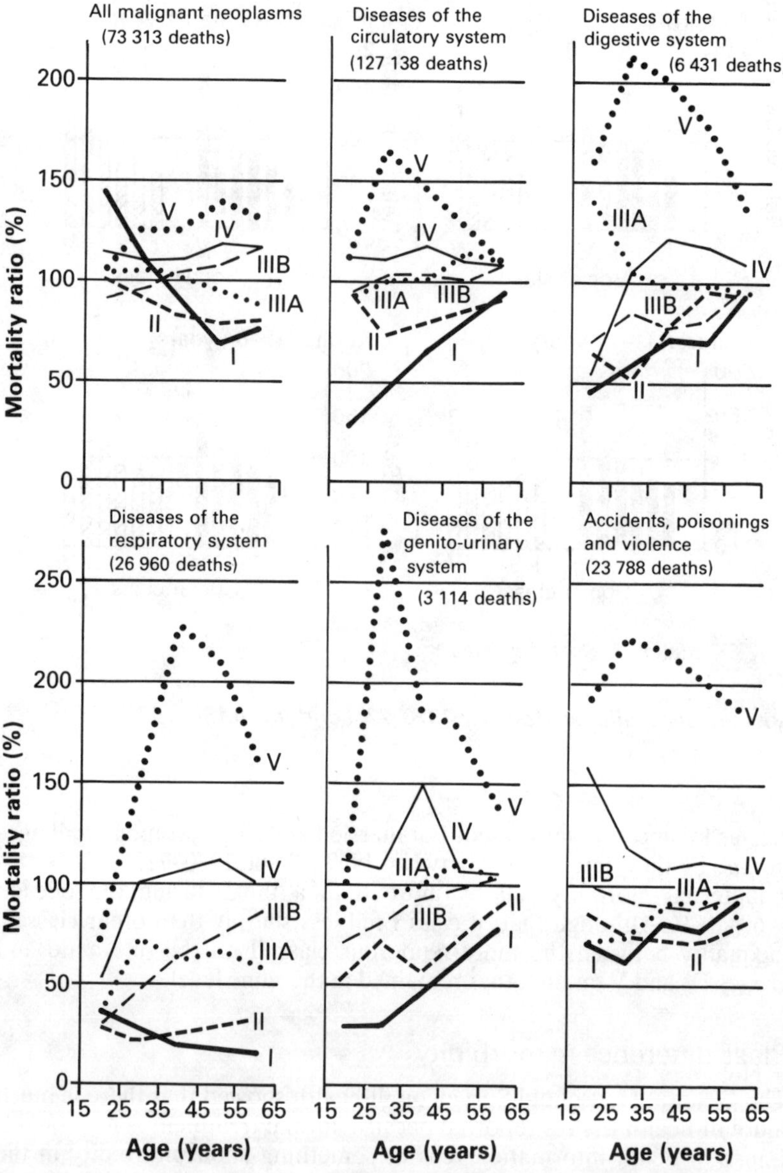

(source: *Occupational Mortality 1970–72, London, HMSO 1978*)

Table 4 Death rates by sex and social class, England and Wales 1971. Rates are per 1000 population between the ages 15–64 years.

Social class	*Males*	*Females*
I	3.98	2.15
II	5.54	2.85
IIINM	5.80	2.76
IIIM	6.08	3.41
IV	7.96	4.27
V	9.88	5.31
RATIO V/I	2.5	2.5

Source: adapted from Townsend and Davidson *Inequalities in Health* p 57

Table 5 Perinatal and infant mortality rates by social class of father, England and Wales

	Social class of father					
Perinatal mortality rate	*I*	*II*	*IIINM*	*IIIM*	*IV*	*V*
1970–2	16.3	18.6	20.6	22.1	23.9	32.1
1976	12.7	14.3	15.6	17.1	19.2	24.9
1978	11.9	12.3	13.9	15.1	16.7	20.3
1979	10.3	11.8	12.7	14.3	16.5	18.7
1980	9.7	11.1	11.8	13.0	15.0	17.0
Infant mortality rate						
1970–2	11.6	13.6	14.5	17.0	19.6	30.7
1976	9.4	10.5	11.2	12.9	15.3	22.3
1978	9.8	10.1	11.1	12.4	13.6	17.2
1979	9.8	9.7	9.8	11.4	14.3	18.7
1980	8.9	9.5	10.2	10.7	13.5	16.0

Source: adapted from *Social Trends 1983*, HMSO 1982 p 92
Perinatal mortality refers to stillbirths and deaths of infants under 1 week old per 1000 live and stillbirths. All rates in the table refer only to legitimate births.

demonstrates a clear association between certain types of illness as well as other causes of death, and social class. This association is particularly strong for males and for respiratory diseases and infective or parasitic diseases. Males in social class V suffer particularly badly from diseases of the digestive system such as stomach ulcers (which are four times as likely to lead to the death of a class V male than a class I male). Even where the correlation is less strong, as with cancer, some types particularly hit class V – cancers of the stomach are twice as frequent for men aged 15–64 than for similar men in class I.

Not all types of ill-health increase as one moves down the social scale. Because those in the upper sections of the scale tend to live longer, they have a higher incidence of chronic degenerative diseases such as rheumatoid arthritis. Cardio-vascular disorders also appear to be higher in the non-manual sector, probably because of the sedentary lifestyle, greater stress of work and possibly richer food. In America the incidence of heart disease has sharply declined in the past decade with greater awareness of the importance of exercise and low-fat diet. The factor of age will sometimes upset the clear class gradient. For example, while incidence of mental illness correlates closely with social class, there are higher rates of its incidence for lower social classes among young patients. This means the incidence gradually levels out in the older patients, and actually reverses itself above the age of 65 years.(70)

Explanations for inequalities in health

The Labour Government in 1974–79 set up the Black Working Party under the chairmanship of Sir Douglas Black, then Chief Scientist at the DHSS. Its members included Professor Peter Townsend, author of *Poverty in the United Kingdom*. Its remit was to assemble information on the social distribution of health and to look into the causes of any differences in health chances between the social classes. The Black Report was published in August 1980 but was given only a limited circulation. It was later published in a Penguin edition under the title *Inequalities in Health*(71). In the foreword to this edition the Secretary of State for Social Services in 1980 states that he considers implementation of the Report's recommendations too expensive and probably ineffective. The account which follows is largely drawn from *Inequalities in Health* which outlines four types of explanation for the persistence of such inequalities between the social classes.

The artefact explanation

This maintains there is no real problem about inequalities in health. The groups in poor health are a declining section of the population (the proportion of people in social class V declined from 12.9% in 1931 to 8.8% in 1971(72)). Upward social mobility caused by the expansion of jobs in the service sector has saved most people from this form of inequality. Even for those who remain in social class V, the general level of health is improving and if this gap remains between them and other sectors, this is only because the health of those sectors too is getting better. The future will see further diminution of social class V and a general increase in health standards. Therefore there is no real cause for concern about this problem which is, anyway, largely seen as such due to a misreading of the statistics.

A number of problems arise with this account that cast doubt on its optimistic perspective. While social class V *has* been declining as a proportion of the total population, in absolute numbers it has been increasing (from 13.247 million in 1931 to 15.668 million in 1971(73)) so their health problems are not disappearing.

Secondly, relative ill-health is not confined only to Class V. Townsend writes:

> "Mortality indicators for class IV, relative to other classes, have shown some deterioration between the early 1960's and the early 1970's, but perhaps the most important general finding is the lack of improvement and, in some respects, deterioration of the health experience of *both* class V and IV relative to class V, as judged by mortality indicators, during the 1960's and early 1970's."(74)

Thirdly, recent findings about the extent of social mobility suggest that very little of it occurs from social class V, most being confined to the middle range of the class structure(75).

The social selection explanation

This argues that the reason for the poor health of the lower social classes is a result of social selection processes. Those individuals who suffer ill-health are not selected for top jobs with responsibility and pressure and so find themselves at the bottom of the class structure. This approach assumes that modern industrial society is based on meritocratic selection procedures in education and at work, and that ill-health is an important criterion of selection. Such an argument clearly has its roots in functionalist perspectives on the nature of advanced industrial societies such as those of T Parsons(76) and K Davis and W E Moore(77). The functionalist view of the nature of social stratification is that to function efficiently, advanced industrial societies *must* be meritocratic and that education institutions perform a 'sifting and sorting' procedure to allocate the right people for the various levels of jobs so that jobs are done well enough to keep the social system going. Ill-health would mean poor performance and so the sick cannot be allocated such jobs.

Criticism of the social selection explanation involves a more general criticism of these functionalist arguments. These have been dealt with in the development chapter. Briefly, these say that more important factors than health operate in the selection of membership of the different social classes, especially the top and the bottom parts of the hierarchy. Moreover, many health problems occur in individuals long after they have been allocated their social positions and so cannot be a causative factor in that allocation.

The cultural/behavioural explanation

This sees the inequalities in health between the social classes as related to their different cultures, particularly the norms of behaviour which may be harmful to health. It blames ill-health among members of social class V on their dietary and leisure activities, for example. These individuals are perceived as being inadequately educated about healthy living and are unreceptive towards such education. Norms of behaviour have developed or been allowed to continue which in higher social classes have been abandoned as harmful to health. The lower social classes smoke more than the higher, and their rate of decline in smoking is slower (see footnote 96). They are more likely to eat white bread rather than the more beneficial brown. They are more likely to be spectators rather than participants in sport:

> "One could summarise these findings on the relationship between social class and the way in which people use their free time by concluding that whilst the working class trend to spend their leisure time passively, being entertained by professional sportsmen and broadcasters or just relaxing, the middle classes are more inclined to adopt active leisure interests . . . that demand some degree of mental or physical activity."(78)

The lower classes are less likely to take advantage of preventive health care, vaccination or ante-natal care (see for example the evidence in J W B Douglas's *The Home and the School*) and are more likely to eat non-nutritious or even harmful food and to give such things to their children. They are less likely to breastfeed, though cows' milk and commercial baby food have been shown by *some* medical experts to be less nutritious than mothers' milk and to deprive children of protection from disease. Even the higher rate of death from accidents for social class V can be accounted for under this theory by reference to the suggested greater carelessness, irresponsibility and lower parental monitoring among the lower social classes. This would explain why the risk of a child being hit by a motor vehicle is five to seven times greater for social class IV than I and the gap increases for deaths by fires, falls and drowning(79).

Just as the previous explanation had clear links with functionalist social theory, so this one has links with the culture of poverty explanation of the continued existence of poverty in affluent societies which puts blame squarely on the poor themselves. The culture of poverty thesis has been widely criticised by sociologists(80) and this theory of health is open to much the same kind of criticism. Perhaps the most telling is the Marxist critique which holds that cultures and sub-cultures are not created in a vacuum but are responses to and reflections of the prevailing economic conditions. To blame culture for the ill-health of the poor is to put the cart before the horse. The economic circumstances of the poor create both culture and ill-health. We need to ask *why* the culture is as it is. In respect of dietary and sporting norms, for example, the simple factor of *cost* is a clear answer. Reasons for the greater levels of cigarette smoking require more sophisticated analysis. We will see how Marxists do this in the next section.

The structuralist explanation

This stresses the importance of the organisation of the economy and the techniques it employs as well as the social structure which, partly at least, is a product of it. As such it is subscribed to by Marxists, but other theorists would agree with some of the points made; even, in some cases, doctors themselves. We will deal with a number of the factors which induce ill-health at least for some under modern economic and social conditions, beginning with work conditions. Table **3** demonstrates that, for the causes of death shown, the gap between social class V and other groups is widest during years of work, which implicates conditions at work as a causative factor.

1 Work and health

Industrial accidents are a greater cause of ill-health and death for manual than non-manual workers. Mining, quarrying, deep-sea fishing, construction and transport are particularly dangerous occupations(81). While the total number of people killed at work is around 600 per year, the number of injuries is considerably more. Half a million per year is one estimate(82). From the Marxist point of view these figures are not surprising. In capitalist society the search for profit comes before safety at work so technology is employed which generates a profit but may be hazardous, and workers are pushed to produce more in less time so that safety margins are cut. Unions do little to alleviate the situation: they tend to demand more money for dangerous conditions rather than seeking to improve safety.

Toxic substances at work are a second cause of ill-health and death, though one which is difficult to isolate with certainty. Statistics tend to come from successful court and tribunal cases over compensation payment and therefore probably seriously under-represent the actual numbers involved. Again, miners and quarrymen were two and a half times more likely to die of chest complaints as members of the general public. Furnace, forge, foundry and rolling-mill workers were one and a half times as likely to die from malignant neoplasms (cancer) of trachea, bronchus and lung, and nearly twice as likely to die from bronchitis, emphysema and asthma(83). In 1973, 367 deaths were officially declared to be due to pneumoconiosis and 700 *new* cases are diagnosed every year. Particular toxic substances include beta napthylamine and vinyl chloride monomore, both of which can cause cancer many years after exposure. Asbestos has also received a lot of attention as a cause of cancer. One disturbing fact about substances such as these is that not only do the workers in the rubber, cable, plastic or asbestos factories suffer their effects but their families do too:

> "Last year Selikoff's group (at the Mount Sinai Medical Centre in New York) started to look at the families of Paterson Asbestos workers

who received slight exposure to fibres brought back by the wage earners in their hair and clothing. To date, the team has X-rayed 210 and the results are disturbing indeed. Almost 40% of the subjects were found to possess abnormalities in their lungs of the type common to asbestos workers. Even more alarming is the fact that some of the abnormalities have shown up in the lungs of the subjects whose asbestos industry kin spent no more than a few days at the Paterson plant."(84)

A third work-related health hazard is stress. Job insecurity, the pace of work, the competitiveness, the noise and rush of city life, the need to do everything quickly and on time, the disruption of family life caused by overtime and shift work, the monotony of assembly-line production are all stress-inducing for working and middle class alike. Stress has effects on both mental and physical health. The social and sexual distribution of mental illness suggests that such social rather than purely personal factors are the cause. If one rejects the mechanistic dualism of Western medicine (which sees mind and body as distinct) as Marxists and others do, then emotional instability, stress and depression can be regarded as causes of physical problems. The precise relationship between stress and the aetiology (causation) of disease is not fully understood. It is clear that when one undergoes stress certain identifiable physical changes occur in the body. The heart rate and blood pressure increase, the distribution of blood in the body alters; glucose, fatty acids and adrenalin are released into the blood stream. It is thought that these reactions, while useful for a rapid response to danger in a life-threatening situation, are harmful to health if repeated too frequently. Reduction of resistance to infection and of the body's ability to repair damaged tissue(85) are two of their effects.

Some interesting studies have been done on stress which demonstrate the artificiality of the separation of mind and body. R J Meyer and R J Haggerty(86) studied streptococci (a type of bacteria) in fifteen middle class Boston families with two or more children over a one-year period. Tests were conducted on their children every two or three weeks and at times of throat infection to establish the presence of streptococci in their throats. In 21% of tests new, and therefore threatening, strains were identified but these resulted in clear signs of illness in only half of the cases. It was found that they were four times more likely to result in overt illness after a distressing life event (as recorded in diaries and interviews with the mother) than before it. Surprisingly, even the acquisition of streptococci without illness was also four times more likely to occur after such events. Furthermore, in those families who had a higher level of general stress (as measured in 17 areas of life, including personal relationships and adequacy of income) it was found that presence of the bacteria was more likely to result in overt physical symptoms than those with low levels of stress.

This study presents interesting evidence against disease theory which, as we saw earlier, suggests that diseases strike more or less at random. In fact we are all exposed to infection much more often than we become ill. As Ian Kennedy in *The Unmasking of Medicine*(87) says: "disease theory has induced a sort of medical tunnel vision" and this has prevented modern medicine from seriously examining the role of the circumstances of the patient in inhibiting or facilitating the onset of disease.

Meyer and Haggerty's work can be criticised for its small sample size, the possibility of the operation of the Hawthorne effect and its exclusion of extra-familial stressors, which would have been of more direct interest to us here. A larger scale study comes from L Srole(88) which found that 23% of a sample of 1660 people living close to the centre of New York were psychiatrically impaired. There was a strong correlation between parents' occupation and the proportion rated psychiatrically impaired (from the highest to the lowest status groups: 17.5%, 16.4%, 20.9%, 24.5%, 29.4% and 32.7%). Stress-causing factors were also linked to the chances of psychiatric impairment(89).

For Marxists the causal chain is clear: exploitative nature of capitalist profit-seeking stress at work and in home life→mental and physical illness. Some non-Marxists (including progressive doctors) would agree, with the proviso that it is in the nature of industrial society in general, not capitalism, to produce stress and this may be inevitable. Studies like those above, while establishing *correlations* which lend support to both cases, do not clarify the nature of causation. Until this is done, neither case can be said to be proven. Once again the theory of social selection could prove as adequate an explanation for such correlations. Moreover, the process by which one becomes identified as suffering from mental illness is not immune from interference by social factors, so correlations which include people who have been labelled as psychiatrically ill or impaired need to be treated with some caution.

Market Liberals and Social Democrats would disagree with the Marxists' contention that death and ill-health caused by work conditions is an outcome of the capitalist mode of production. For Market Liberals such as Friedman, unhealthy work conditions are an unfortunate but largely unavoidable consequence of industrialisation which harms the few for the benefit of the many. Compared with non-industrial and early industrial society, these causes of death and ill-health are now of minor importance. The general levels of morbidity and mortality, including work-related cases, have declined tremendously during the course of this century. Social Democrats stress the role of the state in acting to control the worst excesses of industrialists. They point to important legislation such as the 1833 *Factory Act* and later ones, the 1897 *Workmen's Compensation Act*, the 1909 *Trade Boards Act* and, more recently, the *Health and Safety at Work Act* 1974, which have improved work conditions at the expense of profitability. Marxists reply that these developments have occurred within the limits set by a capitalist economy. They make no drastic changes to fundamentally dangerous conditions. A truly socialist economy would not consider allowing unhealthy work conditions to continue. It is unclear how far such an economy would really be able to reconcile the competing imperatives of healthy working conditions on the one hand, and such things as consumer demand and the requirements of high technology which are generally seen as providing the foundations of socialist society.

2 Housing

Colin Thunhurst, in *It Makes You Sick*, suggests that poor housing can affect health in several ways. Overcrowding leads to ill-health because it facilitates the transmission of contagious diseases between members of the family. After the Second World War overcrowding was shown to be significantly related to the incidence of pneumonia and TB. Conversely, isolation in high-rise blocks as well as other housing circumstances have been demonstrated to increase stress and the risk of suicide. The greater number of accidents at home suffered by social class V than any other class may be due to the use of cheap but sometimes dangerous equipment such as paraffin heaters and to the general lack of space and poor design of homes at the lower end of the housing market. Older housing and dilapidated housing can result in a physical environment which is harmful. Lead poisoning comes from flaking paint and old water pipes, while bronchial problems result from the damp which affects old or cheaply built housing. Poor housing in a depressing environment can cause stress and depression which have more serious mental and physical effects.

Women spend more time in the home than men(90) and this may partially account for the higher incidence of depression and mental illness amongst women(91). It is extremely difficult to prove this conclusively. While it is easy to show a correlation between poor housing and poor health, the precise causal mechanisms are unclear. A variety of factors working together make identification of specific causes difficult to validate. Recently, there has been general improvement in the standard of housing. J W B Douglas, in *The Home and the School*(92) reports that:

> "During the 11 years of this survey, home circumstances improved greatly. 30% of middle class families moved to houses with better amenities . . . and only 7% moved to worse . . . There has been an even greater improvement in the housing of manual working class families."

For the middle class this improvement was largely brought about by home purchase, while for the working class it was due to the greater availability of good council housing. There has been a steady increase in both of these categories of housing and a decline in the sector with the lowest standards of accommodation, the privately rented sector, as the following figures demonstrate:

Table 6 Tenure of households in permanent accommodation in Great Britain

	1961 *percentages*	*1981* *percentages*
Owner occupied	40	56
Rented from local authority/new town	25	31
Rented privately	34	13

(Source: *Social Trends 1983*. HMSO 1982 OPCS)

The general improvement in the standard of housing and sanitation, particularly water supply and sewage disposal, have been seen by some as doing far more than any developments in modern medicine to cut the death rate and improve health(93). In this respect, the evidence appears to support the Market Liberals' argument that capitalism can benefit the relatively badly off; as well as the Social Democrats' case that the state's activities instigate the worst effects of capitalism by organising the provision of generally high quality housing for the poor. Market Liberals point to the expansion of house ownership to include the working class in support of their case; Social Democrats emphasise the increased provision of council housing and rent and rate rebate schemes.

3 Diet and smoking

Marxists and culture of poverty theorists agree that the consumption habits of the poor are unhealthy. For the former this is due to the mode of production which directs and controls consumption patterns; for the latter it is a result of bad habits induced in childhood or during later life. However, it is not just the working class who suffer from the so-called diseases of affluence. All sectors of the community in advanced industrial societies are subject to health problems which do not occur in simpler, rural societies, or occur to a much more limited extent. These include cirrhosis of the liver, appendicitis, certain types of cancer (deaths from all types increased from 92 214 in 1949 to 142 874 in 1977 in Great Britain), ulcerative colitis, arteriosclerosis, diabetes, hypertension, dental cavities, diverticular disease, duodenal ulcers and varicose veins(94).

A recent report of a sub-committee of the National Advisory Committee on Nutrition Education(95) blamed the Western diet which is low in fibre and high in fat, sugar and salt, for many of these ailments. Many wholefood eaters would agree, but for Marxists, our diet is not an accidental product of a particular culture; it is dictated by the demands of capitalist industry. The food industry is increasingly dominated by huge multinationals such as Rowntree Mackintosh, Mars, Rank Hovis, McDougal, Spillers and Allied Bakeries etc. The search for profit may sometimes influence questions of health or nutrition. The production of bread in Britain provides an interesting example. Bran is removed from wholemeal flour in bread production to produce white flour and white bread. This removes fibre which is essential to good health. The reasons for the removal of the bran and the production of white rather than brown bread as the norm are, according to Marxists, connected with the techniques of bread production and with its consumption. The 19th century introduction of the steel roller mill allowed bran to be removed from flour. Once removed, the bran could be sold separately as animal feed, thus enhancing profitability. White bread is far less filling than brown and so one needs to buy more of it; a clear advantage from the producer's point of view. These two factors led to the gearing of bread production technology towards white bread from imported American wheat. To change back to brown bread would involve considerable re-investment in machinery. The producers' response to greater public demand for the healthier brown bread is simply to spend money on advertising campaigns proclaiming the virtues of the white product. In general, the producers' argument is that the demand for brown bread is limited and they produce white because that is what people want.

The move towards processed foods has also been made in the interests of the capitalist companies according to Marxists. To establish brand identity and to prevent waste, a product must be easily transportable from the processing plant, must be storeable and must be identical wherever it is purchased. This means that artificial flavourings, preservatives and colourants are added which may be dangerous when they build up and combine with each other in the body. Butylated hydroxytoluene, an additive which prevents fats and oils going rancid, has been banned in many countries, but is still used in Britain. A further point is that manipulation of flavours and creation of new foods allows the food industry to constantly expand. These commercially created foods are often high in sugar and low in, or lacking, nutritional value.

Given the nature of the food industry, it seems that we are all exposed to potentially harmful foods. Only those who are aware of the importance of diet, have access to shops which sell 'healthy' food and can afford to buy it escape its effects. Not surprisingly, these people are generally among the more affluent as the following table suggests:

Table 7 Household food consumption by income groups (oz/person/week) Great Britain 1979

Income Group	*white bread*	*brown, incl. wholemeal*	*sugar & preserves*	*potatoes*	*fresh fruit*
A	17	5.3	11	39	25
B	22	4.5	12	40	20
C	26	4.3	13	48	16
D	29	4.3	15	48	15

(Gross weekly income of head of household: A = £145, D = less than £56)
Source: *Household Food Consumption and Expenditure* HMSO quoted Townsend and Davidson p 119

Smoking is more prevalent among the lower than the higher income groups, and this is becoming more pronounced as time goes on(96).

Marxists blame the continued desire to smoke amongst some people, and the increase in the habit amongst women on the advertising in the tobacco industry. This amounts to perhaps £1 million per week(97), and is more persuasive than any counter-measures from the Health Education Council, with a total annual budget of around £4 million. Despite the ban on TV advertising, the tobacco companies get plenty of TV coverage through their sponsorship of sporting events and personalities. Marxists maintain that the government has little incentive to prevent people from smoking: the tax revenue was approximately £1500 million in 1975(98); the savings in pensions not paid because people died from smoking-related diseases must be enormous. The newspaper and tobacco industries would suffer (the former depends to a great extent on cigarette advertising) and many jobs would be lost. On the plus side, the NHS would save in the region of £300 000 every day, though this does not really compare with the losses.

The response of the Market Liberals to these arguments is that the food and tobacco industries simply supply people's demands. People are aware of the hazards of smoking and yet continue doing it. As far as food is concerned, its quality has improved tremendously since the beginning of the industrial revolution when it was scarce, of poor quality and adulterated, leading to malnutrition and vitamin and mineral deficiencies. Advanced industrial societies are able to provide a wider range of foods of better quality than any other social formations.

The Social Democratic standpoint is much the same as this, but adds that the government has passed extensive legislation on the content of food, truthfulness in advertising, the use of additives and health warnings on cigarette packets and advertisements. However, the response of the government to the report on the British diet by the sub-committee of the National Advisory Committee on Nutrition Education suggests that wholehearted commitment to healthy diet is not among the government's most important aims. Its publication was blocked by the Department of Health for two years. The *Sunday Times* reporter, G Cannon, links this to the opposition of the British Nutrition Foundation to the recommendations contained in the report that we should cut our intake of fat, sugar and salt while simultaneously increasing the amount of fresh fruit, vegetables, brown bread and fibre in the context of an overall reduction in the amount we eat. The British Nutrition Foundation is 98% funded by the food industry.

4 Unemployment

For some, including Marxists, not only does employment cause ill-health and early death, as we saw earlier; but so does *un*employment. In view of the currently high rate of unemployment world-wide, this is a disturbing claim.

In a society in which the Protestant work ethic is strong and is reinforced by the major socialising institutions, the effects of exclusion from paid work and the sociability and financial reward it generates will clearly be disturbing and stressful for most people. Stress and disrupting life events have effects on health, and so we could expect unemployment to affect health. Research evidence is sparse, of poor quality and generally inconclusive. Perhaps the best known is the work of M H Brenner(99). He searched for correlations between fluctuations in the economy of the USA and changes in the mortality statistics and other health indicators. His conclusion was that as the economy declines, and particularly as unemployment increases, there is an increase in the national mortality rate after a gap of two to five years. The causes of death which increase most are cardio-vascular disease, cirrhosis of the liver, suicide and homicide. The rate of mental illness also goes up, at least as measured by the number of people entering mental hospitals for the first time. This kind of research has a number of problems (as does Durkheim's study of suicide with which it has similarities). The method where data are analysed in search of a correlation between two or more variables, called factor analysis, is an apparently useful but in fact highly dangerous tool. Even if the correlation between factor A (say, increase in unemployment) and factor B (say, increase in deaths from arteriosclerosis) is found to be 1.0 – ie they move exactly together after a time interval – we are not justified in saying "A caused B." The relationship between them might be an indirect one, ie some third factor caused by A and causing B intervenes. In the end any explanation of the cause of the correlation is going to be little more than speculation. Economic decline and increased unemployment have a number of consequences, any one or any combination of which may result in poorer health in the population. Brenner's explanation is stress, but an obvious alternative one is that unemployment leads to low income, thus poor diet and susceptibility to ill-health and early death.

A more recent study linking unemployment to increased mortality is that by J Fox and D Goldblatt(100). Taking a 1% sample of the adult population it demonstrates that unemployed males of working age have a 30% higher mortality rate than the whole group of such men. The major causes of death are accidents, violence and suicide, while cancer deaths are 40% higher in the unemployed group. Again, the problem is that unemployment is likely to hit the unskilled and unhealthy more anyway, so little is learned from such figures. Furthermore, the trends for women seem to work in the *opposite* direction: those registered as unemployed live longer than those in paid employment.

As regards morbidity amongst the unemployed, statistics are unreliable due to the fact that they have more time to dwell on minor ailments and to visit the doctor, which will increase consultation rates. On the other hand, they will not need a sick note and are less likely to find it easy to visit the doctor due to transport difficulties which will decrease the rates. S Kasl and S Cobb(101) conducted periodic tests on a group of men made redundant from one factory and a group still working there. The redundant group had higher blood pressure, higher levels of serum cholesterol and uric acid in the early period of their redundancy, but these later declined. As the theorists of natural and social selection argue, the health of workers will play a large part in the decisions about who is to become unemployed in the first place, so the results are by no means conclusive.

There is little firm evidence of a causative link between unemployment and ill-health. As those most vulnerable to unemployment are also the least healthy section of the population for any given age, the most we can say is that employed or unemployed, their health chances are poor.

In concluding this section, let us examine the implications for social policy of each of the four types of explanation we have examined. If the government accepts the artefact explanation it will see no necessity for action as, from this perspective, no problem exists. Subscription to the social selection explanation would again involve no change in policy as relative poor health for the lower sections of the class structure is an inevitable consequence of the meritocratic workings of a modern industrial society. On the other hand, if the government accepted the cultural/behavioural explanation the policy options would include an attempt to re-socialise the working class into healthier habits. The formal education system, the media, an extension of the work and budgets of bodies like the Health Education Council, would be central elements of such a policy, as would provision of facilities, particularly in working class areas, to facilitate a healthier lifestyle. From the structuralist persons perspective, such initiatives would have little effect because they in no way alter the basic structure of advanced industrial or capitalist society which cause ill-health and health inequalities. Only a rethinking of the priorities of this type of society, an abandonment of the profit motive as the prime consideration and its replacement by questions of health and happiness, would lead to a healthier and fairer society. For the Marxist this could only result from a change in the economic substructure.

The following section deals with the topic of mental health as viewed from the sociological perspective. In it we will review the work of R D Laing and Thomas Szasz. Much of what has been said up to this point has attempted to show that the division between mental and physical health is in many ways an artificial one and that the mechanistic view of the body is unhelpful. Stress and related psychological problems can lead to physical ill-health, while physical sickness can produce symptoms of mental illness. In the light of this it would seem paradoxical to devote a *separate* section to the sociology of mental health. However, as many writers deal with this as a distinct subject area it seems wise to deal with it in this way but to bear in mind its essential indivisability from other areas of health studies.

Mental health

R D Laing: The family and mental illness

Mental illness may be divided into two basic types: psychoses (insecurity) and neuroses (ie what most people know as 'nerves'). Laing mainly looks at one particular example of psychosis – schizophrenia. The symptoms of schizophrenia are bizarre and are not necessarily associated with the split personality which normally comes to mind. The sufferer may have delusions and hallucinations, hear voices and become wildly excited for no apparent reason. Sometimes he/she will go into a catatonic state, a stupor in which no movement is discernible other than pulse and breathing.

Laing's career as a theoretician of schizophrenia has gone through a number of stages. At first, while working as a psychiatrist in a NHS mental hospital in Glasgow, he held the conventional view that schizophrenia was possibly an organic disease (ie having a *physical* cause), but he developed original and unconventional methods of dealing with it. He organised the patients into sociable groups and found that as they interacted with each other, they became less withdrawn and their symptoms were alleviated, at least temporarily. This is the period during which Laing wrote *Self and Others*(102). The second stage in his development marked his attack on *the family* as the reason for the label schizophrenic being attached to particular individuals. He now denied that schizophrenia existed or, at least, that if it did, it was the patient's family who suffered from it, not the patient. This is the period during which *Sanity, Madness and the Family* was published(103). The third stage saw a movement from the psychiatric/sociological to the mystical. He began to see the behavioural characteristics normally regarded as schizophrenia as manifestations of a spiritual journey:

> "in and back and through and beyond into the experience of all mankind, of the primal man, of Adam and perhaps even further into the being of animals, vegetables and minerals: the temporal standstill . . . to aeonic time . . . back into the womb of all things."(104)

This is a journey which Laing was recommending to all of us, one which was a prerequisite of a sane society. The books *The Politics of Experience and The Bird of Paradise* and *The Dialectics of Liberation*(105) were written during this period. The most recent point in Laingian theorising has seen a complete reversal of direction; a return to medicine and a rejection of the second and third perspectives. Of the third stage he says:

> "I'm sorry if I put [the idea of schizophrenia as marking a passage to a desirable state] into people. I would not recommend madness to anybody."(106)

Now he implicitly rejects the second stage by including a poem which praises the family in a new edition of *The Politics of the Family*, a collection of essays. The poem begins:

> "A family,
> a place of peace and quiet,
> a place to laugh and cry and dance and sing,
> a place to eat one's bread in gladness,
> a space for love
> where one is cherished by those one cherishes."

In this section, we are only concerned with the more sociologically interesting second stage, the critique of the family.

Sanity, Madness and the Family presents us with a series of case studies of schizophrenics:

Sarah Danzig's case is perhaps typical. Until seventeen years old, she was a 'good girl' but at that age she began to lie in bed all day, getting up only at night to brood and read the Bible. Her attendance at college became infrequent and until the age of 21 she failed at all the jobs and examinations she tried. She began to claim she heard voices on the telephone and believed that someone was listening to her calls. She saw people on TV talking about her. She became listless, apathetic and quiet, but sometimes raged against members of her family. Sometimes she made bizarre statements, claiming that she had been raped, that people read her letters and tore them up, that people in her father's office (where she worked) talked about her and did not want her to work there. Her reading of the Bible, often at night, continued.

As Laing looked into Sarah's home situation, he began to see that much of Sarah's illness was in fact a fairly accurate perception of the domestic situation. Her father had a habit of coming into her bedroom unannounced while she was undressed, insisting on tidying it up. He listened to phone calls and intercepted letters and, while both parents encouraged her to go out with boys, they watched her every move in this respect so that she felt she had no privacy. She became muddled about whether or not it was right to go out with them. Her mother had a strangely ambivalent attitude; she would insist that Sarah got out of bed in the morning, but would cook her breakfast whenever she actually chose to get up:

> "The more her parents did things for her, the more they wanted her gratitude and the more ungrateful she became. Searching for gratitude, they did even more to help her. Thus, while expecting her to grow up, they treated her as a child, and she, while waiting to be considered as an adult, behaved more and more as a baby. Her parents then reproached her for being spoiled by them, and she reproached them for not treating her as an adult."(107)

Laing sees much of her behaviour as perfectly reasonable in these circumstances. It is the parents' definition of it as mad that is problematic for him. The following quotations illustrate his belief that the wrong person had been defined as ill:

> "Sarah's 'thinking' worried them a great deal. Mrs Danzig knew that 'thinking', especially a lot of 'thinking', was liable to make you have peculiar thoughts, because it 'turns the brain.'"
>
> (Mrs Danzig said) . . . "sitting up all night in a blue nightdress in the kitchen – just the lights on, nobody making a sound. She's thinking and thinking – goodness knows what the heck she's thinking about . . . Not that we particularly want to know what Sarah's thinking or doing, although it's only natural that a mother should be curious."
>
> Laing writes: "Reading the Bible was also a very doubtful activity, especially for a girl. Religion was one thing, but reading the Bible was another. The Bible was possibly all right to glance through . . . but to want to sit down and read it and make a fuss if it was missing from its usual place . . ."(108)

Laing interprets her Bible reading as an attempt to throw light on her present experience and as a search for clear guidance on the rights and wrongs of life, given her parents' ambivalent attitudes.

This family, then, is at least partly a cause of behaviour which is not mad at all. By taking her to the psychiatrist, they have succeeded in fixing that label on her when, if anything, it belongs to them. The progression through the good-bad-mad set of labels attached to Sarah as she got older is, according to Laing, the usual pattern of election of an individual into the role of madness by the family.

One of the problems in assessing Laing's work is that the changes in direction lead to contradictions or ambiguities in earlier and later writing. For example, in one place, Laing says that many of schizophrenics' utterances are nonsense; in another, he says that everything they say has some sort of meaning or intention behind it. It is unclear, also, whether *all* families are implicated in the destructive role he gives to ones like the Danzigs, or whether it is only a few 'odd' ones which cause schizophrenia. If the latter is the case, Laing's work is silent on the question of the differences between normal and abnormal families. In fact, a comparison of families with and without schizophrenic children would have been very helpful in both clarifying the causes of abnormal behaviour and in testing Laing's theory. If the interaction patterns were the same, we would have to seriously question the theoretical basis of his work. From a feminist point of view, Laing has completely missed the real source of oppression within the family – the fact that it reflects in a personally damaging form the wider patterns of patriarchy. Similarly, for the Marxist, the tensions within the family reflect the pressures on its individual members generated by an exploitative economic system. To blame the family is to be blind to the real cause – a society which creates families like the Danzigs.

Thomas Szasz and the myth of mental illness

Szasz's main premise is that 'mental illness' does not exist as an illness at all. It is a label we place on someone who cannot cope with the demands of life:

> "In short, while medical diagnoses are the names of genuine diseases, psychiatric diagnoses are stigmatising labels."(109)

He attacks traditional psychiatry which treats mental illness in the same way as medicine treats infectious diseases – as the product of random attack from outside:

> ". . . hysteria, neurasthenia, obsessive – compulsive neurosis, depression, paranoia and so forth (are) . . . regarded as diseases that *happened* to people."(110)

He adds that we have come to regard phobias, delinquencies, divorce, homicide and addiction as psychiatric illnesses. In so doing, psychiatry legitimises the abnormal, childish and irresponsible behaviour of the 'mentally ill', rewards it and so encourages it:

> "By implication, those who exhibit effective, self-reliant behaviour need not be helped. They may even be taxed, burdened or coerced in various ways. This *rewarding of disability* – however necessary it may sometimes be – is a social practice fraught with complex, unanticipated and often undesirable consequences."(111)

One of the consequences is that we make the patient more helpless by helping him/her. More important though, is the fact that successfully labelling a person as mentally ill permits us to incarcerate them in mental hospitals against their will. In this way, psychiatry has become a means of social control:

> "Agoraphobia is illness because we should not be afraid of open spaces; homosexuality is illness because heterosexuality is the social norm; divorce is illness because it signals the failure of marriage."(112)

The ultimate sanction against these deviants is the mental hospital. Szasz argues that there are clear parallels between the Soviet practice of putting dissidents (deviants) in mental hospitals and our own techniques of social control.

Let us look more closely at Szasz's theory of the origins of mental illness. He considers the behaviour patterns we associate with mental illness to be another form of the game playing which he says characterises all social interaction. When we interact with others, we do so on the basis of shared rules and behave in accordance with them. This approach has much in common with the functionalists' notion of role playing except that Szasz's focus is microscopic while that of the functionalists is macroscopic (they see roles within the context of the larger institutions and these as occupying a particular functional situation within the society as a whole). In Szasz's reading hysteria, which he sees as representative of all types of mental illness, game playing is based on the 'wrong' rules – ones which are different from those of the person the hysteric is interacting with. In the hysteric's game, coercive strategies take precedence over the co-operative ones:

> "The patient's relatives, for example, tend to be deeply impressed by (the abnormal behaviour of the hysteric), often much more deeply than they would be (if the person had tried to get what they wanted in the normal way). The display of sickness or suffering is thus useful for coercing others. This feature of hysteria, more than any other, accounts for its immediate and immense practical value to the patient."(113)

Unable to get what they want in the normal way, some people change the rules and adopt hysterical behaviour because it succeeds where other strategies have failed. The therapeutic consequences of this theory are particularly interesting. It is necessary for the therapist and the patient to agree on the desired changes in the patient's rules of the game because even the normal rules are only generally accepted ones; they are not 'right' in any objective sense. After this has been done, then they can decide what will constitute a 'cure':

> ". . . changes which might be labelled 'improvements' or 'cures' by some may occur in any one of the following directions: more effective coercion and domination of others; greater submission to others and increased preoccupation with suffering . . . withdrawal from the struggle over interpersonal control by progressive isolation from real-life relationships . . . and, finally, learning the goals and strategies of other games and becoming invested in some of them."(114)

Because of this need for agreement between patient and therapist on what will constitute an improvement, it is vital that they co-operate on a roughly equal footing and share the same goals, working together in private and in secret. This can only be done on a fee-for-service basis, and not in a national health service where the therapist will be operating as an agent of social control:

> "In traditional charity practice, the physician was not principally the patient's agent. Sometimes he was not the patient's agent at all. Accordingly, a truly confidential relationship between patient and physician could not develop. The physician was technically and legally responsible to his superiors and employers . . . It is often maintained nowadays that removing the financial involvement with the patient enables the physician better to concentrate on the technical task in hand . . . while this might be true in thoracic surgery, it is assuredly not true in psychoanalysis."(115)

This perspective clearly places Szasz amongst the Market Liberals, which makes it rather strange that he has been acclaimed as a radical theorist, especially by the left. Not only does he ignore the problems which private practice presents for the poor, he ignores the real suffering which the hysteric and other mentally ill people undergo. Coming from a doctor, his view of mental illness as merely coercive behaviour or malingering seems a particularly unsympathetic attitude. Old and really incapable patients need the constant care and attention which only non-profit making institutions can provide for the poor. Returning them to their families would cause familial disruption, and many of them have no families anyway. As for his point that NHS psychiatry is merely a form of social control by mental institution, the fact is that most hospitalised mental patients are there voluntarily. Lesley Garner estimates that 95% of them are theoretically free to discharge themselves, though often this is impossible or unsuitable for practical reasons(116). A further difficulty with Szasz's solution to the problem of 'mental illness' is that many patients become emotionally dependent on their psychiatrist. This factor alone invalidates his claim that fee-for-service treatment would create an equal and co-operative contractual relationship between the two. The opportunity for financial or other manipulation by the psychiatrist would still exist, even outside the context of state medicine.

Finally, from the Marxist position, Szasz's analysis suffers from the same problem that all phenomenological work does. It ignores the wider structures that condition and control interpersonal behaviour. Szasz never asks why some people can cope in normal games and others need to resort to hysterical behaviour. The answer, according to Marxists, is that the dice used in the game are loaded in favour of some and against others. If physical illnesses are exacerbated by stress, living conditions and loneliness, how much more is this true of mental illness?

Medicine and advanced industrial societies

During this chapter we have explored some of the reasons why the health service is not effective in achieving many of its aims, especially that of eliminating inequalities in health and provision within the context of generally improving health levels. In this section, we will examine two views of the role of the medical profession in furthering or hindering these aims: that of Talcott Parsons in *The Social System*(117) and I Illich in *Limits to Medicine*(118).

Talcott Parsons

The doctor's role is a highly technical one, demanding great skill and knowledge. As a result, selection for that role must be based on *merit*, not social position, in order to select the best quality people. Like other roles in modern society, the doctor's is based on achievement, not ascription (although in Britain 33% of medical students come from public schools, which are attended by only 3% of the school population, and a further 13% from grant-aided schools. Many present doctors are the sons and daughters of doctors(119).) The doctor's role must have no emotional content, so that decisions such as whether or not to administer a painful but probably effective course of treatment can be objectively made. The role is also universalistic; the doctor is judged not on personal qualities or characteristics but on objective and universally accepted standards. The role is also a specific one; it is so demanding in terms of time and effort to train and maintain competence that no other role can possibly be played by the same person. However, in one respect, the doctor's role is like the roles played in traditional societies – it is collectivity-orientated rather than self-orientated as is that of, for example, the businessman. The doctor works for the benefit of the community, not him/herself. Parsons writes:

> "The ideology of the profession lays great emphasis on the obligation of the physician to put the 'welfare of the patient' above his personal interests, and regards 'commercialism' as the most serious and insidious evil with which it has to contend . . . this attitude is, of course, shared with the other professions, but it is perhaps more pronounced in the medical case than in any single one except perhaps the clergy."(120)

This collectivity-orientation is protected by a series of practices which, according to Parsons, means that the physician cannot act in a self-interested way:

> "He cannot advertise . . . He cannot bargain over fees with his patients – a 'take it or leave it' attitude is enjoined upon him (and them!). He cannot refuse patients on the grounds that they are 'poor risks' . . . The general picture is one of sharp segregation from the market and price practices of the business world, in ways which, for the most part, cut off the physician from many immediate opportunities for financial gain . . ."(121)

The collectivity-orientation is necessary for a number of reasons:

1 The sick role involves co-operation between doctor and patient. The doctor has to have authority over the patient and this authority cannot be legitimised unless the patient believes that doctor is working in the patient's interests.

2 Therapeutic success, especially in psychotherapy, is impossible unless the patient trusts the physician. In a society where self-interest is the norm, someone who retreats into the role of mentally ill because he cannot cope with the egoism inherent in this type of society would benefit little from the attentions of a doctor who was also out to get everything he could for himself. Even non-psychiatric medicine has elements of psycho-

therapy in it – talking to the doctor about your problems makes you feel better – and for this reason collectivity-orientation is important.
3 The doctor is necessarily accorded privileges (status and income as well as the privilege of being allowed to examine others' bodies, to inflict pain and to take control of others' bodies). These privileges must be justified by reference to the fact that the doctor is working for the collectivity.

It could be argued, however, that the organisation of the medical profession is merely a particularly effective way of disguising self-interest as selflessness. The restrictions on competitive practices placed on doctors by their own professional body could be seen as a way of keeping prices high in the private sector. The deliberate limitation of the number of students allowed to qualify could be seen as a way of ensuring high demand and low supply of doctors. This is a situation which ensures high rewards for them but is against Parsons' perception of the public's interest.

Ivan Illich and the limits to medicine

In sharp contrast to Parsons, Illich is nothing but critical of the medical profession and the practice of medicine in the West in general. He argues that there are three forms of 'doctor-caused' (iatrogenic) injuries: clinical iatrogenesis, social iatrogenesis and cultural iatrogenesis.

Clinical iatrogenesis refers to damage to individual health caused by the application of medicines by doctors. Recent improvements in health have resulted from better hygiene, housing and nutrition. Medicine has merely introduced drugs with harmful side-effects and which are often addictive and frequently ineffective. They also prolong suffering by keeping hopeless cases alive. The diagnostic procedures used by doctors are often harmful themselves. Illich says out of the 20% of people in research hospitals who suffer iatrogenic disease, 10% of cases result from diagnostic procedures while another 50% result from the drug therapy. Unlike Marxists, Illich does not blame the drug companies' desire to push drugs for these ill-effects or for addiction to therapeutic drugs:

> "To blame the drug industry for prescribed drug addiction is . . . as irrelevant as blaming the Mafia for the use of illicit drugs. The current pattern of overconsumption of drugs . . . can be explained only as a result of the belief that . . . in health care . . . technology can be used to change the human condition according to almost any design."(122)

The mechanistic approach to the human body adopted by modern medicine is harmful. It is fundamentally unsuitable because we do not really know enough about ourselves.

Social iatrogenesis is a product of the bureaucratisation of health care. People are no longer in control of their own illnesses, they are put into hospital and forfeit all control over their own bodies. Discussion of their problems is done by others who ignore them as people and speak in a language they cannot understand. This has resulted from the tremendous authority (regarded by Parsons as necessary) we have given to the medical profession. They have used it to take control of us, to dominate us. Recently feminists have taken up this argument in respect of childbirth. Hilary Graham and Ann Oakley(123) show how the views held about the nature of childbirth by obstetricians on the one hand, and mothers on the other, are quite different and lead to conflict. For the obstetrician, childbirth is a medical problem, not distinguished from other aspects of medical work. Women are treated as cases, to be taken charge of (even to the extent of inducing childbirth in some instances to fit the hospital's need for efficiency in bed utilisation). They are dealt with as quickly as possible and given very limited information about their condition. For the women, childbirth is natural rather than medical. It is an important life event. They desire control over it and over their own bodies, but this is denied by doctors who have adopted a relationship of control. Medicine has alienated women in particular and, for Illich, people in general from their own bodies.

Cultural iatrogenesis "sets in when the medical enterprise saps the will of people to suffer their reality." People can no longer accept the inevitability of pain and death. Instead they become cowards, seeking every means available to avoid these unpleasant facts of life. Consequently, they are reduced as people because, for Illich, facing pain gives inner strength, both to individuals and to whole cultures. The attempt to escape from pain and death through drugs and surgery destroys our moral fortitude and Illich says we are worthy only of contempt.

In general, mankind has tried to improve its own lot, in health and in other areas, but the effect has only been to make things worse:

> "Our prevailing ailments, helplessness and injustice are largely the side-effects of strategies for more and better education, better housing, a better diet and better health."(124)

Mankind has been too proud and we are now suffering the consequences. Green revolutions fail, creating infertile deserts and hunger. Industry creates social inequality and pollution. Medicine engenders drug addiction and ill-health, a society of weak-willed cowards. Illich contrasts this with his non-industrial ideal:

> "A world of optimal and widespread health is obviously a world of minimal and only occasional medical intervention. Healthy people are those who live in healthy homes on a healthy diet in an environment equally fit for birth, growth, work, healing and dying; they are sustained by a culture that enhances the conscious acceptance of limits to population, of ageing, of incomplete recovery and ever-imminent death. Healthy people need minimal bureaucratic interference to mate, give birth, share the human condition and die."(125)

Chapter review

This chapter began by demonstrating that the definition of health and ill-health is not so easy as it might at first appear. There are three very different ways of looking at the question of ill-health; mechanistically, as a definition applied selectively according to criteria which in some ways are more economic than medical, and as a social role which has a function within the total social system.

The following sections moved on to summarise the development of the NHS so that the reader would be able to assess the competing theories of three different perspectives on its nature; the Marxist, the Market Liberal and the Social Democratic. We paid considerably more attention to the Marxist perspective than to the other two as it is of more direct relevance from a sociological as opposed to a political or social policy point of view.

The next section showed how health and ill-health are closely related to social stratification in Britain. While most people think of ill-health as disproportionately found amongst older people (those at the top of the age structure), few also think of it disproportionately affecting those at the bottom of the *class* structure. We examined some of the information available about this and looked at four theories which seek to explain it; the artefact, the social selection, the cultural/behavioural and the structuralist theories.

Next we studied the work of two of the most well-known modern writers on the social sources of mental illness: R D Laing and Thomas Szasz. In each case we criticised some of the flaws, assumptions and gaps in their work while at the same time we introduced knowledge of other areas of the discipline in order to criticise these two writers.

The final section looked at two very different views of the medical profession, from the functionalist Parsons and the libertarian anarchist Illich.

Bibliography

(1) Evan Stark *Introduction* to the special issue on health in Review of Radical Political Economics vol. 9, no. 1 Spring 1977. Quoted in L Doyal *The Political Economy of Health* Pluto Press 1979 p. 35

(2) L Doyal op. cit. p. 28

(3) N Jewson *The disappearance of the Sick Man from Medical Cosmology, 1770–1870* Sociology vol. 10 no. 2 1976 pp. 225–44

(4) *General Household Survey* HMSO 1978 quoted in *Society Today*, New Society, 5 March 1981

(5) P Sedgwick *Psycho-Politics* Pluto Press 1982 p. 29, 30, 32

(6) L Doyal op. cit. p. 35

(7) T Parsons *The Social System* Routledge & Kegan Paul 1951 pp. 430–31

(8) Ibid. p. 436

(9) Ibid. p. 437

(10) Ibid. p. 437

(11) Ibid. p. 437

(12) It is difficult to see how the institutionalisation of the sick fits in here. Wards in hospitals seem like universities of illness. Goffman has demonstrated this very clearly (see, for example, M Haralambos *Sociology: Themes & Perspectives* University Tutorial Press pp. 316–19

(13) Open University *Inequality Within Nations* 1976 Unit 13 *Patterns of Inequality*

(14) L Doyal op. cit. p. 146

(15) *Annual Abstract of Statistics* Central Statistical Office HMSO 1981

(16) L Garner *The NHS: Your Money or Your Life* Penguin 1979, p. 70

(17) Ibid. pp. 63–4

(18) Report of the Royal Commission on the NHS Research Paper number 2 *Management of Financial Resources in the NHS* HMSO 1978 pp. 34–5

(19) Ibid. p. 178

(20) J Tudor Hart *The Inverse Care Law* The Lancet vol. 1, pp. 405–12 1971

(21) L Garner op. cit. pp. 34–5

(22) National Federation of Women's Institutes – evidence to the Royal Commission on the NHS 1977, quoted in Garner ibid. p. 35

(23) See Open University op. cit. p. 15 (per capita expenditure on General Hospitals) and p. 19 (Distribution of General Practitioners)

(24) Figures from D Widgery *Health in Danger* Macmillan 1979, pp. 145–6

(25) D Widgery ibid. p. 146

(26) L Doyal op. cit. p. 199

(27) Ann Howlett and John Ashley *Selective Care* New Society 2 Nov. 1972

(28) A Howlett and John Ashley ibid. p. 270

(29) A Cartwright *Human Relations and Hospital Care* Routledge and Kegan Paul 1964

(30) J Westergaard and H Resler *Class in a Capitalist Society* Heinemann 1975 p. 183

(31) Ibid. p. 183. See also G Room *The Sociology of Welfare* Basil Blackwell, and Martin Robertson Oxford 1979, pp. 152–60 for findings of research into the social distribution of medical care

(32) J Westergaard and H Resler op. cit. p. 178

(33) L Doyal op. cit. p. 39

(34) J Westergaard and H. Resler op. cit. p. 63 and 61

(35) J C Kincaid *Poverty and Equality in Britain* Penguin 1975, see particularly pp. 98–100

(36) F Field, M Meacher, C Pond *To Him Who Hath* Penguin 1977, see p. 58

(37) *Dispensing of Drugs in the NHS* HMSO 1983

(38) Figures from D Widgery op. cit. p. 91

(39) L Doyal op. cit. p. 40 quoting from the Haslemere Group *Who Needs Drug Companies?* Haslemere Group 1975

(40) C V Vaitsos *Patents Revisited: their function in developing countries* in C Cooper (ed) *Science Technology and Development* pp. 76–7, Frank Cass 1973

(41) C Thunhurst *It Makes You Sick* Pluto Press 1982

(42) The percentage of the total NHS bill spent on drugs moved from 8.4% in 1950 to 10.1% in 1969. In 1977 the drugs bill was £596 million, the number of prescriptions written per person by GP's rose from 4.96 to 6.99 between 1949 and 1974. Sources: Widgery op. cit. p. 85, Lancet Volume II 1978 p. 946 and DHSS Health and Personal Social Services Statistics for England, 1975

(43) I Kennedy *The Unmasking of Medicine* Allen and Unwin 1981

(44) I Illich *Limits to Medicine* Marion Boyars London 1976

(45) L Doyal op. cit. pp. 268–9

(46) J Rakusen in H Roberts (ed) *Women, Health and Reproduction* pp. 75–109 Routledge & Kegan Paul 1981 argues that it is used in the Third World because, being injectable, it does not rely on women taking it themselves. It can be administered by the authorities in their own interests

(47) In Columbia in 1968 the imported chemical constituent of Valium was overpriced by 6584%, according to C Vaitsos op. cit. p. 86 and drug prices in India are 357% higher than in Europe, according to Thunhurst op. cit. p. 42

(48) D Widgery op. cit. pp. 91–2

(49) L Doyal op. cit. p. 36

(50) L Garner op. cit. p. 177

(51) D Widgery op. cit. p. 97

(52) L Garner op. cit. p. 176 relates how the number of hysterectomies performed in Saskatchewan jumped by 72% after the introduction of an insurance system which reimbursed the doctor. The operation was simply done, more often in patients *already* in care

(53) L Doyal op. cit. p. 180

(54) G Room op. cit. p. 100 quoting D Lees *Economics and Non-Economics of Health Services* Three Banks Review number 110 1976 p. 12

(56) R M Titmus *War & Social Policy* 1963 pp. 85–6 Allen & Unwin London, quoted Room op. cit. p. 64

(57) G Room op. cit. p. 102

(58) Particularly J O'Connor *The Fiscal Crisis of the State* 1973 St Martin's Press NY

(59) G Room op. cit. pp. 44–5

(60) R Miliband *The State in Capitalist Society* Weidenfeld & Nicholson 1969

(61) N Poulantzas *The Problem of the Capitalist State* in R Blackburn (ed) *Ideology in the Social Sciences* Fontana 1972 pp. 238–62

(62) Ibid. p. 295

(63) H Wilson *The Labour Government 1964–70: A Personal Record* Weidenfeld and Nicholson & Michael Joseph 1971

(64) Ibid. p. 37

(65) Garner op. cit. p. 61

(66) For example V Carstairs et al. *Distribution of Hospital Patients by Social Class* Health Bulletin Vol. 24 No. 3 1966

(67) P Townsend & N Davidson *Inequalities in Health: The Black Report* Penguin, Harmondsworth 1982 p. 51

(68) Ibid.

(69) The following information comes from Townsend op. cit. p. 74

(70) Information from W Logan and A Cushion *Morbidity Statistics from General Practice* London HMSO 1958–62 Quoted in Room op. cit. p. 154

(71) P Townsend & N Davidson *Inequalities in Health: The Black Report* 1982 Penguin Harmondsworth op. cit.

(72) Source Table 1 p. 217 ibid.

(73) As above

(74) Ibid. p. 74

(75) See, for example, Goldthorpe et al. *Social Mobility and Class Structure in Modern Britain* Clarendon Press Oxford 1980

(76) T Parsons *The Social System* The Free Press New York 1951

(77) K Davis and W E Moore *Some Principles of Stratification* in R Bendix & S M Lipset (eds) *Class Status and Power* RKP second edition 1967

(78) K Roberts *Leisure* Longman 1970 p. 27

(79) Townsend & Davidson p. 127 op. cit.

(80) P Townsend in *Poverty in the United Kingdom* criticises Oscar Lewis, one of the main subscribers to this theory, on the grounds of merely vaunting middle class prejudices, of imprecision in his deliberation of the culture of poverty, of using poor methodology, of reaching conclusions inconsistent with evidence, and of not really identifying a sub-culture at all but merely a set of norms and values which are a short-term response to a particular situation rather than being the product of socialisation.

(81) In 1980, 48 miners were killed, 128 construction workers, 109 merchant seamen and 17 quarry workers. The total number of fatal accidents was 700 (*Annual Abstract of Statistics*, 1982 p. 90, HMSO)

(82) 1972 Report of the Committee on Safety at Work. Patrick Kennedy in *The Hazards of Work* Pluto Press 1973 estimates *10* million per year

(83) From the *1970–72 Decennial Supplement on Occupational Mortality* OPCS HMSO 1978 – figures based on the 1971 census

(84) Doyal op. cit. p. 76 quoting from *New Scientist* 3 Oct. 1974

(85) J Gray *The Psychology of Fear and Stress* 1971 Weidenfeld London

(86) R J Meyer and R J Haggerty *Streptococcal Infections* in Families Pediatrics 29: 539–44 1962

(87) Op. cit. p. 21

(88) L Srole *Medical Health in the Metropolis* McGraw-Hill NY 1962

(89) T S Langer & S T Michael *Life Stress and Mental Health* Collier-Macmillan 1963 – a second volume on the same study written by some of the original researchers. These authors chose 10 possible stress-causing factors, including parental quarrelling and divorce, work and money worries, friendship patterns and so on

(90) Men spend 55%, working women 71% and other women 87% of their weekday time in the house – M Young and P Willmott *The Symmetrical Family* Routledge & Kegan Paul 1973

(91) 47 women compared with 20 men in every 1000 suffer from anxiety neurosis, for example, according to Lesley Garner's estimate – op. cit. p. 73

(92) J W B Douglas *The Home and the School* Panther 1969 p. 61 (first published 1964)

(93) T McKeown in *The Role of Medicine* Basil Blackwell 1979 demonstrates this: see table p. 92

(94) J Rowles *On the Limitations of Modern Medicine* Science Medicine and Man Vol. I 1973 pp. 1–30 – quoted Doyal op. cit. p. 60

(95) The Committee was set up in 1979 with representatives from the medical and scientific committees as well as the DHSS, Food and Agriculture

Department and nutritionists. The report is detailed in the *Sunday Times* 3 July 1983

(96) Though the percentage of people who smoke in all social classes has gone down since the early 1970's, the average number smoked per person has gone up, especially for women (Social Trends 1983 op. cit.) J Townsend *Smoking and Class* New Society 30 March 1978, shows that the richest 20% of couples without children spent 3.6% of their income on cigarettes in 1961 and 1.9% in 1975, while the poorest spent 4.4% in 1961 and 4.0% in 1975. Couples with one child/two children also saw an overall drop but an increased gap between these years. Deaths from lung cancer and bronchitis have increased among married women (who are smoking more) and remained stable or decreased among men (who are smoking less) between 1961 and 1971

(97) *New Scientist* 17 April 1975 p. 115

(98) P Wilby *Smoked Out by Numbers* New Society 11 December 1975, p. 590

(99) M H Brenner *Foetal, Infant and Maternal Mortality During Periods of Economic Instability* International Journal of Health Services 3, 1973, 2 and *Estimating the Social Costs of National Economic Policy* Joint Economic Committee US Congress, US government printing office Washington DC 1976 and *Health Costs and Benefits of Economic Policy* International Journal of Health Services 7, 1977, 4

(100) J Fox and D Goldblatt *1982 Longitudinal Study – Socio-Demographic and Mortality Differentials* 1971–75 OPCS HMSO

(101) S Kasl and S Cobb *Physiological Changes in Men Whose Jobs were Abolished* Journal of Psychosomatic Research Vol. 18 1974

(102) R D Laing *Self and Others* first published in 1961 by Tavistock Publications. Also *The Divided Self* Tavistock Publications 1960 expounded these theories

(103) R D Laing and A Esterson *Sanity, Madness and the Family* Tavistock Publications 1964

(104) R D Laing *The Politics of Experience and the Bird of Paradise* Harmondsworth Penguin 1967 p. 104, 106

(105) Laing ibid. and *The Dialectics of Liberation* Penguin 1968

(106) Interview with *The Times* 4 Oct. 1972

(107) Laing *Sanity, Madness and The Family* op. cit. p. 121

(108) Ibid. pp. 127–9

(109) T Szasz *The Myth of Mental Illness* Paladin 1973, first published by Secker and Warburg Ltd. 1962

(110) Ibid. p. 27

(111) Ibid. p. 30

(112) Ibid. p. 58

(113) Ibid. p. 241

(114) Ibid. p. 255

(115) Ibid. p. 69

(116) L Garner op. cit.

(117) T Parsons *The Social System* Routledge & Kegan Paul 1951

(118) I Illich *Limits to Medicine* Marion Boyars 1976

(119) D Widgery *Health in Danger* op. cit. quoting a reply to a Parliamentary Question and evidence in New Society 15 Jan. 1976, p. 112 *Who Becomes Doctors?* K. Cruickshank

(120) T Parsons op. cit. p. 435

(121) Ibid. p. 464

(122) I Illich op. cit. p. 73

(123) H Graham and A Oakley *Competing Ideologies of Reproduction: Medical and Maternal Perspectives on Pregnancy* in H Roberts (ed) *Women, Health and Reproduction* Routledge and Kegan Paul, 1981

(124) Ibid. p. 264

(125) Ibid. p. 275

I acknowledge my indebtedness to Peter Sedgwick's book *Psycho-Politics* Pluto Press 1982 for many of the comments in the section on mental illness.

5 The sociology of the mass media

Introduction

The mass media have been defined as comprising:

> "the institutions and techniques by which specialised social groups disseminate symbolic content to large heterogeneous and geographically dispersed audiences".(1)

Some writers date the birth of the mass media from the beginnings of the mass-circulation press in the last century, others date it from the invention of the printing press with moveable metal type in the mid fifteenth century. The interpretation of the word 'large' in the definition is the cause of the disagreement. Whichever point of view is correct, it is clear that the media in their various forms are an important part of modern industrial society.

Television ownership has become the norm in Britain: in 1951, 1.5 million TV licences were issued, by 1978 there were 18 million. Television viewing now forms the largest single leisure time occupation, though this differs across the age structure as the table shows:

Average number of hours of TV viewed each week(2)

Age Group	*1975*	*1976*	*1977*
5–14	24.0	22.0	22.0
15–19	19.3	18.4	17.6
20–29	18.2	19.1	18.2
30–40	18.4	19.0	17.9
50+	19.6	20.4	20.0

The rise of television has led to a parallel decline in cinema-going. The seating capacity of British cinemas dropped from 3.8 million in 1934 to 1.8 million in 1966, with a corresponding drop in regular attendance across the social class scale(3).

Long-term information in radio listening is difficult to acquire, but between 1976 and 1980, there has been an upward trend. This is probably due to the growth of local radio stations. By October 1982, there were 37 independent and 36 BBC local radio stations in the UK. The four BBC national programmes have most listeners. The average amount of time spent listening to the radio per week was 8 hours and 44 minutes in 1976 and 9 hours and 20 minutes in 1980(4).

Book sales, too, have increased dramatically since the war. The increase has been eleven-fold in the 30 years to 1964, to give a total of over 77 million books sold in that year. Readership of newspapers is large but relatively stable. *The Sun* had a circulation of 3.9 million in 1981, *The Mirror* 3.4 million, *The Express* 2.2 million, *The Mail* 1.9 million and *The Star* 1.4 million. The major weekly women's magazines each have a circulation approaching 1.5 million, while monthly magazines achieve nearer 0.5 million on average. Children's and young people's magazines sell between 100 000 and 400 000 per week. The Beano was the top seller in the second half of 1980 with a circulation of 374 000.

Overall expenditure on books, newspapers, and magazines seems to be dropping (£985 million in 1971, £916 million in 1981 in the UK at 1975 prices). Weekly magazines in general, have suffered about a 40% drop in circulation during the last 16 years, a fact which must account for most of the reduction.

Recent technological and commercial developments are likely to change the nature of media use. Video cassette recorders, for example, were found in more than 12% of homes in Britain in 1983. This seems to have led to a drop in the audience for broadcast programmes. In 1981 the average viewing figure per person was 23.1 hours watching broadcast television; 1982 saw this fall to 20.3 hours, and the figure is still falling.

This chapter is divided into two main sections. The first examines research into the effects of the media on behaviour, particularly on *violent* behaviour. This topic is currently the subject of public debate. The concern is that ease of availability of 'video nasties' will lead to an increase in the levels of real violence. As well as reviewing attempts to answer the question of whether viewing violence on the TV screen leads to its practice in real life, we will use this section to contrast psychological, laboratory-based approaches to the question with sociological field studies. This comparison should help students appreciate the differences between the two disciplines, and provide useful examples on the relationship between academic perspective, methodology and the validity of the research results.

The second section examines work concerning the influence of the media on attitudes. The distinction made between attitudes and behaviour is in some ways artificial, as attitude change often leads to behavioural change. However, the 'attitudes' studied by different researchers are of many different kinds. This means that a separate examination of this question will allow us to chart some of the changes that have taken place in mass-media research and theory in recent years. We will divide our examination of the relationship between the media and attitudes into four parts as shown in the following diagram(5).

	Short term effects of exposure to the media on the individual	Long term effects of the media on the political culture
Deliberate attempt to influence attitudes by the originator of the message transmitted by the mass media	**1**	**2**
Non-deliberate influence on attitudes	**3**	**4**

In box **1** we will review some of the early work on the influence that party political broadcasts have on voters' attitudes. We will also present a case study of the deliberate use of the media by a politician who attempted to influence people's attitudes on the issue of race and immigration. These are both situations where there is a conscious effort to use the media to influence people, even though the effect may be short lived.

In box **2** we will try to assess the influence of newspapers' political perspectives (which do not pretend to be neutral) on their readership, and hence on the British political culture.

Boxes **3** and **4** will concentrate on the unconscious bias which, it is suggested, comes from within the media institutions themselves. Box **3** will examine the proposition that because of its procedures for selection and presentation of news and because of the world view of journalists, editors and programme makers, the effect of the media, particularly TV exposure, on the individual is to structure his/her perception of the important issues of the day. In the final section we will deal with the question of whether the media sustain the present socio-political system in this country and abroad by a *consistently* biased and 'ideological' output.

We are aware that there is some artificiality in dividing individual attitudes from political culture and the short term from the long. Political culture has been defined by Alan Ball, in his *Modern Politics and Government*, as comprising "attitudes, emotions and values of society that relate to the political system and political issues". It would seem clear that changes in individuals' attitudes will both reflect and promote change in those 'of society'. At the same time, what may appear transient changes often have long term implications in a variety of areas. We will see this when we examine the effects of Enoch Powell's 'Whip Hand' speech which had a temporary effect on attitudes towards immigration and race but more lasting results in terms of the British political culture as well as Powell's own career.

We present the material in this way, then, not so much in the belief that media effects naturally fall into such a scheme but for pedagogical reasons. We believe the presentation of a general structure prior to consideration of the details will enable the reader to acquire an overall view of the issues and, using this as a 'map', to achieve more accurate and rapid understanding and recall.

The mass media and behaviour

The media, particularly cinema, TV and 'video-nasties', have been the subject of considerable criticism concerning their adverse effects on people's behaviour, especially with regard to sex and violence. We have read of people who, on watching sex or violence on TV, went out and copied what they had seen. H J Eysenck and D K B Elias in *Sex, Violence and the Media*(6) quote the case of Ian Brady and Myra Hindley who were convicted of torturing and murdering a ten year old girl (having recorded her screams and pleas in the process). They were in possession of sadistic literature at home. Another case involved a man who, while trying to rape a woman, was making the guttural sounds he had heard in the film *The Exorcist*. Another example concerned a 16 year-old boy who armed himself with a knife, broke into a neighbouring house and attacked a sleeping woman in her bedroom. An identical event had occurred in a *Starksy and Hutch* episode on TV just hours before.

When we read of such cases in the newspapers, we are often led to believe that the literature, film or TV programme 'caused' the behaviour in question. Things are not so simple. Often, this interpretation is one put on the events by the defence counsel in the court case that follows in order to shift the blame from the accused on to the media. The question arises as to whether similar acts would have been committed *without* exposure to the medium concerned. Furthermore, the causal factor which such stories imply – imitation – is only one of several possible responses to media exposure. A second possible response is *sensitisation* to violence or perversion, ie one is shocked by the scenes and the likelihood of indulging in them oneself is also reduced. The *cathartic* effect would also lead to a reduction in such behaviour. Catharsis is the release or dissipation of strong emotion, here through exposure to violence or sex scenes which act as an outlet for our own energies in these directions. On the other hand, two further responses are possible which would lead to a tendency to commit violent or illegal sex acts and which are not normally discussed in explanations of events like those described above. These are *de-sensitisation* and *disinhibition*. The first suggests that exposure to media sex and violence makes one unfeeling about the humiliation and pain involved. The second assumes that our 'natural' instincts are curbed by inhibitions that stop us realising them and that these inhibitions are broken down when the media portray the things we would really like to do as normal and acceptable. We begin to think of them as not so bad after all. With these two responses the effect of the media is thought to be the same as with imitation (more violence, etc.) but the relationship between exposure and action is both less direct and less immediate. Let us examine some of the more rigorous attempts that have been made to explore the links between the media and violent behaviour.

Experimental laboratory studies

Bandura, Ross and Ross(7) conducted an experiment into imitative behaviour with ninety-six 3 to 6 year-olds from a university crèche. These children were each randomly allocated to one of the following four experimental conditions:

a Control – children saw no aggressive adult.
b Children viewed real adult attacking a bozo doll with a mallet.
c Children viewed a 3.5 minute colour film of an adult attacking a bozo doll with a mallet.
d Children viewed a 3.5 minute colour film of an adult dressed as a cat attacking a bozo doll with a mallet against the background of brightly coloured trees and butterflies (a cartoon).

(A bozo doll is a 150 cm high self-righting inflatable doll.)

Immediately after this experience, the child was put in a room with a variety of toys. These were removed when the child had begun to play with them in order to produce feelings of frustration. The child was then placed in a room with dart guns, balls, a bozo doll and a mallet. After a brief settling down period, the adult left the room.

The idea was that the children would not normally think of attacking the bozo doll with the mallet and therefore if they did, they were clearly imitating the violence they had seen in real life or mediated by film.

The results were as follows:

In Group **b** 88% of the children copied the posture, words and actions of the bozo attacker;
c 88% of the children copied the posture, words and actions of the bozo attacker;
d 79% of the children copied the posture, words and actions of the bozo attacker;

Bandura's argument is that film models are as effective in teaching aggression as real life models, and these results seem to confirm this. Girls were found to be less imitative of both real and film models than boys. This might have been due to stronger inhibitions about expressing aggression.

In another experiment involving reward and punishment for the filmed bozo attacker, Bandura found that children are more likely to imitate aggressive behaviour they see rewarded than that which they see punished.

On the face of it, Bandura's results lend credibility to both the imitation and disinhibition theories of the effect of screen violence. The problems are as follows:

1 It is unclear whether the effect of a film viewed alone in a laboratory is the same as that viewed at home with parents or peers(8).
2 The group studied in these experiments, middle class nursery school children, were not representative of the population at large.
3 A bozo attack is hardly representative of the violence committed either in the media or in real life by either children or adults. It remains an open question as to whether aggression against a human would be similarly imitated.
4 The Hawthorne effect is clearly a problem here – the children are anxious to please and, although it is unstated, it will be clear what is expected of them so we should not be surprised when they do it.
5 It would seem obvious that even the children who have had no model to imitate will pick up the mallet and hit the bozo doll – what else *can* one do with a self-righting bozo doll?

Similar results to Bandura's have been obtained by other laboratory studies. One example is A E Siegel's comparison of children's behaviour after watching a violent Woody Woodpecker cartoon and a non-violent film(9). Another is M A Hanratty's study of children copying a filmed attack on a human clown and a host of others(10). In general, it is true to say that the laboratory-based studies tend to demonstrate that exposure to filmed violence will produce it in the subject. However, the criticisms of Bandura also apply to the rest of them. In addition . . .

> ". . . there appears to be considerable confusion as to what is filmed aggression. For some it is an adult hitting a bozo doll, for others a prize fight, and for [others] . . . it is Westerns or war shows. Few investigators, if any, seem to be concerned that different types of filmed aggression will have different effects on different types of children."(11)

Field studies

Hilde Himmelweit with her book *TV and the Child*(12) provides one of the classics of the 'effects of TV' research effort in this country. Originally intended to be an investigation into the effects of TV on children's schoolwork and homework, it was quickly adopted by those who wished to show that TV did *not* produce violent behaviour as evidence to demonstrate exactly this. Himmelweit compared two sets of children matched for age, sex, intelligence and class who lived in London, Portsmouth, Sunderland and Bristol. The first set of children were TV watchers of at least 3 months' standing. The second set were non-viewers. The total number of children studied was 1854 in two age groups – 10 to 11 and 13 to 14. In a second survey, a group of children was studied over a one-year period during which time they began watching TV (due to the setting up of reception facilities in the locality). In this way she was able to avoid any possible differences between the two groups in the earlier experiment which were unrelated to TV viewing. The children in both studies were given questionnaires designed to assess personality, maladjustment and emotional stability. They were also asked to keep a diary which gave the researchers information about hobbies and homework. Teachers were asked to assess the sociability of the children and parents, teachers and children were interviewed by the researchers.

Few 'effects' were revealed: those with and without TV were very similar. Viewers tended to go to bed later but spent as much time asleep as non-viewers who would read in bed. Viewers were more interested in ready-made entertainment (such as comics and clubs) but this was probably not caused by TV – rather it was a reason for acquiring one. As far as violence was concerned, there was no evidence of a cathartic effect. Indeed, there were signs of tension and anxiety while the children watched violence and they claimed to have difficulty in falling asleep and to have nightmares after watching violent programmes. However, there was no evidence of an increase in violent behaviour either.

Eysenck and Elias, strong proponents of the 'violent effect' school, argue that there are serious flaws in Himmelweit's study:

1 Viewers did not see much violence in these strictly controlled days of early TV broadcasting. Conversely, non-viewers were exposed to violence in the cinema and in comics.
2 As TV had only just been introduced, there was no chance of long-term effects showing up. The effects of disinhibition and desensitisation take some time to become apparent.
3 As the major focus of Himmelweit's research was not on violence, this aspect received only superficial attention. The only measure of aggressiveness was teachers' responses to a closed-ended questionnaire about behavioural characteristics.
4 In a field study of this type it is impossible to control the variables in personality characteristics between those with TV's and those without them sufficiently well to allow accurate assessment of the effect of the variable of interest, ie exposure to TV.

A field study which was *specifically* orientated to the question of TV and violence was conducted by L D Eron(13). He interviewed the parents of 875 children between 8 and 9 years of age about their children's viewing habits. Their answers were scored according to the number of violent programmes watched. Eron then asked the classmates of the same children a series of questions designed to measure the amount of aggressiveness displayed by the subjects in school. There was an association between having a preference for violent programmes and being aggressive at school, but the correlation was only 0.21 (0 = no correlation, 1.0 = total coincidence of the two factors) and only for boys. For girls there was no significant correlation. Interestingly, those who watched *least* TV were identified most often as aggressive. This fact could be used to support the sensitisation or catharsis arguments were it not for the findings about the type of programme viewed. The probable reason for it is that children who prefer violent programmes are simply more selective in their viewing habits.

The main problem with this study is the fact that the identification of a correlation does not establish causation. That watching violence on TV causes aggressive behaviour is only *one* way of interpreting the findings. Another would be that more aggressive boys prefer violent TV programmes. The only way to get round the problem of establishing the direction of causation is to conduct a *longitudinal* study (ie one which studies changes over time) in order to discover which came first – aggressiveness or viewing TV violence. If violent TV programmes cause aggressiveness, early exposure to them should result in such behaviour in real life later on. Recognising these difficulties, Eron conducted a longitudinal study ten years after the first(14). He located 427 of the children in the earlier study who were now between 18–19 years of age. The same technique was used, though this time they identified their own favourite programmes and the questions asked of peers were slightly modified. The findings were that there was indeed a correlation (of 0.31) between early preference for violent programmes and later aggressiveness, but no correlation between early aggression and later preference for TV violence. The graphs on p. 238 illustrate the relationship between the two factors.

Again there was no correlation at all between the two variables for girls. Eron now felt able to assert that TV violence *does* cause aggressiveness in males, and suggested that imitation or modelling is the reason for this. The absence of any significant correlation for girls could be explained by the relative sparseness of aggressive females on TV for the girls to imitate. An alternative explanation would be that their gender role may inhibit displays of aggression amongst the girls.

A number of flaws exist in Eron's work which critics have been quick to identify(15):

1 The people in the second study who identified themselves as liking TV violence were usually different from those who were identified by their parents as liking it in the first study. This suggests that the measures involved in the studies were inaccurate, particularly parental assessment of the child's viewing habits.

2 Eron's categorisation of programmes as violent or non-violent seems to

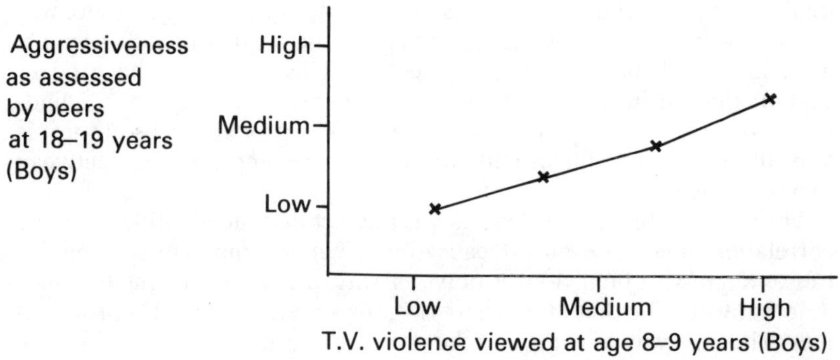

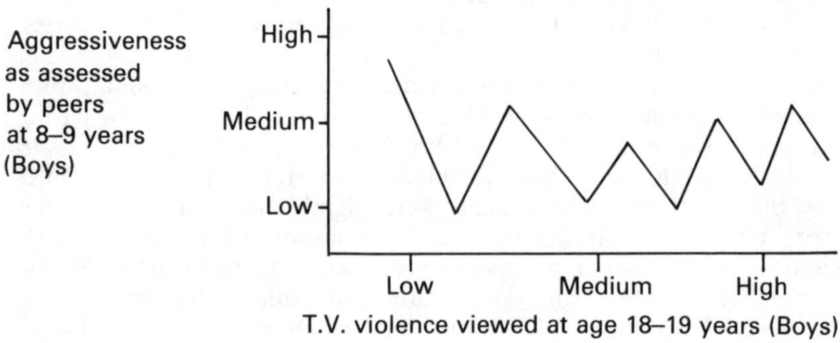

be rather idiosyncratic – *The Lone Ranger* and *Perry Mason* are non-violent, *Have Gun, Will Travel* and *77 Sunset Strip* are violent, according to him. A rather careful content analysis of all programmes would be necessary to improve on this intuitive approach.

3 It is unclear how the child would imitate the behaviour of the characters in *77 Sunset Strip* in the classroom. Aggressive behaviour, as identified by school mates, included "does not obey the teacher" and "gives dirty looks and sticks his tongue out at other boys" – behaviour which is rarely seen displayed by the heroes of American serials. Eysenck at least is happy to concur with the overall findings of the study in spite of these methodological difficulties(16), it is difficult to see any grounds for this other than the fact that Eron's findings happen to coincide with his own view.

A study by J D Halloran and others(17) entitled *Television and Delinquency* attempted to assess the role of TV in producing delinquent behaviour by comparing the viewing habits of delinquents and non-delinquents. They selected a sample of probationers from the Midlands between the ages of 10 and 20 years. In all, there were 281 males and 53 females. A matched sample of working class adolescents was also selected. The first group was interviewed by their probation officers about TV viewing while the second was interviewed by Halloran and his team. The findings were as follows:

1 Both groups watched TV for about 5 hours per day (the girls watched less.)
2 Both groups liked broadly similar types of programmes.
3 Both groups stated the same reasons for watching TV (mainly for information, then for relaxation.)
4 Fewer probationers stated that they watched TV in order to talk about it later with friends.
5 More male probationers than male non-probationers stated that they liked exciting programmes. On specific questioning about aggressive, murder and war films, there proved to be no significant difference between the two groups.
6 Fewer male probationers than male non-probationers stated that they watched educational and cultural programmes.

These findings are inconclusive. The only difference of real interest between the two groups is the *stated* avoidance of informative programmes and preference for exciting ones among male probationers. Noble(18) interprets Halloran's data as suggesting that probationers might be using the characters on TV as a surrogate family. Delinquents were found to watch soap operas such as *Coronation Street* and *Crossroads* more frequently than non-probationers. As delinquents tend to have poor relationships with their own families(19), this preference could allow the probationers to "enjoy at least surrogate interaction with the characters they feel they know".(20) We learn very little about TV and violence, and we should be wary of assuming too much about the differences in behavioural characteristics of delinquents and non-delinquents. Interactionist approaches to deviance stress that there is not really much difference between those who have been *labelled* as deviant and the rest of us, normal people are simply those fortunate enough not to have been stigmatised.

A more recent study was conducted by W A Belson and published under the title *TV Violence and the Adolescent Boy*(21). Belson interviewed 1565 London boys between 13 and 16 years of age. They were asked about the number and type of violent acts they had committed over the previous 6 months and then about how much TV violence they had been exposed to over the previous 12 years (by estimating how often they had watched 68 programmes which had been assessed for the degree and type of violence depicted). The direction of causation problem was avoided by this retrospective examination of TV viewing habits: above average exposure to violent programmes in the past could explain present aggressive behaviour, all other things being equal. It was found, in fact, that the boys with high exposure to violent TV were more likely to have committed violent acts. Those boys with high exposure and violent acts were then compared to boys with low exposure and few or no violent acts to try to eliminate other violence – affecting factors from the study. After this process had been completed, the correlation between exposure and violent acts was reduced but still significant. The conclusion of the study was that violence becomes viewed as a legitimate problem-solving device when heroes (such as Starsky and Hutch) are seen to use it in this way. It becomes seen by the boys as a normal fact of life. Desensitisation, disinhibition and imitation can all be said to be occurring.

The main problems with Belson's work are methodological. The boys were asked to remember the amount and type of TV programmes they watched up to 12 years prior to the study. This is a different task and one which allows room for other factors to affect the process of recall (an aggressive boy might recall watching violent programmes more than non-violent ones). Furthermore, self-reporting of acts of violence is prone to more deliberate exaggeration or minimisation on the part of the boy who might either want to boast about or be ashamed of his exploits. It seems clear that the results of any study into the effects of exposure to TV violence will depend largely on the methodology employed by that study, as those we have examined here demonstrate. Reliance on laboratory experiments tend to indicate an effect while field studies tend to be more equivocal in their findings and often contradict each other because of the differences in method.

The key problem which field studies face is that of controlling the variables to ensure that it really is exposure to the media which has caused an increase in real violence. Measurement of even the two main variables being examined presents profound difficulties. In the laboratory, the attempt to control all the variables has created a highly artificial environment in which subjects know they are being watched, they have a good idea what is expected of them and factors which might affect their behaviour in the real world are not present.

The debate between laboratory versus field is part of a broader debate between the disciplines of psychology and sociology. Psychologists argue that a true understanding of the effects of the media can only be achieved through in-depth study of particular individuals. Sociologists, they say, adopt a perspective which is too macroscopic to yield useful results. Proper explanation requires reference to and attempts to prove or disprove theories about the motivation behind an individual's behaviour. The problem with sociological research is that there is "an almost complete absence of psychological theory in the design of the experiments or interpretation of the empirical data".(22)

Experimental laboratory studies allow all the factors to be measured and controlled so that theories can be tested, revised and finally confirmed.

For the sociologist, a laboratory experiment such as Bandura's does not tell us very much about who watches violent programmes (or any other type) in real life or why. Viewing and reading habits, as well as responses to media exposure, are shaped by socialisation in infancy and by experiences in later life which are themselves the products of social forces, often class or gender related ones. An individual's response to a violent scene will largely depend on his or her prior attitudes to violence which will be the result of socialisation into norms of behaviour and values about displaying aggression. Belson shows, for example, that 38% of the lower working class boys he interviewed reported committing acts of serious violence in the 6 months prior to the interview, compared with only 13% of middle class boys. Microscopic psychological methods are not particularly suited to revealing the reasons for this difference, which is rooted in macroscopic social processes.

A further point is that an interpretation of the media violence which may or may not cause real violence as being *only* people hitting or killing each other is too simplistic. In a competitive and materialistic culture such as ours or the American one, a programme like *Sale of the Century* may heighten desire for material things, produce envy, increase frustration and lead to greater levels of theft and violence. Similarly, the *real* violence on the news (whose effects are rarely studied) may have a far greater impact than pseudo-violence:

"If the media are playing a role in the alleged escalation of social violence, it is almost certainly not *Z Cars, The Virginian, Callan* or *Codename* which are 'responsible' . . . It is, for example, the only too real bodies of only too real Vietnamese floating down an all too real Cambodian river."(23)

By the same token, in extracting violent episodes from the context in which they are found, the psychologist may ignore the overall 'message' of a programme. Fiske and Hartley write:

"TV violence can be thought of as essentially conservative in its effect rather than destructive. This is because it is difficult to avoid resolving a fist fight or a shoot-out: the conflict is resolved one way or another, usually of course, in favour of the socially esteemed morality. Often one or two esteemed but expendable personae (such as women) are done away with before the ultimately inefficient villain gets what's coming to him in the last scene. But this merely enlarges his threat and therefore puffs up the satisfaction that is felt when he drops groaning out of camera shot . . . TV violence too often disposes of really intractable sources of social tension, dislocation or conflict with a neat, bloodless hole in the villain's heart."(24)

These broader social issues and effects are missed by the psychologist whose vision is limited by the four walls of the psychology department laboratory. The adoption of what sociologists themselves regard as a broader perspective results in quite different findings. It is hoped that the contrast between the psychological and sociological approaches presented here will be of use to the student not only in the study of the mass media, but in connection with more general issues concerning academic disciplines, perspectives and the methodologies consequent upon them.

The mass media and attitudes

The sociology of the mass media is surely one of the most diversified fields within the discipline. While some studies have concentrated their attention on the audience, others have examined the media institutions themselves and the process of content-production. Further studies have traced patterns of ownership and control of the companies involved to establish how this might affect production. The effects which the media have can be considered either at the level of the individual or at a broader societal level. Of particular concern at the first level have been questions of the power of the media to change attitudes and (more recently) the effect which previously held attitudes of the audience have on that power. At the second level the role of the media in promoting or inhibiting political and social change have been major issues. Some authors have studied output originating from with media institutions (editorials, articles, fictional programmes), others have concerned themselves with situations in which the media merely transmit a message which has originated from outside (eg a party political broadcast). The much-studied subject of news production includes elements of both, for while news happens outside the media institutions, those institutions must select and process it. To impose some order on this confusion of perspectives, this section will be divided into four. As we explained in the introduction, these are the four 'boxes' created by the twin axes of (**1**) deliberate-non-deliberate attempts to influence attitudes through the media, and (**2**) short-term, individual effects-long-term effects on the political culture.

Let us begin, then with the first of our four boxes.

Deliberate attempts to influence the attitudes of individuals in the short term through the media

Much of the work of political scientists in this area has concentrated on the success of electoral campaigns in the media in changing people's attitudes to parties, politicians and policies. J Trenaman and D McQuail conducted a study of the 1959 election for just this purpose. Entitled *TV and the Political Image*(25), it is seen as a classic because that election marked the beginning of TV electoral coverage. Reporting of electoral campaigns did not begin until 1958 and until the 1959 election, news bulletins and programmes which might have affected the outcome were cancelled. This, combined with the fact that large-scale television ownership also began at about this time, meant that a new and potentially very important development had occurred which demanded academic attention.

Trenaman and McQuail's method involved careful measurement of attitudinal change among a panel of respondents in two Yorkshire constituencies to see how it correlated with exposure to Labour and Conservative Party political broadcasts. The results showed that the impact of the campaign was modest. TV did not change what people considered to be the important issues in the campaign, nor did it dramatically change people's support for the parties. The only discernible effect was that people became better informed about the respective party policies.

This study adopted what has since been called the hypodermic approach to media influence, common in early research. The media, in this case the television, are seen as 'jabbing' the audience with a message which they, the audience, do or do not react to. Most studies which adopted this approach tended, like Trenaman and McQuail's, to discover little effect in terms of attitudinal change. It became clear to social scientists working in the field, that this was too simplistic. The audience cannot be considered as an homogeneous whole because different people *selectively* expose themselves to the media for different reasons and react differently as a result. People might watch TV because they wanted entertainment, information, relief from the tedium of everyday life or simply because they could not be bothered to switch it off. They might give it great attention or very little, or perceive and remember only those parts they agree or identify with. As a result of this (far from astounding) discovery of selective exposure perception and retention, a new technique was established called the uses and gratifications approach. As well as asking what the media do to people it asked what different people do with the media.

A second study of the same two constituencies was undertaken during the 1964 election which took this new development into account as well as seeking to replicate the findings of the earlier study. Jay G Blumler and D McQuail's *TV in Politics: Its Uses and Influence*(26) also took a panel of respondents from the electoral register, 748 of whom were successfully interviewed on three successive occasions; before, during and after the campaign. The enquiry was deliberately limited to short-term effects produced by party political broadcasts, the long-term influences of TV exposure being considered too difficult to assess accurately. Adopting the uses and gratifications approach meant that they needed to ask questions which the earlier study had not:

1 Why do people bother to watch party political broadcasts?

2 Do the different motivations for watching affect people's susceptibility to influence?
3 Do viewers look for confirmation of their own views or are they judging between competing policies?
4 Do viewers really follow arguments or are they only interested in personality clashes?

On each of the three occasions they were interviewed, respondents were asked about their knowledge of party policies and of issues, their attitudes towards the parties and towards the party leaders. In addition they were each questioned about which political programmes they watched (in order that attitude change could be correlated with degree of exposure to party political broadcasts across the group of respondents), about their degree of interest in the campaign and about their reasons for watching the campaign coverage.

While the earlier study had not sought to distinguish between members of the panel other than in terms of differential exposure to TV and changes in attitude, this one found that there were significantly different types of viewer. There were, for example, vote guidance seekers who used the TV as a source of information by which to judge between the three parties (the Liberals being included in this study). There were the people who wanted their own views reinforced or confirmed. Others had a mixture of motivations and just over half had no political motive, watching political broadcasts because of inertia or because they felt it their duty. While reinforcement seekers (who constituted just less than one quarter of the respondents) tended to watch only the broadcasts of *their* party, the rest watched a mixture. This indicates that party broadcasts do not merely preach to the converted, as many American studies have suggested, but reach the uncommitted and therefore, may have an effect.

The findings on the effects of TV political coverage clearly demonstrate the superiority of the uses and gratifications approach over the hypodermic because it *was* found that the initial predispositions of the individual influenced the effectiveness of the message. Only a uses and gratifications approach can take these into account. Taking each of the four areas of study in turn (knowledge of party policies, knowledge of issues, attitude to parties and image of party leaders), the authors found that knowledge of policies increased as a result of exposure to party broadcasts. While this is far from surprising and confirms the finding of the earlier study, what was interesting was that those who were most knowledgeable prior to the campaign gained most new information from it and that party political broadcasts were more effective than any other source in communicating party policies. As far as motivation for watching and increase in knowledge is concerned, Blumler and McQuail write:

"The detailed figures show that those vote guidance seekers who

> saw relatively few party broadcasts actually learned more about party policies than did some of their more highly exposed counterparts. In this case it seems that those voters for whom information was relevant to a *choice* they had to make managed to obtain it even if their opportunities to do so were limited."(27)

On knowledge of issues, the researchers found that exposure to new issues through party broadcasts and attempts by parties to bring particular issues to the fore had little effect on people. For the public, *social welfare* issues were most important (pensions, housing, employment) and they remained so despite Labour's attempt to push the issue of economic growth and the Conservative's, that of the nuclear deterrent. Reinforcement seekers, though, *were* more likely to acquire knowledge of the new issues and to begin to see them as important.

Concerning attitudes to parties, Blumler and McQuail found that the Liberal Party benefited most, though they had only three broadcasts to five each for Conservative and Labour. Even news coverage of the campaign was beneficial for the Liberals – 27% of the panel either changed allegiance, decided late or did not vote and most of those who changed or decided late moved towards the Liberals. They tended to be individuals with a medium or weak motivation to follow the campaign. Blumler and McQuail write:

> "Three general conclusions may be drawn from these results. Firstly, in promoting favourable impressions of the Liberal Party, TV was a more important medium than, say, the press or the local campaign. Second, in facilitating this shift of opinion, the two most powerful TV variables – the news bulletins and the Liberal broadcasts – worked to a considerable extent in harness, each doing more or less the same job as the other. Third, when the extra contribution of each variable, beyond the area of overlap with the others, was assessed, only TV news proved distinctively effective."(28)

So TV news proved even *more* effective in promoting the Liberal cause than their own broadcasts, an interesting finding in the light of studies to be examined later. Blumler and McQuail explain this fact by the argument that the Liberals were able to reach a large number of uncommitted voters for the first time in 1964 – those who had acquired a TV set. Even for those who had had a TV set for some time the dosage of Liberalism increases dramatically at election time because being such a small party, they are not generally news-worthy. People who were uncommitted would favour the 'middle of the road' Liberal case and would be persuaded to align themselves with Liberal policies and vote for the Party. Similarly, those who had low motivation to watch the broadcasts, who simply watched through inertia, were also more amenable to a moderate line of argument:

> "Whereas opinions of the strongly motivated voters were influenced

by major party propaganda, the politically less keen electors responded favourably to presentation of the Liberal case . . . their receptivity to Liberal Propaganda may have arisen from mistrust of the dominant forces in British politics, which they found embodied in the Conservative and Labour parties."(29)

On the last issue, the images of party leaders, it was found that TV exposure did lead to a reassessment of the relative strengths of the Party leaders. Sir Alec Douglas-Home lost standing and Harold Wilson gained it as did Jo Grimond.

The major new finding of the study, then, was that:

"Public attitudes towards the Liberal Party and its leader became more favourable during the campaign, and in the greater part of the sample this movement of opinion was associated progressively with exposure to election TV."(30)

This was a positivist study in the tradition of what is significantly called political science. While it established correlations on a reasonably accurate basis, its *explanations* (eg of the reasons for Liberal gains) took the form of unsupported hypotheses. It treated the media as neutral carriers of a message originating from the parties themselves, even when it was found that the news programmes were more effective than the Liberal Party at carrying the Liberal message. The study concentrated on the audience rather than the media institutions or personnel. While it escaped the narrow hypodermic approach of the earlier study, one which tended to seriously underestimate the power of the media, Blumler and McQuail's still adopted a restricted definition of effects.

An account of deliberate use of the media to produce short-term changes in individual attitudes (this time about race) was Colin Seymour-Ure's analysis of the effects of Enoch Powell's speech about immigration made in April 1968 when Powell was still a Conservative Midlands MP(31).

Powell made the speech to 85 Birmingham Conservatives but, according to Seymour-Ure, deliberately timed and organised its release so that it would get extensive media coverage. Surveys at the time showed that shorty afterwards, 96% of the population had heard about it. It is also suggested that Powell wrote the speech in such a way as to make it appeal to media personnel as 'newsworthy'. He used anecdotes about the personal experiences of his constituents and strong images which would appeal to the popular imagination. Powell spoke of one constituent whose sons would be leaving the country in 15 or 20 years' time because by then "the black man will have the 'whip-hand' over the white man." Another constituent, a woman, was afraid to go out because of the "wide grinning piccaninnies" who jeered at her and because of blacks who allegedly pushed excreta through her letter box. Powell considered that the high rate of black immigration would lead to a swamping of the country in the near future and civil war between black and white. Immigration must be stopped or Britain would become like the "River Tiber foaming with much blood."

The Press picked out the colourful anecdotes and gave them headline treatment, the speech quickly becoming referred to as 'the Whip-hand speech.' They also picked up the conflict about the content of the speech between Edward Heath, leader of the Conservative Party in opposition, and Powell, an excellent illustration of the media's preference for personalities rather than ideas. The effect on people's attitudes was immediate but short-lived. Gallup polls showed strong support for Powell's views after the speech despite the fact that race and immigration were issues about which there had been little public discussion prior to the speech. This support gradually declined over the following two years. Seymour-Ure writes:

> "Powell's speech, by its very attractiveness to the media in terms of their traditional news values, at least confirmed existing prejudices and possibly invigorated them by its emotive style."(32)

In terms of effects of behaviour, the coverage of the speech led to marches by several groups, including London dockers and LSE students, either for or against the views expressed in the speech. Powell was thrown out of the Shadow Cabinet and was from then on a "newsworthy personality." It is alleged that the speech may also have led to a harder Conservative Party line on immigration.

These findings seem to confirm Peter Golding's comment that:

> "In the short term public opinion may be stirred or moulded almost entirely by the mass media, particularly as a result of campaigns or purposive attempts to rouse feelings on issues where public knowledge may be minimal or dormant."(33)

Seymour-Ure has added the issue of *media preferences* to the assumed media neutrality of Blumler and McQuail. Media personnel themselves have ideas about what makes 'a good read', sells newspapers and constitutes 'news'. The media dislike 'quiet' elections and political harmony. They liked clashes and conflicts, especially ones which can be interpreted as being between personalities. They like issues to be clear-cut and the sides to be clearly divided. They devote their attention to questions like nationalisation, nuclear disarmament and immigration, excluding less contentious ones. Seymour-Ure claims that they also have an obsession with forecasting results which can itself affect people's attitudes and subsequent behaviour. It is not enough, then, to study how the media are 'used', because the media themselves have their own influence on selection and interpretation of content.

In the next section, we will go beyond their search for 'news', and examine the view that the media have an implicit political/ideological standpoint of their own which shapes the political culture in quite a deliberate way in support of sectional interests.

Deliberate attempts to bring about long term changes in the political culture through the media

At this point it is necessary to make a clear distinction between the different types of media because some, such as radio and TV, regard themselves as politically neutral (and have a legal obligation to be so) while others, particularly the press, maintain no such impartiality. As far as party politics is concerned, the TV channels must try to ensure fair coverage for all sides, especially during election periods. From the earliest days the BBC was obliged to refrain from expressing its own opinion on party political matters while the 1954 Television Act required that the commercial companies do the same and also decreed that there should be a balance of opinion represented in televised discussion and debate. Until 1959, television coverage of elections was considered to be anti-democratic, but since that campaign, balance has been carefully maintained by control of the air time given to each party's broadcasts. In the mid-1960's, it became accepted that an 'unbalanced' programme could be transmitted if it was followed by another which presented the other parties' cases. Although television has moved away from the strict counting of minutes devoted to each side (with the exception of party political broadcasts which are still controlled), the various channels still attempt to retain balance and impartiality in party matters. On broader issues such as industrial relations and international affairs, the TV channels are expected to maintain 'due impartiality', ie not to take sides except where the 'public interest' is involved. Thus, no channel is expected in a discussion of Northern Ireland's troubles to give equal weight to the case of an IRA terrorist and that of the British Government.

No such restrictions relate to the press. Most newspapers are Conservative in their political standpoint, with only *The Mirror* being a consistent Labour supporter and *The Morning Star* supporting the Communist line. Some, like *The Guardian* and *The Times*, try to sit on the fence. It is sometimes said that the former tilts to the left and the latter to the right. Polls show that most people (including its readers) believe *The Sun* to be a Labour newspaper. In fact, it is not; the confusion probably stems from the fact that its readership is predominantly working class and the assumption is, made that it supports 'the party of the working class.'

The press, then, generally adopt a right-wing stance and tend to take up the 'establishment' line on crime, strikes and current events (such as the Falklands dispute), as well as supporting the Conservatives. They do not objectively report the facts, if such a thing were possible, but state their views on them and consistently over-report some areas while under-reporting others. *The News of the World*, devotes disproportionate attention to sex crimes and solved crimes(34). Drug offences and football hooliganism are consistently over-reported and it is commonplace for sex and sensational stories involving well-known personalities to figure largely in the popular press. Women are generally represented as occupying one of a limited number of roles; mother, housewife, wife or sexual object. They are often the subject of ridicule in popular newspapers' cartoon pages(35). Stuart Hall et al in *Policing the Crisis*(36) document how the papers seized on the 'new' crime of mugging (which in fact, was not new at all, it was merely a new label for a number of different crimes) and, for a period, consistently over-reported its occurrence and whipped up public concern over its purported increase.

There are two currents of opinion on the reasons for this multi-faceted bias on the effects it has. The first can be termed the *market theory* and is held by the press themselves. The second is the *manipulative theory*, and is adhered to by some (but by no means all) Marxists. Let us deal with the Market Theory first. This states that though the press is generally allied with one party, does sensationalise and trivialise, does treat women as sex objects, is pro 'law and order' and so on, this is only because this is what the public wants. Journalists and editors merely cater to public demand in order to sell their newspaper – its content is what the particular section of the public who buy it want to read about. All the tastes which are present in society are catered for by a wide range of newspapers (as well as TV channels, books, films.) The individual merely selects what appeals to him or her and rejects what he/she does not agree with or dislikes. The corollary of this view is that the press have *no guiding influence* on attitudes either in the short or long term. Attitudes may be confirmed but not changed; Communists read *The Morning Star*, Conservatives *The Daily Telegraph* and neither cause is promoted or hurt by the existence of these newspapers. A one-time editor of *The News of the World* writes:

> "What's wrong with a laugh and a joke? Men and women need to escape from hard work and household chores. They enjoy a joke [as well as] . . . a story that is racy, colourful and true . . . An editor wants to sell papers. He has to. If he doesn't, the paper folds up, and he gets fired . . . he wants to amuse and inform you; and he wants to place on the breakfast table a newspaper which is attractive to look at and is part of life."(37)

The problem with this theory is that the press respond unequally to consumer demand. If the audiences is either large or affluent then it will be catered for because the paper can expect either a large circulation or a substantial revenue from advertisers who are willing to pay for access to an affluent audience. This leaves non-affluent sections of the population which have minority tastes in whole or in part uncatered for. These people are least likely to be influenced in their attitudes by the imposition of views, sterotypes and definitions of 'what is important' which they did not hold prior to exposure. Thus, for example, *The News Chronicle* and The Daily Herald, each with a readership of between 1 and 2 million, died because they had a high proportion of poor and elderly readers who, despite their large numbers, were not an attractive proposition to advertisers. Graham Murdock and Peter Golding in *Capitalism, Communication and Class Relations*(38) point out that where market forces kill off those parts of the media which cannot attract large circulations or advertising revenue:

> ". . . dissenting or oppositional views are eliminated, not merely by the disappearance of organs willing to voice them, but by the economic needs of those who survive."

The survivors must aim at the *centre* of opinions at the expense of minority tastes and views to get maximum circulation. The concerns of the press devolve to the lowest common denominator and present a consensual picture of Britain. Their effect is to minimise conflicting elements within the political culture. Even the BBC has to attract large audiences in order to persuade Parliament that it has earned an increase in its licence fee and to show that it is competing with the IBA in its audience ratings. As a result its programmes have become orientated to light entertainment and trivial presentation. It seems, then, that far from catering for all tastes and views, the media increasingly ignore minority tastes and adopt a style of presentation designed to offend as few people as possible.

A second problem with the market theory is that it assumes that editors and journalists somehow magically know what the public wants. Journalists on *The Sun* and other 'populars' argue that the public does not want, for example, foreign news, but how a reader of these papers could develop an interest in foreign affairs on the diet they are fed is a moot point. Public tastes can be developed if the press and other media try to cultivate them. In practice, individuals working on newspapers have to go on their own judgment, the past experiences of the paper, the views of other members of the paper (particularly more senior ones) and contact with readers either in person or by letter. Someone with editorial experience on *The Times*, *The Daily Telegraph* and *The Economist* wonders whether . . .

> "readers guide newspapers or is the opposite true? It is impossible to give a hard judgment. I am inclined to think that in the long run newspapers guide readers, at any rate, the more serious ones. Each day the newspaper thrusts 10 or 20 pages in front of its reader; he will write or telephone to the editor at the most 50 times a year – and that would be a record. The newspaper can influence the reader by a multitude of stories, ideas, recommendations and services. The reader can only refuse his pennies."(39)

This is supported by the findings of a study by Butler and Stokes(40) into changes in political orientation among a panel of newspaper-reading respondents between 1964 and 1966. They found that 73% shifted their opinions towards the party supported by the newspaper they were reading, while 27% actually changed their party allegiance in that direction. The authors concluded that:

> "We may . . . attribute to the Press some role in changing the relative strength of the parties in the short run as well as in forming and conserving more enduring allegiances."(41)

These findings indicate that the market theory's claim that the press has no influence on public attitudes is unfounded and that on the contrary, the political culture of a society may be shaped in the long term by the press.

The third and most serious criticism of the market theory is that the press does not exist in a vacuum, able to respond at will to cater to the whims of public taste, but operates in an environment of private ownership and control. This fact may have important repercussions for the content of the papers which, it has been argued, are a product of the demands and interests of the owners.

This brings us on to the *manipulative theory* of press influence on the political culture. There has been a long term trend towards concentration of ownership of the press, and other media, in the hands of a few companies and individuals. With the exception of *The Guardian* and *The Daily Telegraph*, all national newspapers are owned by UK conglomerates or foreign-based multinationals. Six companies publish 80% of all Daily and Sunday newspapers in Britain. They are Reed International (*The Mirror, Sunday Mirror, Sunday People, Sunday Mail, Scottish Daily Record* and IPC, the company that publishes many of our magazines), News International (*The Sun, The News of the World, The Times, The Sunday Times, the Times Supplements* and several evening and weekly newspapers), Pearson Longman (*Financial Times* and *Economist*), the Thompson Organisation (a chain of important regional newspapers all over England, Scotland and Wales), Trafalgar House (the *Daily* and *The Sunday Express*, *The Daily Star*, *The Standard*) and Associated Newspapers (*The Daily Mail* and several provincial newspapers)(42). The following three tables show that there are considerable interconnections between the various media in terms of shareholding directorships and diversification by particular parent companies(43).

From the Marxist point of view, at least a strictly deterministic version of Marxism, this economic structure allows the capitalist class to use the newspapers, especially, as mouthpieces for their own conservative views and as organs to drum up support for Conservative policies. The trivia which the popular newspapers are full of as the modern version of 'bread and circuses' – Bingo competitions, sex scandals and the monarchy – take people's minds off their own pauperised and immiserated state. Interestingly, it was Rupert Murdoch, head of Associated Newspapers, who fired Stafford Somerfield from his post as editor of *The News of the World*

Television programme company	Parent company	Turnover derived from television programming as a % of total turnover	Parent companies other interests							
			TV set rental	Commercial radio	Films/ cinema	Music industry	Publishing Press	Publishing Books	Electrical equipment/ electronics	Leisure/ entertainment[b]
London Weekend Television Ltd		95				●			●	
Yorkshire Television Ltd; Tyne Tees Television Ltd	Trident Television Ltd	82	●	●	●	●				
ATV Network Ltd	Associated Television Corporation Ltd	43		●	●	●			●	●
Granada Television Ltd	Granada Group Ltd	27	●	●	●	●		●		●
Thames Television Ltd[a]	The British Electric Traction Company Ltd	7	●	●	●	●	●	●	●	●
	EMI Ltd	6		●	●	●			●	●

Figure 2. Patterns of diversification: leading commercial television companies' other communications interests.
Note: a) Since Thames Television is jointly owned by EMI and BET both corporations are included as 'parent' companies.
(b) The category, 'leisure entertainment' includes 'live' theatre, social clubs, sports facilities and catering.

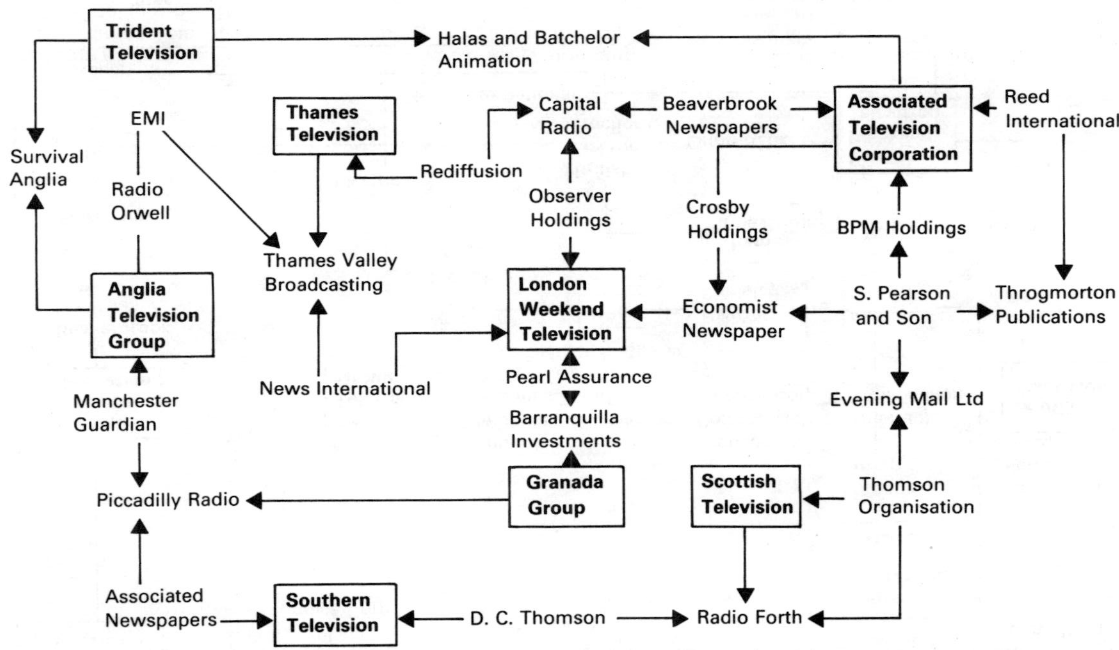

Interlocking shareholdings: selected linkages among commercial television companies and other communications corporations (arrows indicate direction of the holding).

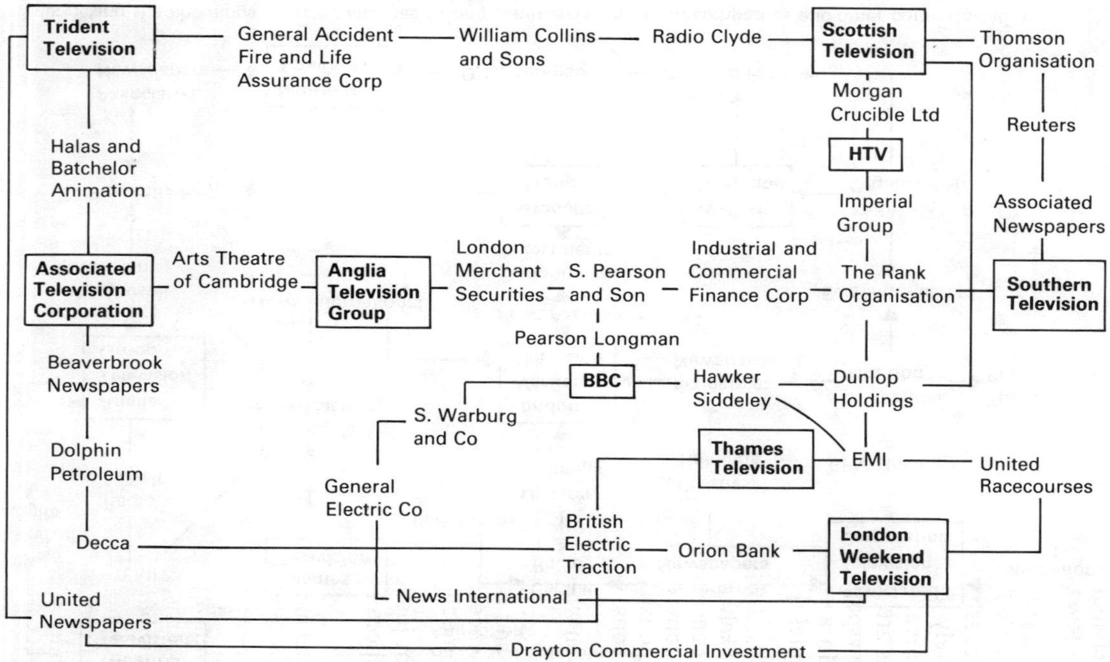

Interlocking directorships: selected linkages among television companies and other corporations.

because the latter could not agree that the owner of a newspaper should determine its content:

> "Murdoch . . . wanted to read proofs, write a leader if he felt like it, change the paper about and give instructions to the staff. I wouldn't allow that."(44)

Somerfield was briskly replaced, presumably by someone who *would* allow it. Other owners have taken a similar line to Murdoch's: Lord Beaverbrook told the Royal Commission on the Press: "I run the paper purely for the purpose of making propaganda, and with no other motive." Modern examples who would appear to have the power to do this are 'Tiny' Rowland of LONRHO, Lord Rothermere of Associated Newspapers and Lord Thompson before his death in 1977.

In a chapter entitled "the process of legitimation" Ralph Miliband argues that:

> ". . . those who own and control the capitalist press media are most likely to be men whose ideological dispositions run from soundly conservative to utterly reactionary . . . [in the past, such men] closely controlled their editorial and political line . . . and turned them, by constant and even daily intervention into vehicles of their own personal views."(45)

Even where editors and journalists *are* given a free hand:

> ". . . ideas do tend to 'seep downwards' and provide an ideological and political framework which may well be broad but whose existence cannot be ignored by those who work for the commercial media."(46)

Not just the owners but also the advertisers in the press and on TV will expect a certain tone from the media they patronise:

> ". . . the 'business community' will, at the least, be accorded a degree of indulgence which is seldom, if ever, displayed towards the labour interest and trade unions: *their* displeasure is a matter of no consequence at all."(47)

Even a large circulation will not protect a newspaper from closure if advertisers cannot be found, as the experience of the left-wing *Sunday Reynolds News*, with a circulation of between one and two million, shows.

From this perspective, then, the media (and particularly the press) are under the direct control of the capitalist class who use them to kill off opposition and nurture support for their own self-interested perspective among the population as a whole. A number of problems exist which cast serious doubt on the validity of this approach, though. Firstly, if it *were* true, then journalists and editors in this country would see themselves as puppets manipulated by the owners. In general, however, they do not, despite the occasional contrary example. Secondly, when the media *are* directly controlled in this way (as in the Eastern bloc countries), the content of the media is quite different from our own. Happy, smiling workers and usually good news predominate, in sharp contrast to the diet of strikes, crime and disasters with which we are fed. A third problem with the theory, and one which a 'market theorist' would raise, is that the public are attracted to the media in general. They must appeal to the interests and deal with the concerns of most people, something which would not be the case if the media were the organs of manipulation and control. Finally, critics of this theory have pointed to the 'ombudsman' role of the press and TV, ie the investigative journalism which often uncovers scandal, fraud and exploitation in the upper echelons of society. This would not be allowed to continue if the media were really expressing the interests of the capitalist class.

From the market theory perspective, then, concentration of ownership is limited by the professional independence of journalists and by other shareholders who are interested only in *profit*, not the effects of the media on the political culture. In the light of the criticism made earlier of the market theory, it would appear that neither approach is very satisfactory. What evidence there is suggests that newspapers can at least help to shape the political climate, but it is far from proven that there is a *deliberate* attempt to do this in Britain.

The situation is quite different in the Second and Third Worlds where the media tend to be state-controlled and are often used to build up a political and/or national consciousness to promote social stability, foster development or preserve ideological priority amongst the population. P Golding and P Elliot in *Making the News* note that the writings of Kwame Nkrumah, once President of Ghana . . .

> "extol the virtues of the press as a political weapon in the struggle to organise the masses in the fight against imperialism. 'The drumbeat of the African revolution must throb in the pages of the newspapers and magazines; it must sound in the voices and feelings of our news readers. To this end, we need a new kind of journalist for the African revolution'."(48)

Golding and Elliot report that in Nigeria this became translated into the use of the press and broadcasting media to obtain national unity, often by stifling opposition – especially after the outbreak of civil war in 1967. That country's broadcasting service quoted:

> "The importance of broadcasting as a medium for the creation of national consciousness came sharply into focus . . . not only were rebel lies about the true position of things in Nigeria being effectively debunked, the case for a united Nigeria was also forcefully put across to the world."(49)

Even after the end of hostilities in 1970, the wartime role of broadcasting continued, with an extremely close association between NBC and the state which Golding and Elliot describe as 'accommodation' rather than mediation or intervention. In their press, too, journalists who write stories based on what they consider to be intrinsic newsworthiness rather than on government interest can expect conflict with both the newspaper and government authorities.

In the USSR the relationship between the media and the state is an extremely close one. Strict control is maintained over output to prevent harmful material from reaching the page, screen or ear. The broadcasting media are state agencies and another agency 'Glaviit' exists as a censoring body for publishing houses. Newspapers are under strict control, though journalists and editors come to know what is expected of them and operate a form of self-censorship. The possibility of there being a 'maverick' editor or journalist is very slight as they are carefully selected by the party officials by a process called Nomenklatura (nomination). The media in the USSR are very useful agencies to the government and party. They publicise and 'sell' the latest change in policy, inform the population about the latest events in international relations (and pushing the Soviet line on them), and encourage effort to fulfil the requirements of current five-year plans. In this kind of situation, the deliberately induced effects of the media are quite different from those in a country like Britain, where the media are free from at least such overt controls. Let us now look at the effects which our media may have on attitudes which are *not* deliberately brought about.

Non-deliberate short term influence of the media on individuals' attitudes

The following two sections will examine work on the media which looks at the sources of non-deliberate influence on attitudes. The question of consistent but unpremeditated bias within the media is central to this discussion. This section concentrates on the effects on the individual, particularly on the way the media structures how he/she views the world. The next section will be devoted to the effect on the political culture which the media may have, both here and in the Third World. It looks at arguments suggesting that media bias is *consistently* in the interests of dominant groups acting to preserve the status quo, and hence is ideological.

The way the news is produced has been looked at by many sociologists. The thrust of each of the arguments has been that there is an unwitting bias in the selection of events that are considered to be 'news', in the *interpretation* of these events and in their presentation to audience. All these combine to structure both the individual's view about what is 'important' (and what is not), and the way he/she thinks about these 'important' things. Two central concepts here are the *gate-keeping* role of the news media and their *agenda-setting* function. Gate-keeping refers to the process of allowing some events, views, people and interests access to the media to the exclusion of others. Agenda-setting refers to the prioritisation of issues by the media which sets the framework for thought and discussion among the audience.

The series of studies conducted by the Glasgow University Media Group and published under the titles *Bad News*(50) *More Bad News*(51) and *Really Bad News*(52) provide the most detailed account of consistent bias in broadcast news production. The first two books report the result of recording and analysing 6 months of news programmes from January to June 1975. Though they are self-declared socialists, the Glasgow Media Group felt that by careful positivist content-analysis (ie careful measurement and classification of the content of the news) they could 'prove' bias in the news while avoiding allegations of political bias themselves. One of the problems with views on the media has been that all political angles claim that the media take the opposite view to their own (whatever they are). Many Conservatives think that the BBC for example, is dominated by leftist intellectuals; Socialists see it as run by establishment figures who are well to the right of the political spectrum. The group's method was to carefully time each news item, the number and type of items were noted, as was the type of presentation (eg studio or outside broadcast, library film, visual displays, interview, newscaster talking). Where non-media people appeared, details of who they were and their point of view was noted so that the amount of time devoted to high and low status people, to men and to women, to left and right, to trade unionists and businessmen was accurately measured. The time and day at which the broadcast went out were noted so that any patterns of change in these respects could be identified.

The group found there was no correlation between the amount of time devoted to a particular strike (strikes were the main focus of attention that year), and its severity in terms of hours of production lost. Strikes in the car industry were consistently over-reported, while those in the shipbuilding industry received much less attention. This left the impression that some industries were more 'strike-prone' than was actually the case. In the reporting of strikes, excessive coverage was given to their effects on the public rather than to the background of the dispute. The coverage of a Scottish refuse-collectors' strike concentrated on the health hazard presented by uncollected waste rather than on the pay and conditions of the men. The group also found that there was a hierarchy of access to the media: managers, professionals and 'experts' get more coverage than trade unionists or ordinary members of the public. Furthermore, the treatment of high status people was very different; they were often interviewed in an office or the studio and allowed to make their point quietly and at length. Trade unionists, were often seen standing outside in the cold in groups. They had to shout over the sound of noise around them or, were frequently voiced over by a news commentator. Another aspect of the hierarchy of access was the uncritical use of *government* statistics in the news. For example, statistics on wages and prices were derived from government sources to make the point that inflation is the product of wage demands. While in a sense this is true, the trade unions would have produced statistics on other factors (cost of fuel, dividends to shareholders) to explain inflation.

The use of particular words to set the tone of a news report was also picked up by the group. Words like 'trouble', 'radical', 'made idle', 'ransom', 'pointless strike' and even "and now, rubbish" (to introduce a story on the strike referred to above) were used in reporting industrial disputes and they subtly influence the viewer's attitude to the material presented. A further finding was that a selection process occurred which blamed the workers for causing strikes and presented management in the role of victim. Harold Wilson (the then Prime Minister) made a speech in which he said that a strike at the Cowley car plant was "manifestly avoidable" and blamed the financial management at the plant as well as the workers for the stoppage. The evening news bulletins had him blaming *only* the workers. Similarly, wage claims were blamed by TV news for the rapid inflation and economic decline experienced by the country at that time while other contributory factors such as foreign competition, huge increases in oil prices and bad management were ignored.

To summarise, then, the agenda which is set is one which gives priority to the discussion of 'pointless' and 'harmful' strikes by workers who have no real cause for complaint and who are unreasonable. The gate-keeping process systematically excludes alternative definitions to this one by not giving people who would present them a suitable opportunity to do so. The reasons for this consistent bias are a combination of a number of factors, primarily the nature of the people who work in the media and of the media institutions themselves. Media personnel are middle class, affluent people who tend to take a 'reasonable', consensus-orientated view of most issues. Meanwhile, there is also internal pressure from within the media institutions not to 'rock the boat'. On the first point, the authors of *Bad News* approvingly quote Stuart Hood, a former editor of BBC news, who writes:

> "A bulletin is the result of a number of choices by gate-keepers. Each of the gate-keepers accepts or rejects material according to criteria which obviously . . . [are] determined by a number of factors which include his class background, his upbringing and education, his attitude to the political and social structure of the country."(53)

This leads to the expression of a consensus view of politics which appears to be impartial but in fact ignores inequality and exploitation within society. Journalists' own 'class-bias' is reinforced by secondary socialisation into journalistic values; they learn from their colleagues how strikes should be treated, which words to use and which not to, who is suitable for interview and who is not, and so on. On the second point the authors of *Bad News* point out, as does Stuart Hood, that the boards of governors of the BBC and IBA (the controlling bodies of the various commercial companies) are appointed by the Prime Minister and are the establishment figures who would strongly disapprove of any radical content in TV output. Furthermore, the Director-General of the BBC has to think about the necessary increases in the cost of the licence fee and whether Parliament will allow them. If he attracts the displeasure of the powers that be, there may be difficulties placed in his way in that respect. Examples of institutional pressure in operation is the displeasure of Channel Four's board of governors caused by the radical *Friday Alternative* programme (which has now been taken off the screens) and government pressure on the BBC in negotiations about the new licence fee in 1979 because of interviews conducted by them with members of the IRA group who killed the M.P. Airey Neave(54). These constraints filter downwards and journalists come to know what is expected of them. The Glasgow Media Group write:

> "All kinds of benefits and privileges accompany the upward path through the hierarchy (of the BBC). Breaches of conformity can be punished by removal to obscure managerial shuntings (and) . . . the real threat of redundancy. I spoke to one or two who thought that potential non-conformists were noted by the management – 'they turned down the left-hand corner of your file' – 'and you get discreetly pushed'."(55)

This form of direct control, though, is only a rare occurrence . . .

> "since most top journalists share a similar social and cultural background with the hierarchies of the state. More importantly, the routine working practices of journalists are informed by the class assumptions of the society in which they live."(56)

The Glasgow Media Group summarise the main thrust of their argument on the reasons for the partiality of the news by rejecting the idea that there are objective standards of 'news worthiness' and suggesting instead that the relevance and importance attached to events is the result of the world view that these news values express:

> "Our argument, then, is that the world view of journalists will prestructure what is taken to be important or significant. It will do this in two ways. First it will affect the character and content of specific inferential frames used in the news . . . Second it will set general boundaries on where news is looked for, and on who are the significant individuals, the 'important' people to be interviewed, etc."(57)

What journalists are doing, then, is to impose *their* definitions of the 'interesting', 'surprising', and 'unusual', as well as their interpretation of events upon the rest of us.

In *Really Bad News*, a popular rather than academic approach is adopted. More recent case studies of a wider range of issues are analysed. News coverage of the Labour Party is studied. During the 1980 Party Conference, Dennis Healey's views (to the right of the Labour Party) were accorded great respect while left-wingers like Tony Benn were presented as Utopian dreamers and were given only limited access to the medium. A central theme of conference coverage was that there was a left-wing conspiracy to attempt to gain control of the Party. Right-wingers such as Shirley Williams (now a Social Democrat) were given ample opportunity to publicly attack 'left-fascism', 'bullying', 'blackmail' and 'intimidation'. This implicit support of the Labour right – and 'wet' Conservatives demonstrates the consensus view that Journalists have, and their dislike of any form of 'extremism'. Small wonder, that such extensive coverage was given to the setting-up of the Social Democratic Party – the 'natural' party of media personnel according to this account. Blumler and McQuail's finding (see pages 243–6), that news broadcasts influenced uncommitted voters in the direction of Liberalism is also unsurprising from this point of view, though the reasons suggested by the Glasgow Group for this are very different from that of Blumler and McQuail.

The Glasgow Media Group explicitly reject the market model of the media held by journalists themselves. They say that the different news services do *not* compete with each other, offering different products between which the audience can choose. The stories reported, the treatment they receive in both quantitative and qualitative terms is remarkably similar across the channels. Channel Four, with its depth, news and programmes like *Opinions*, appears to be an exception to this, but it is doubtful whether they will be able to withstand the various pressures being exerted on them to move to a more 'normal' approach(58). The group also reject journalists' claims to be reacting to audience demand. They argue that there is no intrinsic reason why investment figures are boring while the amount of car production lost because of a dispute is interesting. Either could successfully be put across; the difference between them is only that the latter appear shocking (and hence, newsworthy) from a middle-class jounalist's point of view, while the former do not. News broadcasts, then, *lead* rather than *follow* opinion, they structure people's attitudes in a very systematic way.

Paul Hartmann and Charles Husband in *The Mass Media and Racial Conflict*(59) agree that the media "play a major part in defining for people what the important issues are and the terms in which they should be discussed."(60) They analyse the way the media and particularly the press set the agenda on the race issue and the reasons for this. There are two main parts to their argument, firstly, that:

> "The British cultural tradition contains elements derogatory to foreigners, particularly blacks. The media operate within the culture and are obliged to use cultural symbols. Hence, it is almost inevitable that they will help to perpetuate this tradition in some measure."(61)

The cultural symbols journalists refer to are stereotypes of blacks such as the missionary in the pot, the fakir on the bed of nails, the snake charmer, etc. A headline such as *Police Find Forty Indians in Black Hole* refers to the symbol of the *Black Hole of Calcutta*, which evokes colonial associations and thus suggests that the appropriate attitude to adopt towards Indians is that adopted in the days of the Empire. Cartoons in newspapers, particularly, make frequent reference to these stereo-typical symbols.

Hartmann and Husband's second point about the media treatment of race is that certain themes around this issue fit in with journalists' ideas about what is newsworthy. The authors suggest that an element of conflict is considered an essential ingredient of a good story and any black-white conflict has inherent newsworthiness. Words like 'invasion', 'fear' and so on will be used to stress the *threat* posed by blacks. A story is also more valuable, from the journalistic perspective, if it can be "interpreted within a familiar framework or in terms of existing stereo-types or expectations." So 'racial' tension in Birmingham is interpreted in the light of the American experience of ghettos and race riots, even when there are few real parallels between the two countries. Similarly, after the coverage of Powell's speech (discussed earlier) later 'race' news is fitted into the context created by Powell – the threat of a black 'invasion' – and stories along these lines are more likely to get into the papers. The authors document a case in 1970 where figures about a decline in immigration were announced 2 months after the publication of figures revealing a high birth rate among immigrants. The two events were given quite different treatment because of their different newsworthiness:

> "Seven of the eight national dailies carried the birth figures, five of them on the front page. Only four carried the news about the reduction in immigration, only one of these on the front page. The average headline for the birth figures occupied four times as much space as the average headline for the low immigration figures . . . Five of the seven papers carried Enoch Powell's reaction to the birth figures, of which only one, The Times, went to the trouble of trying to balance the story by eliciting reactions from other sources."(62)

The birth rate story had the twin attractions of 'threat' and consistency with previous issues, namely Powell's speech and the debate it produced. The immigration story had neither. Hartmann and Husband's conclusions are echoed in J D Halloran's *Demonstrations and Communi-*

cation(63). He showed that a large-scale peaceful rally was portrayed by the media as a violent confrontation parallelling police-demonstrator battles earlier in the year in Chicago and Paris. Interestingly, this line was taken in news bulletins even *before* the rally had taken place.

Hartmann and Husband conducted a study in order to assess the impact of the media treatment of race on schoolchildren's attitudes. They wanted to see whether this differed between those who had real experience of coloured people (because they lived in an area of high immigrant density) and those with littler or no exposure. They interviewed a total of 208 boys and girls in the 11–12 and 14–15 age groups. Half came from the West Midlands and West Yorkshire (areas of high coloured immigration) and half from Teeside and Glasgow (areas of low coloured immigration). Schools were analysed for the proportion of immigrants in them and for each area a high and a low immigrant density school was selected. The final sample looked like this:

		Immigrant density (School)	
		HIGH	LOW
Immigrant Density (Region)	HIGH	52(**A**)	52(**B**)
	LOW	52(**C**)	52(**D**)

Figures refer to number of children studied

The results were that large numbers of children in all areas and schools saw immigrants as a threat and thought that there were "too many here." Children in Boxes (**A**) and (**B**) were more aware of 'realistic' competition between blacks and whites for houses and jobs but (**C**) and (**D**) children were *more* likely than (**A**) and (**B**) children to see conflict as characterising black-white relations. The authors concluded that:

> "Children who live in areas of low immigration rely perforce more heavily on the media for their information about coloured people than do others. Media-supplied information carries the inference of conflict more often than that from other sources. As a result these children are more prone to think about race relations in terms of conflict than are those in 'high' contact areas, even though they (the 'lows') live in places where the objective conditions for inter-group competition or conflict are absent."(64)

J Fiske and J Hartley in *Reading Television*(65) apply semiotic analysis (discussed in Chapter 3) to the study of television. They argue that the media, being run by members of the dominant class, propagate the dominant value system both in news and entertainment programmes. This is not an obvious process, the values are encapsulated in a series of signs or codes. The semiotic analyst can 'read' these codes and expose the message which they carry. For example, news shots of British soldiers patrolling Belfast streets, defending sandbagged positions and operating with a helicopter and armoured troop-carriers are coded messages which say: "one of our lads – professional and well equipped". By having a camera shot over the soldier's shoulder, the director encourages us to identify with him, to share his position. Such use of the camera is, say Fiske and Hartley, a more subtle development of the 'white hat = good, black hat = bad' symbolism of the early Westerns.

Entertainment programmes, too, can be 'read' in this way:

> "The Sweeney tells us that in a period when 'real life' offers us wage restraint, inflation and a fall in living standards, there is no need for class hostility. The Regan/Carter relationship personalises for the TV audience a point of view which places two 'classes' in a hostile environment and shows how working together can produce individual satisfaction for both – though *not* equality for the subordinate 'class'."(66)

In this case the subordinate class is Sergeant Carter, Inspector Regan's junior.

The problem with this kind of approach, though, is that while it is fascinating ('spot the symbolism' is a great game) and often appears fruitful, we are only really left with a personal interpretation of what the programme 'means'. We are exposing ourselves to precisely the criticism which the Glasgow Media Group sought to avoid – our own partiality. In the example just quoted, another reading might be that Inspector Regan is stereotypically working class in manner and accent and has achieved a high position in the Flying Squad; he personalises the opportunities for social mobility based on a personal qualities which exist in our society. Furthermore, the semiotic approach is in danger of reducing the study of the media to the mere documentation of a culturally fluid process of signification, losing sight of the structural relationships which the signs represent and which are the real subject of analysis.

Other authors have pointed out more technical factors which shape the news and set the agenda for the audience. J Galtung and Mari Ruge in *Structuring and Selecting News*(67) point out that only *some* events have a suitable time span for news reporting. Events that happen quickly are easily reported, but long-term processes are not. Building an aeroplane is not a suitable subject for a daily newspaper to report, but a plane crash is easily and successfully dealt with in one issue. They write:

> ". . . the more similar the frequency of the event is to the freqency of the news medium, the more probable it is that it will be recorded as news by that news medium."(68)

Negative news (murders or plane crashes) gets into the media more often because its *frequency* is more like that of news programmes and papers than positive news. One result of this is that the news presents an image of consensus because everyone can agree that such negative news is bad. A positive event (for example the building of a motorway) may be applauded by some and decried by others. Schisms would become exaggerated by this type of content.

The requirements of technology is another factor which shapes news content. Some things come over well on TV, others appear boring because the technology cannot be used to present them in an interesting way. Radio is presented with a completely different set of problems, as are the other media.

Practical constraints like money and time mean that only some events, often predictable ones, are covered. Unpredictable events with no cameras or journalists present simply do not get covered, which explains why so much news is London-based, so little comes from the provinces and very little hard news comes from the Third World. Peter Golding and Philip Elliot write:

> "Lack of time and lack of manpower or other resources are by far the most obvious of the limitations on broadcast news perceived by journalists. Problems such as the difficulty of obtaining access to certain news sources or types of information loom less large."(70)

Lack of time for the journalist to prepare material and do the necessary reading and research combined with lack of air time for in-depth treatment means that the news tends to be superficial, lacking background and explanation.

Factors such as the frequency of an event, time and money, are influences on news content which give it a particular 'slant'. While this is not necessarily the result of deliberate manipulation or the perspective of the journalist, it does structure the viewing audience's view of what the 'important' events of the world are and how they should be perceived. It could be argued that these, combined with audience demand, are the only factors which shape the news. By this account there is no 'journalist's world-view', only a professional appraisal of the possible and the desirable. This of course is the line taken by the journalists themselves. They would reply to the Glasgow Media Group with the argument that the news broadcasts during the Winter of 1975 were only airing the issues and views which were the subject of public discussion at the time. If wage demands were given heavy emphasis, this was only because the Wilson Government was being active in stimulating public discussion on wage restraint. If management came over on television as more rational, this was only because this was the fact of the matter. The journalists argue that they do not affect attitudes, they simply stimulate debate by bringing the important current events to the attention of a wider audience than would otherwise come to know about them.

Non-deliberate long term influence of the media on the political culture

The foregoing discussion concentrated on the selectivity of the media, their gate-keeping and agenda setting functions which, for a variety of reasons, serve to structure our attitudes towards contemporary issues and events. From recent Marxist perspectives this is merely a manifestation of the media's role as a major channel for the propogation of bourgeois hegemony, for diffusing the bourgeois concept of reality throughout society and so for shaping tastes, customs, political views and morality in a fundamental and permanent way. In short, the media fulfill an *ideological* function, using that term in Mannheim's sense as a set of ideas emanating from the dominant class and justifying the status quo. Clearly the Glasgow Media Group see the media in this light as they say:

> "We have empirically established that, at least with regards to industrial and economic stories, the overwhelming use of inferential frameworks, routines and presentational techniques which favour one side of industry rather than the other exist. In this sense, for whatever reasons, the ideology of one particular class, despite contradictions in the output, is dominant and preferred".(71)

However, because of the nature of their preferred methodology, the micro level of close content analysis, they have been forced to concentrate on studying only the short term and specific manifestations of this bias rather than go in depth into its social structural causes and consequences. They are, in fact, quite damning about attempts to analyse the larger scale relationships between society and the media:

> "Whilst agreeing that some general theories of society, especially those that stress the role of the class structure and conflict, are more feasible than others, we cannot agree that such theories at present offer us the concepts to analyse the manifold variations of cultural reproduction in our society".(72)

They suggest that perhaps the best attempt to arrive at such a general position has been made by Murdock and Golding(73) who move uneasily between studying patterns of ownership and cultural monopoly in the media and society and the argument that:

> "A fuller explanation must look for the complex of inter-relationships between the persuasive definitions of industry, the Nation, responsibility and the like, with trends in industrial news practice, the conventions of interview, film and narrative and so on".(74)

This second, of course, is the kind of analysis adopted by the Glasgow Media Group who stress the difficulties involved in moving from the micro to the macro level of analysis, no matter how compatible the basic assumptions behind each approach may be. Peter Golding and Phillip Elliot make an attempt to unite these two levels in their book *Making the*

News. They argue that by analysing the long term, unreflective practises of journalism we come to understand that journalists subscribe to a set of rules which govern their working routines. These rules include both the explicit regulations of organisational charters (such as the BBC's Charter or the requirements that the IBA has to fulfill under the terms of the Television Act 1954) and journalist's concepts of news-worthiness and public taste that we examined earlier. But:

> "When we come to assess news as a coherent view of the world, that is to step up from news values to social values, we enter an altogether more complex and tangled argument. News is ideology to the extent that it provides an integrated picture of reality. But an ideology is more than this; it is also the world view of particular social groups, and especially social classes. The claim that news is ideology implies that it provides a world view both consistent in itself, and supportive of the interests of powerful social groupings."(75)

This combination comes about in two ways according to Golding and Elliot. Firstly, as we have seen, the constraints and demands of news production allow only a partial view of the world. This may or may not coincide with the ruling ideology and therefore the interests of the dominant group(s). However as news has developed as a service to, and is provided by, literate elite groups the goals and values which surround journalism have come to coincide with the needs and interests of these groups. This is illustrated below in the international context when we examine the content of media in the Third World. Secondly, in attempting to appeal to widespread and anonymous audience news (and presumably other media output) draws upon the most broadly held common social values and assumptions, ie the prevailing consensus, in establishing common ground for communication with its audiences. Within a capitalist society, where this consensus represents the viewpoint and interests of the dominant groups, the media automatically come to reflect that viewpoint and those interests. Thus the media act as what Althusser(76) calls an ideological state apparatus which, while formally independent of the state and the ruling class (in Britain at least), in fact serves its interests by masking the real relation of the individual to the relations of production in which he or she lives and thus hiding the exploitative nature of capitalist society. Golding and Elliot note that there are certain *consistently* missing dimensions in news production. Firstly the account of the evolution of events is never given on the news, only the culmination of that evolution. Thus:

> "Industrial relations appears not as an evolving conflict of interest but as a sporadic eruption of inexplicable (and irrational) anger and revolt . . . Similarly the political affairs of foreign lands appear as spasmodic convulsions of a more or less violent turn, while interna-

> tional relations appear to result from the occasional urge for travel and conversation indulged in by the diplomatic jet set".(77)

As a result, the deep seated reasons for such events, based on exploitative relations, are forgotten.

The second missing dimension in the news is *power*. The tremendous power of multi-national corporations, owners of property and that of the rich nations is masked by the media's concern with individuals – "News, and broadcast news in particular, is the last refuge of the great man theory of history" they write. So a view of events which lacks both an appreciation of social process and of power constitutes both a world view *and* an ideology:

> "the absence of power and process clearly precludes the development of views which might question the prevailing distribution of power . . . A world which appears fundamentally unchanging, subject to the genius or caprice of myriad powerful individuals, is not a world which appears susceptible to radical change or challenge".(78)

In addition to portraying a world which is unchanging and unchangeable, the media focus our attention on those institutions (like Parliament) and events in which social conflict is managed and resolved because it is these which provide ease of access and appropriate material for making the news. Finally there are the statutory demands, examined earlier in this Chapter, to avoid partiality or controversy as well as the professional ethic of objectivity, which actually represents the consensual values and beliefs. Thus according to Golding and Elliot the partial nature of media output shapes the political culture in the long term interests of the dominant class, pre-empting opposition to seats of power and the pattern of social process by consistently ignoring these aspects of social reality.

Let us now turn to the influence of the media on the political culture of Third World countries. Here the connection between the relations of production and the diffusion of ideology is perhaps easier to see than it is in the 'advanced' societies. Rosemary Righter(79) documents how the *Western* perspectives is imposed on the news. Latin America gets a blow by blow account of the Watergate Affair but little internal news because of the dominance of the North American news agencies there – United Press International – Associated Press. Golding and Elliot confirm this when they describe the material supplied to Nigerian news organisations by Western news agencies as:

> ". . . irrelevant and too out of date. The agencies cover this problem by supplying many 'soft' (ie general 'state of the country' rather than 'hot news') stories where loss of immediacy is unimportant. Generally there is dismay about the dearth of African stories. Most of all there is concern about the language. African sub-editors tire of substituting 'freedom-fighters' for 'guerillas', 'racist regime' for

'South African government', crossing out 'tribesmen' and so on. Gradually, the Nigerian journalist finds himself seeing his own world as an outsider, the journalist's view of Africa becoming coincident with the Western view."(80)

A Kenyan journalist at the 19th General Conference of UNESCO at Nairobi said:

"Through the power of the Western news media, especially the major international agencies . . . Third World people have come to feel a great sense of impotence over the cultural influences which permeate their relationships with the Western World through the mass media. It is an unrelenting one-way traffic of ideas and values from the Western countries to the Third World with little opportunity given to Third World nations to examine the content of the materials which daily flood their own presses and other media from the West."(81)

The sale of TV serials such as *I Love Lucy* and *Dallas* produced in the Dream Factories of the USA, and even the UK is also likely to affect attitudes towards 'normal life' and the self-perception of Third World audiences. This 'Westernisation' of attitudes is a by-product of the past and present nature of capitalist imperialism, according to the Marxist. Old colonial relationships are perpetuated in present-day dependence and the Third World is used as a vast market for news (produced by Associated Press, UPI, Reuters and Agence France Presse, the dominant agencies), old movies and, through media advertising, goods. For the latter the broadcasting media are perfect for use in the Third World where illiteracy rates are very high. For example, in Mexico . . .

"The officially admitted illiteracy rate is more than 27%, contact with school is for the vast majority of the population fleeting, but exposure to TV and the transistor radio is lifelong. As Lee Bickmore explained to us describing his marketing plans for Ritz Crackers, one does not need to be able to read to get the Ritz message. His point was illustrated a few months later when we encountered an illiterate shoeless peasant in a poor Mexican village riding a burro laden with boxes of Ritz crackers."(82)

Barnet and Müller argue that the transfer of ideology by the global corporations through the media has several disastrous long-term results. By winning over a few relatively affluent people in the Third World to Western eating, dressing and travelling habits, it kills reformist zeal and makes the people who *could* change things complacent:

"In Latin America the university radical who, by his late 20's is obediently sipping beer in front of his colour TV in a comfortable house in the suburbs is a stereotype. Those who rent their comforts through instalment debt, no matter what revolutionary impulses may lie dormant within them, do not like to think about, much less do anything about, social change."(83)

For the poor of the Third World the effect of Western media intrusion is to reduce perceptions of class differences according to Barnett and Muller, just as Althusser and Poulantzas view the media *within* Western nations as masking real conflicts of interest. Barnett and Muller quote the findings of studies by Evangelina Garcia at the Central University of Venezuela into the attitudes of the poor:

> "They think that there are, to be sure, rich and poor . . . but that all have access to the same consumer goods they hear about on the transistor or see on the TV. It is a matter of luck whether they have the money to buy them, and luck can change. Johnson's Wax conducted a study of *marginales* and found that a common reaction in hovels with dirt on the floor was "I don't have a floor to wax, but I can buy the wax if I want to."(84)

The authors point out that the population of Third World countries are encouraged to want things like floor wax and lipstick so that they get psychological satisfaction from buying these rather than the physical benefit of spending money on much needed foodstuffs. Furthermore:

> ". . . the companies' control of ideology through advertising has helped to change the dietary habits of the poor in unfortunate ways . . . studies in West Bengal show that poor families under the influence of advertising are buying patient baby foods at exorbitant rates . . . They had been persuaded (falsely) that the packed food had 'extraordinary food value'".(85)

The Western media in the Third World, then, have important influences on the attitudes of the population on a range of issues through its control of news production, its sale of old programmes and its use by companies to sell products through advertising.

Although this latter is clearly a deliberate attempt to influence people (to buy products), there is a latent and undeliberate effect on the political culture. By making people less conscious of class differences and antagonistic class interests, these advertisements carried by the media serve to cement society together.

Chapter review

The general conclusion to be drawn from our examination of some of the work on the influence of exposure to the mass media on the behaviour and attitudes is that what you discover very much depends on what you are looking for and how you look for it. The laboratory experiments on the media and violence found an effect taking place, but probably because the experiments were set up in such a way that the participants merely did what they felt the researchers required of them. Moreover, the definition of violence is so limited, being a fictional and stylised one, that this seriously qualifies any conclusions reached. Field studies on the media and violence, on the other hand, tended to find no effects or only a limited effect and those that did, like Eron's, had serious drawbacks. The main problem faced by these studies lies in isolating and measuring the variables involved. What constitutes media violence? How much of it have the respondents been exposed to? What constitutes real violence and how much of it have the respondents indulged in? Did the first cause the second, or are above-average exposure to and indulgence in violence both products of the personal characteristics of the individuals involved or of the (sub) culture they were socialised into? These and other unresolved problems made it unlikely that field studies on the media and violence will come up with a definitive conclusion in the future.

With regard to the media and attitudes we examined the hypodermic and the uses and gratifications perspectives on the media's influence on individuals' attitudes. The first assumes that the audience is an homogeneous whole, anonymous individuals sitting in front of the TV set, not interacting with each other and not 'using' the TV message for anything, being only the object of its influence. The uses and gratifications approach regards the audience as diverse, comprising groups of individuals whose motivation for watching TV or using any other form of media may range from escapism to the desire for more knowledge or from wanting to have something to talk about with friends to the search for a sense of belonging to a family or community. Neither approach, though, has found the existence of any significant effect on attitudes. Such a result is hardly surprising in view of the fact that these studies take the media *content* as unproblematic: their focus is very firmly on the audience. If such studies had examined the content of the media and asked what gets in and what gets left out, then the role of the media in defining what is and is not an important issue, and in establishing the framework of discussion about such issues would have been exposed. To take a specific example of non-deliberate effects on the individual, a hypodermic study on the media and race would question respondents before and after seeing several episodes of *It Ain't Half Hot Mum*, *Love Thy Neighbour* or *Mind Your Language* (programmes with racist overtones) using questions such as 'do you think black people are less intelligent than white? Do they pose a threat to white people's livelihoods? The usual result would be the null-effect one. What this sort of study omits is more important than what they include, however. There may have been a strengthening of racist opinions held before viewing the programme, people may become disinhibited about expressing racist views after such views had become at least partially legitimised by these programmes. But more importantly, by screening such programmes the TV has put race onto the agenda and has presented a framework for it to be thought about and discussed. In the three programmes above, the competition between black and white in the home and the workplace and the stereotypical stupidity and dependency of coloured groups are models for thought and discussion.

In the next area of study on the media and attitudes, we examined deliberate attempts to influence attitudes in order to shape the political culture. We examined the manipulative view of the media in Britain, contrasting it with the market theory as well as briefly discussing the use of the media in this respect in the international context. Here the focus has firmly shifted towards the determination of the content of the media and the reasons for it. In the British case it is still unclear how far the ownership and control patterns in the media influence its content but evidence suggests that we cannot whole-heartedly accept the manipulative viewpoint. More subtle factors such as the pressure applied by advertisers and market forces appear to have a greater determining influence on content. Likewise the market theory, while containing elements of truth also cannot be completely accepted. The range of choice available to the audience is a limited one and, in the case of newspapers at least, this appears to be becoming increasingly the case. How far attempts to increase the range of choice such as Channel Four's will succeed in a competitive market remains to be seen, as does the answer to whether the content of cable and satellite TV will be 'more of the same' or will represent an expansion of the range of options open to the viewer. The American experience suggests that cable TV merely provides the same but older and of lower quality.

In moving into the realm of non-deliberate influences of the media we examined in detail the work of the Glasgow University Media Groups. By using quantitative methods of content analysis, a strong positivists' tool, they showed how media content is skewed in certain directions and theorised about the reasons for this. They argued that middle class journalists' values and elements of the structure of the television organisations lead to a pattern of gate-keeping and agenda-setting which reflects only one 'world-view': white, male and middle class. However, they did not study audience response to this, merely assuming that the audience would accept the agenda as it had been set for them. How far the audience ignore, criticise, reject or avoid newscasters' and editors' definitions of the world is a problem not tackled by the Group. Hartmann and Husband attempted to fill this gap in their examination of children's acceptance of the media's definition of the race issue and found that those with little or no *actual* experience of blacks did accept it, while those who had such experience only partially accepted it. Now as most adults have some experience of work, industrial relations and trade unionism, it seems likely that this will affect the reception which alternative definitions of these areas will receive. Another problematic area for the Glasgow Group is how far they have answered the market theory's arguments about public demand. If the media portray only one world-view, why are the media so successful at attracting an audience among people who, initially at least, do not share it? In fact, the audience seems to share journalists' definitions of what is newsworthy and, furthermore, other factors such as the frequency of events, available money and technology and so on, determine the content of news at least as much as journalistic predispositions do.

In the final section we moved beyond the question of agenda-setting into the area of the preservative function of the media for capitalism. In dealing with the ideological role of the media, their propagation of bourgeois hegemony, this section illustrates most clearly the artificiality of the behaviour/attitude distinction adopted here. Ideology promotes certain forms of thinking, attitudes and opinions which themselves promote behaviour which is non-disruptive to the established order. Conversely, a deliberate attempt to influence behaviour (eg to get someone to buy a product) may have an unintended, though not necessarily unwelcome, influence on attitudes towards the social system. This section briefly attempted to show how the bias within the media may be of a consistent and ideological nature, serving to sustain the social structure both in this country and in the Third World.

Bibliography

(1) M Janowitz *The Study of Mass Communication* in D Sills (ed) *International Encyclopaedia of the Social Sciences* Vol. 2 Macmillan Free Press 1963 p. 41

(2) Source of table J Thompson *Sociology Made Simple* Heinemann London 1982 p. 143

(3) See Halsey *Trends in British Society since 1900* Macmillan 1972 p. 560

(4) Source *Social Trends* 1983 HMSO p. 135

(5) This schema is adapted from P Golding *The Mass Media* Longman 1974 p. 79

(6) H J Eysenck and D K B Elias *Sex, Violence and the Media* Paladin 1980, first published by Maurice Temple Smith Ltd., 1978

(7) Bandura Ross and Ross *Imitation of Film-Mediated Aggressive Models* Journal of Abnormal and Social Psychology 67, 627–34, 1963

(8) G Noble *Children in Front of the Small Screen* Constable and Co. 1975 is the source of these criticisms

(9) A E Siegel *Film Mediated Fantasy Aggression and Strength of Aggressive Drive* Child Development 27, 365–78 1956

(10) M A Hanratty et al *Effect of Frustration upon Imitation of Aggression* Journal of Personality and Social Psychology 21, 30–4 1972. See Eysenck and Elias, Chapter 7 for a catalogue of the rest

(11) Noble op. cit. p. 141

(12) Hilde Himmelweit et al *TV and the Child* Oxford University Press London 1958

(13) L D Eron *Relationship of TV Viewing Habits and Aggressive Behaviour in Children* Journal of Abnormal and Social Psychology 67, 193–6

(14) L D Eron et al *Does TV Violence Cause Aggression?* American Psychologist 27, 253–63

(15) For example Noble op. cit. and Eysenck and Elias op. cit.

(16) See Eysenck and Elias op. cit. p. 108

(17) J D Halloran, R L Brown, D Chaney *Television and Delinquency* Leicester University Press 1970 Leicester

(18) Noble op. cit. p. 161

(19) See, for example, the findings of S Glueck and E Glueck *Criminal Careers in Retrospect* NY Commonwealth Fund 1943

(20) Noble op. cit. p. 161

(21) B A Belson *TV Violence and the Adolescent Boy* Farnborough: Teakfield 1978

(22) Eysenck and Elias op. cit. p. 11

(23) Stuart Hall *A World At One With Itself* in S Cohen and J Young (eds) *The Manufacture of News* Constable 1981 first edition 1973 p. 147

(24) Fiske and Hartley *Reading TV* Methuen and Co. 1978 pp. 179–80

(25) J Trenaman and D McQuail *Television and the Political Image* Methuen, London 1961

(26) Jay G Blumler and D McQuail *Television in Politics: Its Uses and Influence* London Faber and Faber 1968

(27) Ibid. p. 167

(28) Ibid. p. 206

(29) Ibid. p. 217 and 219–220

(30) Ibid. p. 263

(31) In C Seymour-Ure *The Political Impact of the Mass Media* Constable 1974

(32) Ibid. p. 126

(33) P Golding *The Mass Media* p. 84 op. cit.

(34) See Bob Roshier *The Selection of Crime News in the Press* in S Cohen and J Young *The Manufacture of News* Constable 1981, first published 1973

(35) See Helen Butcher et al *Images of Women in the Media* in S Cohen and J Young ibid.

(36) S Hall et al *Policing The Crisis* Macmillan 1978

(37) Stafford Somerfield *Banner Headlines* Scan Books West Sussex 1979 pp. 147–8. He was editor between 1960 and 1970. John Whale in *The Politics of the Mass Media* Fontana 1977 agrees, arguing that the media are split into popular and posh because people are. The Royal Commission on the Press, headed by Sir David Ross concurred in its 1949 report (Command 7700 HMSO)

(38) G Murdock and P Golding *Capitalism, Communication and Class Relations* in Curran et al *Mass Communications and Society* Edward Arnold 1977 p. 39

(39) Donald McLachlan *The Press and Public Opinion* in R Rose (ed) *Studies in British Politics* Macmillan 1976 3rd edition (pp. 257–266) p. 262

(40) D Butler and R Stokes *Political Change in Britain* Penguin 1971

(41) Ibid. p. 299, quoted P Golding *The Mass Media* op. cit. p. 81

(42) Information from Jane Thompson *Sociology Made Simple* Heinemann 1982 pp. 151–2

(43) Source of all 3 tables: O U DE 353 *Mass Communication and Society* The Open University Milton Keynes 1977 © The Open University Press

(44) Somerfield op. cit. p. 191

(45) R Miliband *The State in Capitalist Society* Quartet 1973 first published Weidenfeld and Nicholson 1969

(46) Ibid. p. 205

(47) Ibid. p. 207

(48) P Golding and P Elliot *Making the News* Longman 1979 p. 47

(49) Nigerian Broadcasting Corporation Annual Report 1967–8 quoted Ibid. p. 50

(50) Glasgow University Media Group *Bad News* Routledge & Kegan Paul, 1976

(51) Glasgow University Media Group *More Bad News* Routledge & Kegan Paul 1980

(52) Glasgow University Media Group *Really Bad News* Writers and Readers 1982

(53) S Hood *Politics of TV* in D McQuail *Sociology of Mass Communications* Penguin 1975 p. 418, quoted Glasgow Media group *Bad News* op. cit. p. 12

(54) The first reported in *The Sunday Times* Aug. 28, 1983, the second in S Hood *On Television* Pluto Press 1980

(55) Glasgow University Media Group *Bad News* op. cit. p. 83. See also *More Bad News* p. 112 for further discussion of this point

(56) Glasgow University Media Group *Really Bad News* op. cit. p. 138

(57) Glasgow University Media Group *More Bad News* op. cit. p. 113

(58) Financial considerations mean that Channel Four news must use material also used by the other commercial channels, thus limiting its ability to be 'different'. It is, anyway, produced by Independent Television News, the same company which provides news programmes for the others. The need to attract advertisers with high viewing figures will lead to a more "popular", less "heavy" approach to the news.

(59) Paul Harmann and Charles Husband *The Mass Media and Racial Conflict* in Cohen and Young op. cit. pp. 288–302

(60) Ibid. p. 291

(61) Ibid. p. 292

(62) Ibid. p. 296

(63) J D Halloran *Demonstrations and Communication* Penguin 1970

(64) Hartmann and Husband op. cit. p. 300

(65) J Fiske and J Hartley *Reading Television* Methuen and Co. 1978

(66) Ibid. p. 188

(67) J Galtung and Mari Ruge *Structuring and Selecting News* in Cohen and Young op. cit. pp. 52–63

(68) Ibid. p. 53

(69) In the foreword to *Bad News* op. cit.

(70) P Golding and P Elliot *Making the News* Longman 1979 p. 126

(71) Glasgow Media Group *More Bad News* op. cit. p. 414

(72) Ibid.

(73) Murdock and Golding *Capitalism, Communication and Class Relations* op. cit.

(74) Ibid. quoted in *More Bad News* page 414

(75) Golding and Elliot *Making the News* op. cit. p. 208

(76) L Althusser *Ideology and Ideological State Apparatus* in Closer *Education, Structure and Society* Penguin 1972

(77) Golding and Elliot op. cit. p. 209

(78) Ibid. pp. 210–211

(79) L Righter *Whose News?* Burnett Books 1978

(80) Golding and Elliot op. cit. p. 109

(81) Quoted in Righter op. cit. p. 52

(82) Barnet and Muller op. cit. p. 173, (83)–(85) ibid. pp. 174–183

Author index

Author Index

Author Index

Subject index

Subject Index

Subject Index